The Life and Work of
FORD MADOX FORD

The Life and Work of
FORD
MADOX
FORD

by

FRANK MacSHANE

LONDON
ROUTLEDGE & KEGAN PAUL

*First published 1965
by Routledge and Kegan Paul Limited
Broadway House, 68–74 Carter Lane
London, E.C.4*

*Printed in Great Britain
by Western Printing Services Ltd., Bristol*

For
E. M. C. and L. R. C.
with love and gratitude

In a slightly different form, portions of this book have appeared in *The London Magazine*, *The South Atlantic Quarterly* and *The Dalhousie Review*.

CONTENTS

ILLUSTRATIONS

ix

EPIGRAPHS

xi

PREFACE

Of all the figures of twentieth-century English literature who have exerted powerful influences on its development and who have also been imaginative artists of merit, Ford Madox Ford has perhaps received the least attention and credit for the part he played. Certain writers like Ezra Pound and Graham Greene have publicly acknowledged their debt to him, while others like Mark Schorer and Allen Tate have recognized him as one of the most important novelists of our time. Nevertheless, the extent and scope of his literary career is still largely unknown, and his name tends merely to evoke disjointed images of him—as a great editor, or as Conrad's collaborator, or as the author of *The Good Soldier*.

There are several reasons for his curiously nebulous position in contemporary literary history. In the first place, he wrote too much —in all, more than seventy books of all sorts—and this bulk and variety of output has discouraged a proper assessment of him as an artist. Moreover, since he belonged to three quite distinct literary generations, he has never been given a satisfactory niche in any single one.

In recent years, however, Ford has begun to emerge from the past as someone to be reckoned with. Within the last decade his best novels have been reissued both in America and England, and several critical studies of his novels have also been published. The increasing mention of his name in the literary journals also suggests a growing interest in him both as a writer and as a literary figure.

I have chosen to write a biography of Ford rather than a purely critical work because the published facts of his literary career are not so well known that one can assume them, and because a large amount of new material has come to light and needs to be recorded. Nevertheless, what is important about Ford is his work, and I have always attempted to relate the facts of his life to his writings.

I emphasize this point in order to warn readers that my book is in no sense a 'definitive' biography. Thus I have not repeated here much of the information about Ford's personal life that is to be found in previous works about him, notably in Douglas Goldring's *The Last Pre-Raphaelite* and Violet Hunt's *The Flurried Years*. All I have tried to do is to present for the first time a coherent account of Ford's career as a literary figure and to discuss, in this context, his development as an artist and thinker.

From the first, this has been my limited intention, but I must also add that I have been unable to use unpublished letters and manuscripts by Ford. As a consequence, I have only quoted brief extracts from material by Ford that is already in print.

A note must be added about the use of Ford's name. During his lifetime, Ford changed his name a number of times. Most of these changes were minor adjustments of Christian names, but in 1919 he changed his surname from Hueffer to Ford. Throughout this book, however, I have referred to him as Ford—not from a desire to sound familiar, but simply for the sake of uniformity. Occasionally, as in quotations from other writers, he is referred to as Hueffer, and this name is also used in the notes in connexion with the books he wrote before 1919.

For this study a large quantity of new material has been discovered which has been of great help in determining the nature of Ford's literary career. I have been able to examine a considerable amount of unpublished material, and I have been granted interviews by many people who knew him. I am most grateful to all those who have provided me with information.

* * *

In particular I would like to thank the following who not only provided me with much useful information, either through correspondence or by interview, but who have also most kindly allowed me to quote from their letters: Dame Rebecca West, Miss Katherine Anne Porter, Messrs. Joseph Brewer, Edward Crankshaw, Edward Dahlberg, Graham Greene, Ezra Pound and Allen Tate. I am also most grateful to the following who have most generously allowed me to quote from material in their possession: Mrs. Gerald Bullett on behalf of her late husband, Mme Catherine Guillaume, who has allowed me to quote from letters written to me by her late father, Richard Aldington, Miss Jean Stafford, Miss Eudora Welty, Mrs. Florence Williams on behalf of her late husband, Dr. William Carlos Williams, Messrs. Nathan Asch, W. H. Auden and Theodore

Pratt, the Trustees of the Joseph Conrad Estate for permission to quote so extensively from Conrad's unpublished letters to Ford, the Estate of Theodore Dreiser, Melville Cane, the Executor of the Sinclair Lewis Estate and the late Professor Morton D. Zabel.

I am also indebted to the following who not only allowed me to interview them, but who also, in many cases, provided me with useful written material: Miss Léonie Adams, Miss Natalie Barney, Mme W. A. Bradley, Miss Caroline Gordon, Mrs. Oliver Madox Hueffer, Mrs. Jerrard Tickell, Miss Alice B. Toklas, Mrs. Phyllis Vallance, Mrs. Irita Van Doren, the Rev. Mother Mary Matthew, Sir Alec Randall, Sir Frank Soskice, Sir Stanley Unwin, Messrs. Anthony Bertram, Georg Hartmann, Charles Kinross, Harold Loeb, Robert Lowell, John Crowe Ransom, Willard Trask and M. S. Wilde. Before their deaths, Lady Compton Mackenzie, Messrs. Jonathan Cape, A. E. Coppard, Christopher Morley and Lloyd Morris also kindly supplied me with information.

The following took the trouble to write to me, in many cases extensively, about their impressions of Ford, and for the material and information they provided I am most grateful: Mrs. Katherine Hueffer Lamb, Mrs. Helen Rossetti Angeli, Mrs. C. F. G. Masterman, Miss G. B. Stern, the late Miss Harriet Shaw Weaver, Sir Herbert Read, Messrs. David Garnett, Stephen Haweis, Gerard Tetley and Robert Penn Warren.

In addition, I wish to thank the Curators and Directors of the British Museum, the Houghton Library at Harvard, the Huntington Library, the library of the University of Illinois, the National Library of Scotland, the library of Northwestern University, the University of Pennsylvania Library, the New York Public Library, the University of Chicago Library, the University of Virginia Library, the Princeton University Library and the Yale University Library for permission to inspect manuscripts and letters in their possession.

Thanks are also due to Mrs. Ianthe Jerrold Menges, the Rev. H. R. Barton, Messrs. Carlos Baker, Paul Bartlett, J. G. Brennan, Ashley Brown, Stanton Campbell, W. S. Collins, Donald Gallup, John Gordan, Cecil Goldbeck, David D. Harvey, Percival Hinton, John Rodker, Peter Russell, Rupert Hart-Davis, A. J. West, Kenneth Young and the late Charles Bramley, who, together with the Society of Authors and over twenty publishers and literary agents, provided me with much useful information and help.

FORD MADOX FORD

1873–1939

The lobbed ball plops, then dribbles to the cup. . . .
(a birdie Fordie!) But it nearly killed
the ministers. Lloyd George was holding up
the flag. He gabbled, 'Hop-toad, hop-toad, hop-toad!
Hueffer has used a niblick on the green;
it's filthy art, Sir, filthy art!'
You answered, 'What is art to me and thee?
Will a blacksmith teach a midwife how to bear?'
That cut the puffing statesman down to size,
Ford. You said, 'Otherwise,
I would have been general of a division.' Ah Ford!
Was it war, the sport of kings, that your *Good Soldier*,
the best French novel in the language, taught
those Georgian Whig magnificoes at Oxford,
at Oxford decimated on the Somme?
Ford, five times black-balled for promotion,
then mustard gassed voiceless some seven miles
behind the lines at Nancy or Belleau Wood:
you emerged in your 'worn uniform,
gilt dragons on the revers of the tunic,'
a Jonah—O divorced, divorced
from the whale-fat of post-war London! Boomed,
cut, plucked and booted! In Provence, New York . . .
marrying, blowing . . . nearly dying
at Boulder, when the altitude
pressed the world on your heart,
and your audience, almost football-size,
shrank to a dozen, while you stood
mumbling, with fish-blue-eyes,
and mouth pushed out
fish-fashion, as if you gagged for air. . . .
Sandman! Your face, a childish *O*. The sun
is pernod-yellow and it gilds the heirs
of all the ages there on Washington
and Stuyvesant, your Lilliputian squares,
where writing turned your pockets inside out.

But master, mammoth mumbler, tell me why
the bales of your left-over novels buy
less than a bandage for your gouty foot.
Wheel-horse, O unforgetting elephant,
I hear you huffing at your old Brevoort,
Timon and Falstaff, while you heap the board
for publishers. Fiction! I'm selling short
your lies that made the great your equals. Ford,
you were a kind man and you died in want.

—ROBERT LOWELL

Chapter One

———————————«•»«•»———————————

BROWNS AND HUEFFERS

———————————«•»«•»———————————

Because they are sensitive and perceptive, artists are usually more affected by the experiences of their youth than ordinary children are. Often they find themselves in opposition to the pressures of their family tradition and upbringing and, when the opportunity arises, they rebel against all that they have experienced. If they are novelists, they write books like *Main Street, Sons and Lovers* and *A Portrait of the Artist as a Young Man.* Then, having escaped the smothering atmosphere of Sauk Centre, Eastwood or Dublin, they try to make their own lives the opposite of what they experienced as children. They move to New York, Paris or some other great capital and there they spend the rest of their days in the company of other artists.

For the artist brought up in a family where books and paintings are treated with more respect than football or money, the situation will be quite different, however. The young artist, considered perhaps a prodigy, will be encouraged in his talents and will be given opportunities to express himself that one born outside of the artistic milieu would never have. Yet the accessibility of the artistic career carries certain dangers with it. For if he is by nature rebellious, the young artist will find his rebellion seriously circumscribed: he will want to rebel against the atmosphere in which he has so far lived, yet this life is the only possible one for him.

Thus the disadvantages of an artistic youth may easily outweigh the advantages. Caught in a topsy-turvy world of attractions and repulsions, the young artist will sometimes want to escape and pre-

I

tend to be somebody different; at other times he may revert and express pride in his artistic heritage. Almost certainly he will try to become someone other than merely the son or grandson of a famous man.

What has been outlined above was, in rough measure, the situation Ford Madox Ford faced as a child and young man. In addition, he had to cope with a complicated international background and a singularly irregular education.

On the side of his father, Francis Hueffer, who was a transplanted German, Ford had many Continental relatives. According to an autobiography written by his grandfather, Johann Hermann Hueffer, the Hueffer family (or Hüffer as the name is spelled in Germany) had from the early eighteenth century been the proprietors of one of the two great printing presses in Münster, Westphalia.[1] This establishment, the Aschendorff Press, was originally licensed by the Bishop of that city and is to this day owned by the family. The Hueffers were staunch Roman Catholics and leading middle-class citizens, the grandfather, Johann Hermann, at one time himself Chief Burgomaster of Münster. He married twice and had no fewer than seventeen children, of whom fifteen survived childhood. Ford's father, Franz Karl Christoph Johann, was the youngest, and was born on 23 May 1845. With such a brood it was fortunate that the family business flourished, as indeed it must have done, for Johann Hermann Hueffer also found time to be a deputy to the national parliament that was originally held in Frankfurt before being moved to Berlin.

Little is known of Johann Hermann's second wife, Julia Kaufmann, except that her grandfather was a judge in Cologne, while one of her brothers was a poet and the other Chief Burgomaster of Bonn and a member of the Reichstag. She was apparently much loved since a family newspaper, called the 'Julia' in her honour, was established after her death in 1870 to keep the widespread family in touch with one another. The eldest of the Hueffer sons succeeded to the family business, but many of the others left Germany. One, Wilhelm, became a business tycoon who settled in Rome where he erected a palatial house, built the Piazza Cairoli and restored the Termini fountain. At his funeral, three Roman dukes and the German ambassador were pall-bearers and in the newspaper accounts he was referred to as 'Barone Hueffer', even though he apparently preferred to be called 'Mr. Hueffer'. Another son, Leopold, had been

a merchant in New York, but upon Wilhelm's death, moved to Paris
to take over his brother's French interests. Leopold's granddaughter, Barthe, married a French marquess, J. B. d'Oncieu de la
Bâtie. Yet another son, Hermann, after whom Ford was in part
originally named, was the author of a history of the Hueffer family
from which most of these facts are taken. He was a noted historian,
a member of the Catholic Party in the Reichstag, Dean of the
Faculty of Law at Bonn and for a one-year term Rector of the
University. The sisters generally made distinguished marriages to
civil servants and judges, two of them, curiously enough, marrying
in succession the same Dutch merchant, C. W. E. Wilde of Amster-
dam.

That so many of the Hueffer family should have moved from
Germany at a time when the country was becoming unified and
powerful may be attributed to their Westphalian distaste for Prussian
nationalism and to their Roman Catholic dislike of the new Protestant hegemony.

According to his brother, Hermann, Francis Hueffer spent his
youth as a peripatetic student, attending during the 1860's the Universities of Bonn, Leipzig and Berlin. In his reminiscences, Ford
states that his father actually received his doctorate at Göttingen
because of a student prank that enraged the rector at Berlin. 'My
father,' writes Ford, 'occupied a room in a hotel which had a balcony
overlooking the Spree. In the same hotel, but in the next room,
there dwelt the rector of the university, and it happened that one
of the Prussian princes was to be present at the ceremony of con-
ferring degrees. Thus one evening my father was sitting upon his
balcony whilst next door the worthy rector read the address that he
was afterwards to deliver to the prince. Apparently, the younger
members of the institution addressed the prince before the dons. At
any rate, my father having heard it only once, delivered word for
word the rector's speech to His Royal Highness. The result was that
the poor man, who spoke only with difficulty, had not a single word
to say and my father was forthwith expelled without his degree.'[2]
Since it was then possible to take your degree at a sister university
without having established residency, Hueffer took the train to
Göttingen, sat for his examinations and received his doctorate
there.

Shortly after this episode he left Germany for London where he
founded a philosophic journal called the *New Quarterly Review*

whose purpose was to spread the doctrines of Schopenhauer. The review lasted only a short time, but all his life Dr. Hueffer was an enthusiastic supporter of the German philosopher. His brother, Hermann, noted that 'He belongs to Schopenhauer's school of philosophy and believes that man's lot on earth is nothing but misery and misfortune; nevertheless he always regards his immediate circumstances in the most favourable light possible.'[3] William Michael Rossetti observed a different characteristic, however, and described Hueffer as 'a rather bulky but not a tall man, of very Teutonic physiognomy: brilliant ruddy complexion, brilliant yellow hair, blue eyes radiant with quickness and penetration. He was a believer in Schopenhauer; and, though not a melancholy person in his ordinary demeanour, had a certain tinge of hypochondria in his outlook on life.'[4] To this assessment Rossetti's brother, Dante Gabriel, clearly agreed, as his well-known limerick testifies:

> There was a young German called Huffer,
> A hypochondriacal buffer;
> To shout Schopenhauer
> From the top of a tower
> Was the highest enjoyment of Huffer.[5]

In London, Dr. Hueffer had taken rooms in Chelsea and there he had become friendly with Carlyle and Rossetti. It was through their good offices that, upon the failure of the Schopenhauer review, he was appointed chief music critic of *The Times*. Hueffer used this position to defend Wagner's reputation in England, and his book, *Richard Wagner and the Music of the Future* was the first full statement published in English in support of that then unpopular composer. He also wrote articles on many other musical figures, including several for the *Encyclopaedia Britannica*. Although not himself a practising musician, Hueffer was not limited to criticism, and on two occasions he wrote librettos for operas that were later produced in Drury Lane.* Like his son in later years, Dr. Hueffer was also an enthusiastic admirer of Provence. One of his favourite poets was the troubadour, Guillem de Cabestanh, on whose life he based one of his operas. He also wrote *The Troubadors, A History of Provencal Life and Literature in the Middle Ages*, which is still a standard work on the subject.

* The music for these operas was written by Sir Alexander Mackenzie who for years was principal of the Royal Academy of Music.

Not long after his arrival in England and induction into the literary and artistic circles of London, Dr. Hueffer met and married Catherine, the younger daughter of the painter Ford Madox Brown. Compared to the international Hueffers, the Browns were relatively provincial, but from them were to come strains in the character of the future Ford Madox Ford that are even more important than those that may be traced to Germany. Moreover, the Browns were far from being undistinguished. Ford's great-great-grandfather, Dr. John Brown, was a famous Edinburgh 'anti-lancet' surgeon who in his own way was as unpopular amongst medical authorities as his grandson, Madox Brown, was amongst academic painters. Although he was respected by such worthies as Napoleon and Frederick the Great, he died, as Ford later commented, 'in a debtor's prison because he invented and stuck to the surgery of posterity.'[6] Brown was the father of two sons, one of whom became President of the Edinburgh College of Surgeons, while the other, Ford Brown, was a purser in the Royal Navy. After service during the Napoleonic wars, this younger son married Caroline Madox of Kent and retired across the Channel to Calais. There, in a town then famous as the residence of Beau Brummel, they gave birth in 1821 to a son whom they named Ford Madox Brown. In his turn, Madox Brown was destined to outlive two wives. The first, like his mother, was of Kentish extraction, and the child of this marriage, Lucy, married William Michael Rossetti. His second wife, the daughter of a Herefordshire farmer, was only fifteen when she married Brown. Two children were born of this marriage: a son, Oliver Madox Brown, and a daughter, Catherine who, as has been noted, married Dr. Francis Hueffer.

At first glance it would appear that Ford, the first son of this Anglo-German liaison, had an ordinary childhood. He was born in the middle-class metropolitan suburb of Merton, Surrey on 17 December 1873, and was christened Ford Hermann Hueffer. The year in which he was born was certainly unexceptional: Victoria had been on the throne for thirty-six years, the country was satisfied and prosperous under Gladstone and, except for the recent declaration of the German Empire in Paris, the international situation was calm. The American Civil War and Crimea were safely over and the Boer War was still some twenty-five years away. Tennyson and Browning had published the major part of their work, and the Pre-Raphaelite Brotherhood had long since made its mark; Ibsen's reputation had not yet been established in London, and Oscar Wilde was still a student in Dublin. The only artistic excitement there was centred on Wagner, whose English champion was the baby Ford's father. It was altogether an off-season year in which to be born.

Shortly after Ford's birth, his parents moved back to London and settled in a house at 90 Brook Green, Hammersmith. Nothing has been recorded of Ford's infancy, but it may be presumed that it was perfectly ordinary and peaceful. His nurse, Mrs. Atterbury, perhaps introduced a note of the macabre through her uncanny and continual presence at scenes of violent murder and accident, but these notes of adventure were probably sounded against a background of domestic tranquillity and middle-class Victorian ease. As a young child, Ford was frequently taken to his grandfather's house in Fitzroy Square. This house, used by Thackeray as the home of Mr. Newcome, was distinguished by the presence of a huge funeral urn that stood on a pedestal over the front door. It was an intimidating place, full of Brown's blustering Pre-Raphaelite friends and full too of adventures for a small boy. On one occasion Ford was taken to the house to sit as model for his grandfather. The picture in which he appears is that of William Tell's son, and the painting shows him as a wide-eyed child with long blond hair flowing straight down his shoulders. It was also in this house that Ford first encountered Algernon Charles Swinburne who one evening was delivered at Madox Brown's door with the words, 'I've got your master drunk in my cab.' To this assertion, Charlotte the housemaid hotly retorted that *her* master was sitting at the head of his table with his guests. 'That's Mr. Swinburne,' she said, pointing to the figure in the four-wheeler. 'Help me carry him upstairs and put him in the bath.' Apparently, one of Madox Brown's more humane customs was to have his own name and address sewn in the coats of those of his friends whose habits were similar to Swinburne's, with the hope that when the need arose, they would be delivered to his house rather than to the local jail.[7]

How often Ford actually encountered the great figures of the Victorian age is a matter of some doubt. In one of his books of reminiscence, *Ancient Lights*, he wrote that his youth seemed to be hemmed in by big men in top hats forever spouting poetry or art criticism. Certainly as a child he must have encountered a great many poets and painters, since a number of them were relatives. His mother's half-sister was the wife of William Michael Rossetti, the Secretary of the Inland Revenue. Rossetti's brother was the painter-poet, Dante Gabriel Rossetti, and his sister was the author of 'Goblin Market', Christina Rossetti. These constituted Ford's immediate connexions with the Victorian 'great', but as a child he was also introduced to men like Tennyson and Holman Hunt.

On the other hand, many of these meetings must have taken place at a very early age, for by the time Ford was six, Swinburne had retired to 'The Pines' and Mr. Watts's supervision, and both Dante Gabriel Rossetti and Christina Rossetti had become virtual recluses.[8] At about the same time the circle was also temporarily broken by the departure of Madox Brown for Manchester. A year or two before he had suffered the severe loss of his extraordinarily brilliant and talented son, Oliver Madox Brown. 'Nolly', as he was known by everyone, had been a child prodigy, and his sudden death at the age of nineteen greatly saddened his father. Brown stayed in London for only a short time afterwards before going to Manchester to paint his great series of murals in the Town Hall.

In the meantime, the immediate Hueffer family grew and prospered. A second son was born and named from family piety after Oliver Madox Brown, and a daughter, Juliet, was born not long afterwards. As to the tenor of life in the Hueffer household, there is no really satisfactory evidence. As a father, Francis Hueffer seems to have been a calm and righteous man; indeed he was distinguished most in Ford's memory for these qualities. 'He was enormous in stature,' Ford later noted, 'had a great red beard and rather a high voice. He comes back to me most frequently as standing back on his heels and visibly growing larger and larger.'[9] Dr. Hueffer was also respectful of knowledge, and he used to chide his eldest son by calling him 'a patient but exceedingly stupid donkey.'[10] Doubtless the remark, a quotation from Ford's spelling book, was meant as a joke, but the sensitive Ford never forgot it.

Ford's sister, Juliet, has recorded impressions of their mother, 'Cathy' Hueffer. She was a pretty and fair-haired woman, who though timid, was a firm believer in justice. She also had certain artistic traits and, as Juliet Soskice writes, 'made any room pretty she went into.'[11] But with the necessity of looking after her ill brother, Oliver, her own children and then, after her husband's death, the household of her father, Madox Brown, she was never able to continue her early attempts at painting.

How Ford fared in this milieu may be conjectured from his

description of the clothes he wore 'as a very small boy indeed.' 'In those days, as a token of my Pre-Raphaelite origin, I wore very long golden hair, a suit of greenish-yellow corduroy velveteen with gold buttons, and two stockings of which the one was red and the other green. These garments were the curse of my young existence and the joy of every street-boy who saw me.'[12] The accuracy of this description has been denied by one of Ford's Rossetti cousins, but it may be presumed that it at least gives an impression of how Ford felt he was treated. Indeed, it is curious that, except for the respectful mention Ford makes of his parents in his reminiscences, there is little to indicate that they had much influence on him or that he cared for them very much. Such qualities as 'righteousness' and 'justice' are of course admirable, but they are no substitute for family affection and kindliness. Ford believed that his younger brother Oliver was preferred by his parents to himself, and doubtless the baby girl, Juliet, also demanded more attention than he did.

Another element of Ford's early childhood was his love of romance. With his nurse's grandson, Walter Atterbury, he would, as all children do, play games of discovery, turning the kitchen table upside down and imagining it a full-rigged ship on the Spanish Main. 'Certainly,' he later recorded, 'I watched Captain Kidd bury his treasure and equally certainly I heard Nelson say: "Kiss me, Hardy", at the end of Trafalgar day. I heard it, you understand, more clearly than I now hear the wind in my olive trees.'[13] Thus, with an imagination far more vivid than that of most children, Ford early in his life found reality in romance and never, even in his later years, did he entirely overcome his predilection to confuse the two.

The playing of games with the child of a servant also introduced, as it did in the house of almost every English middle-class child, the notion of class distinction. How to treat one's 'betters' or 'inferiors' was strictly inculcated by parents and, in common with all of his class, Ford early learned this code. He was never fully to outgrow it.

At the age of eight, Ford was sent to a boarding school in the South of England. The school chosen by Dr. Hueffer was one run by a Dr. and Mrs. Alfred Praetorius who had come originally from Frankfurt-on-Main. Their school had attracted the attention of the Hueffers because Dr. Praetorius, a follower of Froebel, the founder of the kindergarten, was considered 'advanced' in his educational thinking. Originally the school had been located in Harley Street and thus the children of a number of doctors were in attendance, but by the time Ford and his brother Oliver were sent to it, it had moved to Folkestone in Kent.

At this school Ford first began to realize that his family background was unusual. In his own home or at his grandfather's house, there was a continual mixture of languages and a constant influx of people from the Continent. Although the young child probably thought this normal enough—as normal, say, as being English and having surnames like Rossetti or Hueffer—at Folkestone he saw that his experience as a child was quite exceptional. On the whole, according to one of the masters,[14] Ford's schoolmates came from families prominent in the professions and from the landed gentry. Ford's and Oliver's connexions with the Rossettis and Madox Browns therefore set them apart from the others.

Classes and conversations at Praetorius were conducted on alternate days in French and German and the students were enthusiastic and intelligent. In its sporting and social life, however, the school was quite ordinary, for like many foreigners, Dr. Praetorius was an admirer of much of the public school system. As a result, according to Dame Rebecca West,[15] there was a great emphasis placed on the ephemera of that type of school: reasonably enough, probably, since in Victorian times it wouldn't have done to run a wholly experimental school. Thus the Praetorius School could be summed up by saying that Dr. Praetorius had the almost hopeless ideal of strengthening the intellectual side and encouraging youthful enthusiasms while at the same time producing English gentlemen of the public school type.

Being something of a foreigner in a foreign school had its benefits, and Ford, knowing German, was able to do his studies with ease; on the other hand, he was doubtless anxious to appear English rather than German and so became an enthusiastic cricketer. Self-awareness seems to have been one of Ford's natural traits, and it is probably from his school that he first learned to adopt personae to suit his feelings of the moment, a habit he developed and maintained through his life, to the amusement and occasional confusion of others. A continuing difficulty Ford had to face at school was the rivalry with his brother, Oliver, who it has generally been agreed was the more witty and humorous of the two.

That a certain nervous insecurity was a part of Ford's young life may be gathered from a curious anecdote related by one of his

9

schoolmates at Praetorius. At the age of nine this boy arrived at Folkestone with two larks in a cage. For a while all was well, but with the coming of winter the two birds, frantic to migrate, began to be noisy and conspicuous. 'Ford,' the schoolmate continues, 'as the biggest boy in the school, very fair and very Germanic, felt it incumbent upon him to make a very welcome protest against the sinful cruelty of keeping larks in a cage. He asked that they should be set free. Mrs. Praetorius, in delighted agreement, gave the order that the cage was to be opened in the school-yard and the birds set free at once—in the presence of the whole school. I saw my precious pets depart through a mist of tears. . . .' So far, as the schoolmate writes, so good. But then 'Nature's nobleman and advocate felt that his work was not yet done. He felt obliged to taunt me in the playroom afterwards with my despicable cruelty in contrast with his personal superiority and power, since at a word from him the birds were at once released—ha-ha!'[16]

While this anecdote cannot be taken too seriously, since childish actions are rarely calculated, there are two features it contains which are worth noting. The first of course is the sense of justice and kindness which it suggests Ford possessed, since no other boy had asked that the birds be released. The second is simply an indication of Ford's desire to make himself noticed and respected by others. As a child, he had been told again and again to keep in the background. This training, he later noted '. . . certainly rendered me timid, incapable of self-assertion. . . .'[17] At the same time, he was encouraged to be a 'genius', and when he wrote his first book at the age of eighteen, he was puffed and praised. Thus, while momentarily freed from parental discipline, it is not surprising that he sometimes reacted in a peculiar manner.

One positive result of his schooling, however, was an absence of shyness with women. His familiarity with his female Rossetti cousins doubtless contributed to this ease, but the Praetorius School was also open to young ladies, with the result that as a very young man Ford played chess during the evenings in the headmaster's 'parlour' with, amongst others, the young lady whom he eventually married.

At the end of 1888, when Ford was only fifteen, his father suddenly died from a heart attack following erysipelas. To a family so afflicted by youthful deaths, that of Dr. Hueffer at forty-three was very hard to bear, and deprived of a regular income, they seemed on the verge of a difficult future. Mrs. Hueffer's father, Ford Madox Brown, whose wife had also just died, soon returned from Manchester, however, and took charge of the Hueffer family. One of the most benign and hospitable of men with rough kindly manners and a beard that made him look like the King of Hearts, Madox Brown engaged a spacious and agreeable house at 1 St. Edmund's Terrace, near Regent's Park, and invited his daughter and grandchildren to live with him there. Two doors away lived his son-in-law, William Michael Rossetti, and between the two households there was constant cousinly traffic. Other frequent visitors were the Radford children and the sons of Dr. Richard Garnett, who was the Keeper of Printed Books at the British Museum and a good friend of Brown's.

The father's death meant the withdrawal of the two Hueffer boys from boarding at the Praetorius School, and for a time they were enrolled in the University College School, a London day school then located in Gower Street. At this large school, Ford did not distinguish himself as he had formerly done at Folkestone, and one of his classmates there, Mr. Charles Kinross, has said that there was nothing remarkable about either of the Hueffer boys, both of whom were normally intelligent and agreeable. Quite naturally, Ford excelled at modern languages, and the only incident of life in this school that he has recorded concerns a translation into German of a sentence which he felt to be insulting to the art of music. Although normally a quiet and peaceful student, Ford suddenly became enraged and dressed down the schoolmaster in violent language, ending his tirade by a quotation from Victor Hugo in which the French writer abuses schoolmasters in general.[18]

That Ford should have been moved to such excesses may have been due in part at least to an aspect of his youthful education which was somewhat out of the ordinary. Owing to Dr. Hueffer's position on *The Times*, music played a large part in Ford's young life: he was a frequent attendant at concerts, and in his father's house he often met famous prima donnas and even more famous composers like the Abbé Liszt. On the one hand, these experiences discouraged Ford from becoming a composer himself since he doubted his ability to succeed in so highly competitive a profession. On the other hand, they encouraged him to develop a passion for the sanctity of the arts as almost a priesthood.

This passion, together with a sense of brotherhood amongst artists, was doubtless inherited from his grandfather, whom he now saw daily. Though a kindly man, Madox Brown was given to

extravagant statement and noisy bluster, especially on artistic subjects. He was fiercely independent, refused to have any direct connexion with the P.R.B., and was scornful of academicians. Because
of his outspokenness and because of his refusal to compromise, as
his friend John Everett Millais had done, Madox Brown was never
a financially successful painter, and his name, though respected by
fellow artists, never captured the public as did those of Rossetti,
Millais, or even Holman Hunt. He was also of the older generation
that had been partly eclipsed by the 'revival' of Pre-Raphaelism
under Morris and Burne-Jones.

Thus in some ways Brown was a lonely person and perhaps more
conscious than some of his contemporaries of the position the artist
occupied in society and the duty one artist had towards another.
Looking back on his forebears, Ford has recorded that although the
Pre-Raphaelites and their friends may have quarrelled violently in
private, hotly calling one another fools and liars and engaging in
numerous improbable adventures such as those concerning Charles
Augustus Howell and the exhumation of Rossetti's 'Jenny', they
united in a common front against outsiders, always praising the work
of colleagues before possible picture buyers, and attempting to find
commissions for others temporarily impecunious. This social
responsibility seems somehow, in the episode of the schoolmaster,
to have been passed on to Ford.

That the Pre-Raphaelite tradition made a strong impression on
the young Ford was inevitable, although it would be incorrect to say
that he welcomed it in all its ramifications. The Brown household
was virtually a museum of the Brotherhood: sketches and paintings
by Brown himself, Rossetti and Holman Hunt hung in all the rooms,
and the bookcases were full of inscribed books by Carlyle, Browning
and Tennyson. Of course the literary and artistic movements with
which Brown had been associated had ceased to exist, and Rossetti,
Carlyle and Browning were all dead by the time the Hueffer family
moved into the Brown household; nevertheless they were all alive
as presences. There were, moreover, a number of remnants of the
great age still about, and these Ford encountered from time to time.
He regularly called, for example, upon the executor of his father's
will, Mr. Watts-Dunton, and there at 'The Pines' in Putney, he saw
the once-rebellious, now quiescent poet, Algernon Swinburne. On
occasion Ford also went to see his 'aunt', the poetess Christina
Rossetti. In her later years, this remarkable woman was an invalid

1. 'Tell's Son,' a painting by Ford Madox Brown, 1877;
modelled by his grandson, Ford Madox Ford.

2. Dr. Francis Hueffer and his two sons, Oliver Madox Hueffer and Ford Madox Ford. Line drawing by J. A. Hipkins.

3. Dr. Francis Hueffer, Music critic of *The Times*. Line drawing by J. A. Hipkins.

4. Ford Madox Ford, circa 1895. Line drawing by J. A. Hipkins.

who hardly ever went out, but because of his great admiration for her quiet verse, Ford often visited her. Perhaps most overwhelming of all was the poetess Mathilde Blind who had more or less been adopted by the Madox Brown household. On occasion she would approach the young Ford with literary questions, none of which the young boy was able to answer. As a result, as Ford later noted, 'Miss Blind frightened me out of my life. And rising up and gathering her proof-sheets together, the poetess, with her Medusa head, would regard me with indignant and piercing brown eyes. "Fordie," she would say with an awful scrutiny, "your grandfather says you are a genius, but I have never been able to discover in you any signs but those of your being as stupid as a donkey."'[19]

As well as any other, this anecdote reveals the aspect of the Pre-Raphaelite tradition that most distressed Ford as a young boy. 'That terrible word "genius"'[20] dogged him wherever he went to the extent that he really became obsessed by it. He may have appeared in the eyes of his cousin Helen Rossetti to have been 'a particularly cheerful and normal small boy'[21] but inwardly or at least in retrospect, he dreaded what he later called 'the full educational fury of our aunt'[22] whose sole design seemed to be the training of the young Rossettis and Hueffers as future geniuses. Certainly what contributed to his distaste for the rôle was the precociousness of the Rossetti children who, together with the Hueffers were encouraged by Mrs. William Rossetti to perform and to give public exhibitions of their talents. The effect of these exercises on a small boy who was accustomed to being characterized as a donkey was frequently disastrous. In later years, Ford recalled a typical incident:

My cousins, the Rossettis, were horrible monsters of precocity. Let me set down here with what malignity I viewed their proficiency in Latin and Greek at ages incredibly small. Thus, I believe, my cousin Olive wrote a Greek play at the age of something like five. And, they were perpetually being held up to us—or perhaps to myself alone, for my brother was always very much the sharper of the two—as marvels of genius whom I ought to thank God for merely having the opportunity to emulate. For my cousin Olive's infernal Greek play which had to do with Theseus and the Minotaur, draped in robes of the most flimsy butter muslin, I was drilled, a lanky boy of twelve or so, to wander round and round the back drawing-room of Endsleigh Gardens, imbecilely flapping my naked arms before an audience singularly distinguished who were seated in the front room.[23]

It was thus with a great sense of relief that, after a year or so at University College School, Ford went abroad to Paris to visit some of the Hueffer relatives. Since the Paris branch of the family was wealthy and the Madox Brown household relatively poor, the trip was doubtless arranged in hopes of procuring from Ford's uncle a contribution towards the fatherless nephew's education. The visit was not Ford's first to the Continent, since he had earlier been to Provence to stay with his father's friend, the poet Frédéric Mistral. There he had learned French with a Provençal accent that had horrified his father. Dr. Hueffer, with what may be called a foreigner's sensitiveness to English customs, had insisted that his son speak French in the manner of an English gentleman—that is, fluently, but with a marked British accent.

When he went to Paris, Ford presumably stayed with his Uncle Leopold or with Leopold's granddaughter, who had married the French Marquess. Thus he saw Paris from a pleasant vantage point, attended lectures on market gardening and agriculture at the Sorbonne and was confirmed into the Roman Catholic Church. The Rossettis and Madox Browns were, of course, confirmed agnostics, and therefore Ford's earlier religious training had been negligible. The Hueffers, on the other hand, were staunch Papists, and Ford's confirmation may have been arranged partly to please them and partly to induce contributions for the children's upbringing.

Ford never altered his religion afterwards, but he was not a 'strict' Catholic. Friends of later years remarked that he was more attracted by the stained glass and music of the Church than by its doctrines, but in fact his faith had an intellectual basis derived from his experiences later in life. Much of his early liking for Roman Catholicism, however, came simply from a temperamental dislike of Protestantism which he considered a gloomy, illogical and philistine religion.

This excursion to Paris was but one of several trips Ford embarked on before he reached the age of twenty. On one occasion he went to Bonn where he studied history under his uncle, Hermann Hueffer. This individual, the author of the family history, evidently was the type of the absent-minded professor, and Ford recounts that on one occasion when he was walking with him in Bonn, his uncle observed an attractive lady who smiled as she passed him. 'That is a very attractive woman,' said Uncle Hermann. 'I should like to make her acquaintance.' It was his wife.[24]

14

At Bonn, Ford was exposed to German university life as it was during the hey-day of Prussian militarism. As a student and as a member of a professorial family, he passed his time amongst Social Democrats, whose greatest rivals were the military units, the Bonn Hussars, who were stationed in the town. The experiences he underwent in student riots and in discussing the intellectual shortcomings of the military mind in the company of his fellow-students doubtless contributed to Ford's life-long dislike of Prussian militarism.

On another occasion, Ford travelled through Bavaria with a tutor, staying in small villages and visiting spas. Memories of the Franco-Prussian war were still fresh, and the southern part of the country was sharply divided in its attitude towards what Bismarck had wrought in unifying the country under Prussian domination. So that here again Ford was able to sense something of the true political nature of the country. Indeed his observations at this period must inevitably have contributed to the theory he later propounded to prevent future German military aggression—the formation of a Rhine confederation independent of Berlin.

Altogether, the months Ford spent on the Continent broadened Ford's horizons considerably. They emphasized what he had already expected—that he was not simply a young Englishman, but a young man with roots all over Europe. To many English families, Continental connexions are a matter of course, but for a young man whose childhood had in some ways been oppressive, and who was not entirely English, the visits abroad provided both a relief and a cosmopolitan outlook. On the other hand, they also contributed to the difficulty Ford was later to experience in establishing for himself an intelligible political and social philosophy. The comparative extensiveness of his experiences weakened the firmness of any particular foundation upon which he might later wish to stand.

The immediate effect of these experiences could be seen in the rôle he proceeded to play amongst his cousins and friends in London upon his return from Paris. Partly to please his uncle and partly to assert his international character he styled himself Joseph Leopold Ford Hermann Madox Hueffer and appeared to his sister as 'a fair, clever young man, rather scornful, with smooth pink cheeks and a medium-sized nose like my grandfather's, a high, intellectual forehead, and quiet, absent-looking blue eyes that seemed as if they were always pondering over something. I was nervous with him, because he was very critical and thought that everyone was stupid and not worth disagreeing with. But he was very kind and liked to take me out to tea. He wore a black coat with a cape over the shoulders, and when we took hands and walked along it floated out a little way behind.'[25]

Shortly afterwards, Ford took his sister to have tea with Prince Kropotkin, the famous Russian revolutionary whom he had probably first met through Edward and Constance Garnett. Mrs. Garnett, who was later to be renowned for her translations of Tolstoi and Dostoievsky, had lived in Russia and knew many of the multitudes of Russian exiles who flocked to London during the 'nineties of the last century. Many of these—amongst them the Nihilists Sergius Stepniak and Felix Volkhofsky—were also frequent visitors to the premises of an anarchist journal called *The Torch* which had been published for some time from the household of William Michael Rossetti. The presence of so radical a paper in his own house was a source of continual embarrassment to that august civil servant who found to his shame that he was under scrutiny by Scotland Yard, but Rossetti endured it out of deference to his wife's advanced views. As a matter of course, then, Ford frequently encountered these individuals in his uncle's house and, after his return from the Continent where he had met several students in exile from Russia like Magdalena Schabrowsky, he soon became acquainted with a number of leaders of the English left, like Ben Tillett, Tom Mann and Charles Rowley, the Manchester Socialist, who was also a good friend of his grandfather's.

Yet, despite the status these interesting acquaintanceships gave him amongst his cousins and immediate friends, Ford was never attracted to politics. Almost from the first he had observed that an unnaturally large proportion of political energy was expended in internecine quarrels. Socialists squabbled with anarchists; anarchists squabbled with pacifists, and effective political power seemed more often than not to be in the hands of entirely unscrupulous people such as the Czarist *agent provocateur*, Azev. Moreover, Ford was temperamentally ill-suited to political activity. He much preferred literary work or the desultory study of musical instruments, and thus his only contribution to *The Torch* was a short poem mostly remarkable for its lack of political overtones.

The exciting and romantic acquaintanceships of Ford's youth, together with his experiences on the Continent were doubtless helpful to him in overcoming his youthful feelings of insecurity amongst

16

his immediate friends. But in the long run, they were damaging to his career. In the first place, he had come to know far more about the ways of the world than most young men know, and as a result had no illusions about an artistic career. In a rash moment, when he apparently felt he would rather do anything than become a composer or writer, he even told his grandfather that he wanted to join the Indian Civil Service. Brown, of course, was incensed and horrified, and Ford therefore dropped the idea. The incident, however, is significant in so far as it shows Ford's desire to escape the life of 'genius' for which he had been so assiduously trained. At bottom, Ford's natural inclination was to accede to his grandfather's wish that he follow the artistic life, but he hesitated to act for fear of being a failure in the eyes of his famous relatives. Thus the problem of career still remained unsolved, complicated in Ford's own mind by his doubt that a 'patient, but exceedingly stupid donkey' could in fact become a 'genius'.

Because of the relatively easy circumstances in which the Hueffers and Browns lived and because of the subject's youthfulness, no actual decision was ever made. Instead, Ford seems to have drifted into what came his way. His first book, *The Brown Owl*, published in 1892 when he was only eighteen, was a fairy-story he had written to amuse his sister Juliet. But upon hearing of it, Grandfather Brown provided two drawings as illustrations and placed it in the hands of Edward Garnett who was then the reader for T. Fisher Unwin. Presumably Ford was not hostile to the idea of publication, or to his grandfather's illustrations, but the affair seems to have been engineered more by Madox Brown than by Ford himself. Ford has commented that Unwin paid him £10 for it (of which his mother allowed him to keep but ten shillings) and that, ironically, it sold more copies than any of his subsequent books.

Distressed as Ford may have been at beginning a literary career—for his father had seriously warned him 'Fordie, whatever you do, never write a book,'[26] he at least had the benefit of a model of artistic integrity in his grandfather. After Dr. Hueffer's death, Madox Brown had gradually taken over the rôle of father to Ford, and the grandson has evinced both in his reminiscences and in the official biography he wrote after Brown's death, the tremendous piety and admiration he felt towards the old painter. In 1911 he said quite simply that 'Madox Brown was the finest man I ever knew.'[27]

There are two attributes of Madox Brown that Ford especially admired which constitute a code of behaviour that can hardly be improved upon for an artist. First of all, Madox Brown had standards. He was devoted to the ideal of painting as well as he possibly could and of applying himself wholeheartedly to his art. Compared to that, nothing else really mattered. If an artist is really imbued with this passion then he will not alter his art for any purpose: he will not paint in order to teach a moral lesson, and he will be wholly unable to produce a flattering portrait or to boil a few pots with quickly applied daubs. Instead he will devote all his energies to his art, as Brown did for twelve years on his painting 'Work', and he will probably die impoverished, ignored by his contemporaries and relying wholly on posterity to redress the balance.

The other reason for Ford's admiration of his grandfather may be found in the 'rule of life' he laid down for his grandson. It is worth quoting as Ford has transcribed it:

> Fordie, never refuse to help a lame dog over a stile. Never lend money: always give it. When you give money to a man that is down, tell him that it is to help him to get up; tell him that when he is up he should pass on the money you have given him to any other poor devil that is down. Beggar yourself rather than refuse assistance to any one whose genius you think shows promise of being greater than your own.[28]

These, then, were the standards of behaviour that Madox Brown bequeathed to his grandson. They are applicable to any branch of the arts and, had Ford been an enthusiast, or had he received a training other than that for the nebulous occupation of 'genius' they might have had immediate effect and have embarked him on a full-scale literary career prior to his twenty-first birthday. As it happened, however, the events of the next few years, coupled with his disinclination to follow the career indicated for him by his grandfather, enabled him to put off the truly artistic life for another five years.

He was a longish, leanish, fairish young Englishman, not unamenable, on certain sides, to classification—as for instance by being a gentleman, by being rather specifically one of the educated, one of the generally sound and generally pleasant; yet, though to that degree neither extraordinary nor abnormal, he would have failed to play straight into an observer's hands. He was young for the House of Commons, he was loose for the army. He was refined, as might have been said, for the city, and, quite apart from the cut of his cloth, he was sceptical, it might have been felt, for the church. On the other hand he was credulous for diplomacy, or perhaps even for science, while he was perhaps at the same time too much in his mere senses for poetry, and yet too little in them for art. You would have got fairly near him by making out in his eyes the potential recognition of ideas; but you would have fallen quite away again on the question of the ideas themselves. The difficulty with Densher was that he looked vague without looking weak—idle without looking empty. It was the accident, perhaps, of his long legs, which were apt to stretch themselves; of his straight hair and his well-shaped head, never, the latter, neatly smooth, and apt into the bargain, at the time of quite other calls upon it, to throw itself suddenly back and, supported behind by his uplifted arms and interlocked hands, place him for unconscionable periods in communion with the ceiling, the tree-tops, the sky. He was in short visibly absent-minded, irregularly clever, liable to drop what was near and to take up what was far; he was more a respecter, in general, than a follower of custom. He suggested above all, however, that wondrous state of youth in which the elements, the metals more or less precious, are so in fusion and fermentation that the question of the final stamp, the pressure that fixes the value, must wait for comparative coolness. And it was a mark of his interesting mixture that if he was irritable it was by a law of considerable subtlety—a law that, in intercourse with him, it might be of profit, though not easy, to master. One of the effects of it was that he had for you surprises of tolerance as well as of temper.

HENRY JAMES, *The Wings of the Dove*
(Ford is said to be the model for James's character, Merton Densher.)

Chapter Two

————《◆》《◆》————

MARRIAGE

————《◆》《◆》————

Two events in the early 1890's were especially important to the young Ford. The first was the death, on 6 October 1893, of his grandfather, Madox Brown, and the second was his marriage some seven months later to Elsie Martindale. The painter's death, brought about by apoplexy, once again left the Hueffer family devoid of material support. Ford, the eldest son, was only twenty and his brother and sister were still at school. William Michael Rossetti— who had presided over the funeral arrangements of so many famous men—was of course of indispensable help, and for a while the two households combined. Soon, however, tension arose between them, for Mrs. Rossetti resented the absorption of a second family with her own, and William Michael was too busy to concern himself much with the Hueffers. Thus much of the happiness of the old Madox Brown household evaporated with the death of the old man.

Not long before he died, Madox Brown had become involved in the love affair his grandson, Ford, was conducting with a certain Miss Elsie Martindale, the daughter of Dr. William Martindale, an eminent chemist and assistant of the famous Lord Lister who was the founder of antiseptic surgery and follower of Pasteur. When the Praetorius School was located in Harley Street, 'Mr. M.' as he was known, had enrolled his daughter Elsie, and she had continued on after the school moved to Folkestone. There she met Ford for the first time, and there their romance started. Although frequently separated by Ford's absences on the Continent, they kept in touch with each other, and in due course their romance attracted Grandfather Brown's attention because of the lack of enthusiasm taken towards it by Elsie's father. In his book on Ford, Douglas Goldring put the situation well by likening it to the Browning–Barrett romance. To the eminent scientist, the young Ford, with his artistic connexions and manner, seemed hardly a suitable match for his daughter. He had for example dedicated a book of poems to Elsie, using only the most transparent of pseudonyms. Martindale of course recognized the respectable elements in Ford's family—his uncle's position in the civil service and his grandfather's close friendship with Dr. Richard Garnett. But there was still the artistic heritage to reckon with, not to mention the anarchists. Moreover, Ford was hardly twenty, and Elsie was only seventeen.

Dr. Martindale therefore behaved like the typical Victorian father of fiction, virtually imprisoning his daughter at home and discouraging her love affair with the young artist in every way he could. Such conduct naturally distressed Madox Brown, who himself had married a young girl of fifteen, and so he interfered. He called on Dr. Martindale to make it plain he approved of the romance, but he also assured him that Ford would do nothing to distress him.

Then seven months after Madox Brown's death, Ford and Elsie decided to act. On her way to the country, ostensibly to visit with her sister, Elsie suddenly jumped trains and went to Bath where she made her address known to Ford by the prearranged method of advertising in the newspaper. Ford soon appeared on the scene with his barrister friend, Robert Garnett, and on 17 May 1894, the two were secretly married. The elopement enraged the Martindales and embarrassed Mrs. Hueffer and the Rossettis, but the deed was done, and Ford, not yet twenty-one, and his seventeen-year-old bride went off to live where they had always wanted to settle—near the Romney Marsh in Kent, where they procured a little cottage in the village of Bonnington.

That Ford and Elsie should have made such a decision and one that was guaranteed to irritate and hurt their relatives may seem strange in view of what is known of Ford's character up to that time. Hitherto he seems to have been a young man more acted on than acting, a young man who simply never had to face a decision affecthis life. Indeed, it is difficult even to guess the sort of person Ford was as a young man on the verge of his majority. Without being singular or impressive in any particular fashion, he seems to have been generally agreeable, perhaps a trifle bland. One pictures him

21

as having spent most of his time with his elders where he was more a listener than a talker, and he seems to have been vaguely uncomfortable in the presence of his contemporaries. At bottom then a somewhat lonely young man, he doubtless found in Elsie Martindale someone who could understand his position and who could sympathize with his desires. The evidence of later years also points strongly to Elsie's strength of character, and certainly the elopement indicates her resourcefulness. This attribute tended to make her somewhat rigid in her later behaviour, but doubtless Ford saw in her an element of strength and purpose he himself lacked. Thus with the removal by his death of Madox Brown's protective umbrella, and with the growing disagreeableness of joint living in the household of William Michael Rossetti, Ford's marriage to Elsie provided both an escape from the unpleasant and a new promise of moral support and love.

Bonnington, the village they moved to, was a lonely isolated settlement made up of scattered cottages that ran along a range of hills. Once common land, the area had been settled by squatters who put up mud huts with thatched roofs, planted hedges round their plots and grew potatoes, cabbages and tended their few fruit trees. Ford's and Elsie's cottage was made of wood and thus was slightly more elegant than the others, and they soon imported pieces of furniture famed for their literary connexions. The writing desk had belonged to Christina Rossetti, a large table had been designed by William Morris, and there was a cupboard for paintings that had once been used by Madox Brown. Later on, when they moved to Pent Farm, they hung over the couch in the drawing-room two additional, somewhat gruesome mementoes: the death masks of Dante Gabriel Rossetti and, strangely enough, of Oliver Cromwell.

The years spent at Bonnington seem on the whole to have been cheerful and happy. The Martindales, who had a country place in nearby Winchelsea, soon became reconciled to their daughter's elopement, and Ford later honoured the doctor by using him as a model for the hero of his novel, *The Benefactor*. Although the young people had little money, country living was not expensive in those days, and they were able to spend much of their time in writing. Mrs. Hueffer had a small talent and in later years published a translation of Maupassant's stories and wrote a novel called *Ellen Slingsby*.

Ford's prolonged residence in the country has occasionally been attributed to the teachings of William Morris, but it is probable that personal desires and other influences played a greater part in the move to Kent. Ford of course knew Morris's doctrines and, as a frequent attendant at lectures in Kelmscott House, knew 'Topsy' personally, but to Ford the simple-life philosophy of Morris was always suspect, largely because it promised too much. It was at once backward-looking and Utopian and had little connexion with actuality. More important to Ford than living according to a particular doctrine was the simple and romantic idea of love in a cottage and the freedom this life would give him from relatives and family pressures. For a young man brought up in the city, the country also gave promise of a fresh start free of the gradually debilitating experience of social intercourse in London. In a society caught up with Socialism, Fabianism, Anarchism and the rest, Ford felt himself at a loss. 'I must, personally, have had three separate sets of political opinions,' he later noted.[1] That he could appear as a Tory to his advanced relatives, as an anarchist to his bourgeois acquaintances, yet in general be considered a mild socialist of the Morris variety betokened that he had really no true basis for taking any political stand. In London it was easy to alter one's views for convenience or expediency. This very quality Ford found illustrated in the anecdote concerning a relative of his who happened one day while walking along the Strand to meet a lion that had escaped from his cage. Asked by Ford what he then did, the relative replied: 'Do! Why I took a cab.'[2]

London, in short, provided too many easy ways of escaping the emergencies of life. Moreover, it permitted a writer to descant on the realities of life without actually knowing anything at all about them. If caught out, he could always take a cab. Thus it was not so much the influence of Morris that drove Ford to the pastoral life as that of W. E. Henley and his 'gang' who believed that before a man could write a genuine sentence he had first to be a man of action. In later years Ford believed that the Henley group unnecessarily exaggerated their doctrine: it was hardly necessary to spend all of one's days wandering between California and Samoa. At the same time, the doctrine was a healthy corrective for one who had been 'trained for genius': for that sort of writer, as Ford himself realized, merely looks at life without sharing it. 'This is his calamity; this is his curse.'[3]

Thus it was very much a part of Ford's intention to retire to the

23

country not merely to write but to live a life of action. Of course he never became in the truest sense a country farmer for he was always looked upon by the villagers as a representative of the 'gentry'. But he did plant his own vegetables and prune his own fruit trees. Using the information he had gathered from Professor Gressent at the Sorbonne, he engaged in agricultural pursuits: he dug in the ground with a hoe, he scythed the grass and, with the assistance of one of the villagers, turned his hand to simple carpentry and plumbing. Some of these things were done self-consciously, for Ford desperately wanted to have 'some sort of normal existence,'[4] but he knew that it was only through knowing really well at least a segment of the ordinary life of men that he could write and speak with a definite point of view.

These agricultural pursuits did not of course occupy all of his time, and he must have realized that like it or not he was destined to be a writer. By the time of his marriage, he had published no fewer than four books. Because his first book, *The Brown Owl*, had proved so successful it was followed a year later in 1893 by *The Feather*, a fairy-tale which, like its predecessor, contained a frontispiece by Madox Brown. In addition to the book of poems dedicated to his fiancée, Ford also wrote his first novel, *The Shifting of the Fire* which, like the fairy-stories, was published by Fisher Unwin.

This novel, written during Ford's late teens, shows a remarkable maturity of observation, although it suffers from imperfections in conception of character and motives. The story of a rather spoiled young girl who upon hearing that her fiancé is ruined financially, decides to sacrifice herself by marrying a decrepit old millionaire called Kasker-Ryves in order that she may inherit his wealth and eventually marry the man she loves, it obviously suffers from a basically unlikely situation. Yet in its analysis of the naïve romantic heroine, the lascivious old millionaire who learns her secret and out of sexual jealousy tries to drive her insane, and the rather bland hero, Hollebone, whose stereotyped reaction in 'releasing' his fiancée upon word of his ruin has in fact brought about most of the trouble in the first place, *The Shifting of the Fire* is not without merit. It is an interesting study of three people caught up in a situation in which Victorian codes of propriety, arrant materialism, sexual desires and romantic dreams all play with disastrous and contradicting results on their victims. Both in concept and in some of its means of presentation the book is somewhat crude, but it contains a depth of perception quite astonishing in an author not yet twenty. More than a mere attack on the hypocrisy of the age, it reveals a remarkably acute sense of the psychological implications of mores and a feeling of pity for the unwitting human beings who, having behaved according to their best lights, encounter little but profound misery.

How well the book was received is not known, except that it did not sell so well as his fairy-stories. The result was that the first book he published after his marriage was *The Queen Who Flew*, another fairy-tale, this time illustrated by Sir Edward Burne-Jones. The aptness of its title to Ford's and Elsie's elopement gave the book a certain amount of notoriety. It may have been discouraging to Ford to realize that these children's stories were more successful than his first attempt at serious fiction, but the experience he gained from writing for that most difficult of all human audiences was to prove useful later on. At this stage, however, Ford probably did not consider himself to be in training as a writer. Instead, these early books leave the impression that they were written without much thought of the consequences and that they were produced more because somebody else wanted him to write them than because he was interested in them himself. Ford's upbringing and the impression made on him by the various great figures that crowded his youth led him to prefer to start his career in a minor key. Since he had no difficulty in finding a publisher for his books and the one literary influence upon him as a young man was that of his courtesy aunt, Christina Rossetti, he seems to have emulated her quiet calm rather than to have attempted to create a sensation. Since Ford was only nineteen when his first books were published, it is hardly likely that at that age he should have formed a rationale for serious literary production. As it happened, he was fortunate to be able to try his wings with relatively trivial material, for with a goal only to be amusing, he was spared the necessity of being impressive; he could concentrate on his craft without having at the same time to be 'important'.

To contemporary eyes, Ford's early poems seem somewhat dated, and his first collection, *The Questions at the Well*, signed with the pseudonym 'Fenil Haig', consists largely of pleasant songs, none of them notably original either in subject-matter or technique. The first poem Ford wrote, 'The Wind's Quest' which was originally published in *The Torch*, gives an idea of his early style. Ford was eighteen when he wrote it.

'Oh, where shall I find rest?'
Sighed the Wind from the west;
'I've sought in vain o'er dale and down,
Through tangled woodland, tarn and town,
But found no rest.'
'Rest thou ne'er shalt find . . .'
Answered Love to the Wind;
'For thou and I, and the great grey sea
May never rest till Eternity
Its end shall find.'[5]

The poems Ford wrote during the early years in Kent, which in 1900 were collected for a volume called *Poems for Pictures*, are largely derivative. They contain echoes of Christina Rossetti and Browning, and consciously avoid big subjects. The title itself is a reminder of the Pre-Raphaelites and is copied from D. G. Rossetti's habit of writing poems to accompany his paintings. The influence of William Morris may also be seen in Ford's early tendency to borrow subjects from ancient legends. 'St. Aethelburga' from *Poems from Pictures* and the verse plays, 'Perseverance d'Amour' and 'King Cophetua's Wedding' all reflect this P.R.B. habit. Yet although these subjects and his general manner of writing seem to owe much to the familiar tradition of the Pre-Raphaelites, the experiences resulting from his personal withdrawal from that tradition also affected his work. Thus the best of these poems deal with country life in Kent, describing the marsh, the sheepdowns, gipsies and country characters. One poem in particular illustrates the degree of understanding Ford had attained as a farmer and recorder of country life.

THE PEASANT'S APOLOGY

Down near the earth
On the steaming furrows
Things are harsh and black enough
Death there is and lack enough,
And immemorial sorrows
Stultify sweet mirth
Till she borrows
Bitterness and blackness from the earth.[6]

One influence whose absence in his writing is worth noting is that of the so-called 'Aesthetic Movement' of which Oscar Wilde and Aubrey Beardsley were the leading proponents. Ford did, in fact, publish a poem in *The Savoy*, a magazine founded by Arthur

Symons and Beardsley after their rupture with *The Yellow Book*, but he was never personally associated with this famous movement of the 'nineties. The principal reason for his dissociation from the Aesthetes was his distaste both for their subject-matter and manner. He recognized that they were the successors to the Pre-Raphaelites, but, although he was almost an exact contemporary of Beardsley, he considered that the Aesthetes had 'degenerated into a sort of mawkish flap-doodle'[7] instead of perpetuating the best of the earlier heritage. Rather than write for the generality of mankind, they seemed to be writing in an increasingly mannered fashion for an increasingly specialized audience, and Ford believed that this posed a dangerous threat to English letters. Moreover, since he was himself in revolt against the P.R.B., he could hardly associate himself with the acknowledged successors of that movement.

Essentially, then, what Ford seems to have wanted most was isolation from all literary involvements, and certainly the two principal works of this period have little to do with the dominant literary attitudes of the period. The first of these projects, upon which he had embarked by 1895, was the official biography of his grandfather, Ford Madox Brown, which he had been commissioned to write at the suggestion of his uncle, W. M. Rossetti. A great deal of labour and research was involved in this book: letters had to be obtained from Brown's friends, and reproductions of his grandfather's paintings had to be prepared. Ford's childhood friend, Edward Garnett, acted as his agent, and the correspondence between them illustrates some of the difficulties of the undertaking. Ford originally planned the book as a two volume 'Life' of the sort that was normally produced as a memorial to a great man. The publishers decided, however— long after the book was under way—that one volume would suffice. The necessity of having to recast the whole book was in itself annoying, but Ford also had the disadvantage of writing at a time when his Uncle William was preparing his own reminiscences, which meant that the more interesting letters—like those between Brown and D. G. Rossetti—would be reserved for the older man's work. Yet Ford persevered and after a full year devoted to the work, had the book published in 1896. From the point of view of Ford's subsequent literary career, what is interesting about the book is that although on the surface it was an 'official' biography, and took the traditional form of such works, it also showed a refusal on Ford's part to be completely bound by the tradition. He was humorous when it seemed appropriate to be so, made use of personal knowledge and, within the framework of an official piece of writing, created an original and informal portrait.

The other book which he was then preparing, although it was not published until 1900, was a lengthy description of the Cinque Ports, the five Kentish and Sussex towns which for centuries have been united in this French phrase. Like the biography of his grandfather, this book required a great deal of research, and Ford spent many hours examining the ancient charters of the towns, reading local history and consulting the records of archaeological societies. In a letter to his friend Olive Garnett, he expressed the fear that his continual study of reference books would injure his own style, but the final version of the book was polished and urbane. In addition to his literary researches, Ford visited the five ports and the two 'Antient Towns' of Winchelsea and Rye which he dealt with in the book, and he soon came to know the people who lived in the area. Thus what emerges is not a dry county history but what is essentially a book of impressions. Since in later years Ford was so closely associated with the movement known as literary impressionism, his first attempts in this genre are worth noting. The subject of course lent itself to this treatment, but what is important in assessing Ford's contribution to the techniques of English prose is his early recognition of the need to employ the tools of a novelist in factual accounts so that they would be interesting and readable. The narrative skills he developed as a writer of fairy stories were part of his equipment; in addition, he judiciously mixed anecdote, character study, historical reference and description in order to give a vivid impression of the area.

One result of his observation of country life that was to be important in his later work was his assessment of the country farmer. Sussex and Kent, like most country districts, abound in 'characters' who, with their quaint ways and homely truths, are undoubtedly attractive to artists like Ford and Thomas Hardy. But Ford, like Hardy, was not content merely to record the quaintness of these rustics. As he studied them, he began to see in them some of the admirable qualities of human life that were rapidly disappearing in the metropolis. His admiration for these qualities went deeper than a purely academic approval of 'the simple life', however, for it came from direct observation rather than from hearsay. As he came to know these simple country people—'Meary' Walker, 'Meary'

5. Pent Farm, near Aldington, Kent. Occupied by Ford, 1896-1898, and by Joseph Conrad, 1898-1907.

6. The Little House, Winchelsea, Sussex. Occupied by Ford, 1901-1909. A plaque placed over the front door commemorates Ford's residence.

7. Mrs. Ford
Madox Hueffer,
Katherine Hueffer,
Christina Hueffer
and Ford; Aldington,
Kent, 1900.

8. Ford Madox
Ford, a pastel by
Stella Bowen, circa
1922.

Spratt, Policeman Hogbin, Grocer Rayner and the splendidly named Ragged Ass Wilson—it gradually dawned on him that these were truly exceptional people. He was never sentimental about them for he knew the harshness and misery of their lives; at the same time, he considered them, as he noted in later years, 'the best English people I ever knew. I do not think that, except for the parson and the grocer, any one of them could read or write but I do not believe that any one of them ever betrayed either me or even each other.'[8]

As he grew accustomed to the integrity of his neighbours, Ford became increasingly conscious of the immorality that was gradually seeping into public life. With the outbreak of the Boer War in 1899, political morality seemed to have come to an end, and Ford, in common with the greater part of intellectual England, deplored the opportunism of the Government in general and of Joseph Chamberlain in particular. Afterwards, he looked back on the war and characterized it as a 'chasm separating the new world from the old. Since that period the whole tone of England appears to me to have entirely changed, principles having died out of politics, even as the spirit of artistry has died out amongst the practitioners of the arts.'[9] In *The Inheritors*, the first novel written in collaboration with Joseph Conrad, he dealt explicitly with this abdication of morality on the part of public figures, and ever afterwards—in his *Women and Men* of 1923 as in *Provence* and *Great Trade Route*, two books written only shortly before his death—he pitted the natural goodness of the simple agricultural class against the avarice and inhumanity of the financiers of Birmingham and London. In this way, his experience of country living in Kent was not only to alter his personal life but was also to affect his general outlook as a writer and critic.

Two years after Ford and his wife had gone to live in the country, they decided to move from their cottage in Bonnington to the nearby village of Stanford. There they bought an old house called Pent Farm which Ford, together with the loyal Ragged Ass attempted to restore 'on the most approved lines to its original antique condition of great rafters and huge ingles with rackets and crocks.'[10] Partly the move was occasioned by the need of a larger house, for in July of the following year their first daughter was born and named Christina in honour of the famous poetess. The move was probably also made in order once again to re-establish relationships with London friends. In Bonnington they could hardly entertain at all, and Ford, in his desire to withdraw completely from the life he had known, had really entered into the life of the village, going down to the village shop on Saturday nights for a bit of gossip, or calling on the parson who despite his intellectual gifts had never been promoted to a deanery because he had made the tactical error of marrying his cook. 'The village,' Ford later noted, 'was full of sociability; you chattered over the hedgerow or from orchard to orchard. There was always plenty to talk about and plenty to do.'[11]

It was not a bad life, as Ford conceded; indeed, it was probably 'as good a life as the world had to show,'[12] but it had its limitations for a man who at heart was an intellectual. At any rate, the move to Pent Farm was soon followed by a rash of invitations to London friends to come for a visit. One of the first to be invited was Walter Jerrold to whom Ford extolled the virtues of his new domain: 'The house is a real old farm,' he wrote, 'very jolly and all the rest of it with oak beams and a number of other advantages on ceiling and floor. . . . We've got room for a small army and welcomes for a large one. (This is the old country-gentleman style up to wh. we are trying to live. It is rather difficult. We have only just moved in—last Thursday—and have managed to keep it up so far, however.) . . .' He also urged Jerrold to bring his cycle, saying that it was 'glorious country for that sport. You push up a hill—jump on, ride down—push up and so on for miles and miles.'[13]

Other visitors included Edward and Constance Garnett and their children, one of whom, David, has subsequently provided glimpses of Ford and Elsie during these years. 'At the time I first remember him,' he writes, 'Ford was a very young man, tall and Germanic in appearance, with a pink and white complexion, pale, rather prominent, blue eyes and a beard which I referred to when we first met as "hay on his face" . . .' Ford, he continues, 'was a most charming entertainer of my youth. He would suddenly squat and then bound after me like a gigantic frog. He could twitch one ear without moving the other—a dreadful but fascinating accomplishment.' Elsie, by contrast, 'was tall, high-breasted and dark, with a bold eye and a rich, high colour, like a ripe nectarine. She dressed in richly coloured garments of the William Morris style and wore earrings and a great amber necklace, and I, at the age of five, was greatly attached to her.'[14]

Other signs of a greater involvement with the intellectual world included Ford's preparation, in 1897, of a retrospective exhibition of his grandfather's paintings at the Grafton Gallery. This task, which included the supervision of the exhibition and the composition of an introduction to the catalogue, required a good deal of correspondence and a number of trips to London. Thus for the first time in three years Ford began to spend some time in the metropolis, meeting old friends and making new acquaintances. So enlivening was the experience, after the isolation of life in Kent, that by 1898 he decided to let Pent Farm to the well-known painter and illustrator of children's books, Walter Crane, and move to Limpsfield in Surrey where he took a rough stone cottage not far from the Garnetts' house.

The contrast to Kent was marked: Limpsfield was still country, but by virtue of its proximity to London it was inhabited not so much by simple farmers as by suburbanites. But in addition to the stockbrokers it was most distinguished as the country home of the Fabians. 'Today,' Ford later remarked, 'the Fabian Society is an integral part of the British Government. It was not then. Its members then wore beards, queer, useful or homespun clothes and boots and talked Gas and Water Socialism. They were the Advanced.'[15]

The Hueffers soon found themselves attending meetings addressed by Sidney Webb, Bernard Shaw and H. G. Wells, but on the whole they were not enthusiastic. They had not moved to Limpsfield to become embroiled in the same sort of activities which they had left behind them in London in 1894.

What did attract them, however, were the friendships they soon made with a number of writers who either lived in the village or visited there frequently. These writers represented the new wave whose existence Ford had begun to recognize in his solitary readings in the depths of Kent. As a subscriber to Henley's *New Review* and *To-day* he had come across the writings of Israel Zangwill, Wells, Conrad and Crane, and he realized that here was something entirely new. 'The tone of all this new literature,' he later remarked, 'was of course very different from that of Pre-Raphaelism. It was in many ways more vivid, more actual, and more of every day, just as it was certainly less refined and less precious. And I must confess that I at least revelled in this new note.'[16]

Many of these writers owed a good deal to Edward Garnett who, as an unusually perceptive publisher's reader, had encouraged them and arranged for the publication of their books. Since he had already arranged to have Fisher Unwin publish the first three books Ford had written, Garnett naturally considered Ford as one of his protégés and swiftly introduced him to other members of his circle, including John Galsworthy, W. H. Hudson, Stephen Crane, Stephen Reynolds and Joseph Conrad. Through these introductions Ford also came to know 'The Master', Henry James, who lived in the 'Antient Town' of Rye. After the quiet isolation of Kent, this new society seemed delightfully stimulating to Ford, and he soon became friends with many of the group. There were week-ends at Brede Place, the damp Sussex house Stephen Crane had rented and in which he entertained so hospitably. There were talks and walks with Henry James along the cheerless low road that connects Winchelsea and Rye, and there were frequent dinner parties at the Garnetts with Galsworthy and others in attendance. Altogether, so far as Ford was concerned, the move to Limpsfield introduced him to the world of Edwardian literature.

Of all the men whom Ford met at Limpsfield, the most important was to be Joseph Conrad. Ford had first heard of Conrad in 1894 when Edward Garnett showed him the manuscript of *Almayer's Folly*. From the beginning he was impressed by Conrad's work and, after the two men met, he came to have an immense admiration for the man himself.

After *Almayer's Folly* was accepted by Fisher Unwin, Conrad went off on what was to be his last sea journey. When he returned to England he settled in Essex where he lived in virtual solitude. He first met Ford at Stephen Crane's house, but it was at a second meeting, arranged by Edward Garnett, that he made it known how desperately he wished to leave Essex in order to live in the south where he might have company and intellectual stimulus. As Walter Crane's lease had expired, Ford was able to offer his own house, Pent Farm, to Conrad. This offer Conrad quickly and gratefully accepted.

By September of 1898, the Conrads began preparations to move in amongst the 'relics' of Pre-Raphaelism with which Pent Farm was decorated. Conrad was delighted with the prospect of a new house and wrote Ford that 'This opportunity is a perfect Godsend to me. It preserves what's left of my piety and belief in a benevolent Providence and probably also my sanity.'[17] Three weeks later he wrote again to say that 'Nothing could suit me better than to have you for my landlord. I only hope you won't find me too objectionable. . . . And in any case I could not look upon you as an invading enemy. I hope that whenever we leave Pent Farm for a time you shall step in for a matter of course; and the times also could be arranged to treat both our tribes.'[18] Soon the tone of his letters grew even more friendly, and he wrote his 'Honoured and dear Landlord' that he hoped their proximity would permit them to have further friendly concourse.[19]

ROMANCE

'C'est toi qui dors dans l'ombre, ô sacré Souvenir'

If we could have remembrance now
And see, as in the days to come
We shall, what's venturous in these hours:
The swift, intangible romance of fields at home,
The gleams of sun, the showers,
Our workaday contentments, or our powers
To fare still forward through the uncharted haze
Of present days. . . .

For, looking back when years shall flow
Upon this olden day that's now,
We'll see, romantic in dimn'd hours,
These memories of ours.

—FORD MADOX HUEFFER and JOSEPH CONRAD

Chapter Three

―――――《◆》《◆》―――――

CONRAD COLLABORATION

―――――《◆》《◆》―――――

I

IN one of the letters he wrote to Ford about moving into the Pent, Conrad had added: 'There are other big interests—not mentioned here. No room. They are big—big. The fact is I would be glad of a quiet half hour with you. I have a word for your ear.'[1] What Conrad presumably was referring to was the impending collaboration. By 1898 he had come to realize he needed a collaborator because he wrote so slowly. His English was correct enough, but it was painfully produced and somewhat stiff. He first had to translate his Polish thoughts into French and then recast his French into English. Since this procedure took so long Conrad knew he could not possibly earn a living in England by writing alone. He therefore appealed to W. E. Henley, in whose *New Review* his *Nigger of the 'Narcissus'* was appearing, and Henley must have suggested that he consult Ford. Henley must also have been aware of the dangers the collaboration might have for Ford's literary career, for he urged Conrad not to take lightly the responsibility of entering into the arrangement. To this warning, Conrad replied in part:

I have meditated your letter. The line of your argument has surprised me. R.L.S.—Dumas—these are big names and I assure you it never occurred to me they would be pronounced in connection with my plan to work with Hueffer. But you have judged proper to pronounce them and I am bound to look seriously at that aspect of the matter. When talking with Hueffer my first thought was that the man there who couldn't find a publisher had some good stuff to use and that if we

36

worked it up together my name, probably, would get a publisher for it. On the other hand I thought that working with him would keep under the particular devil that spoils my work for me as quick as I turn it out (that's why I work so slow and break my word to publishers), and that the material being of a kind that appeals to my imagination and the man being an honest workman we could turn out something tolerable—perhaps; and if not he would be no worse off than before. It struck me the expression he cared for was in verse; he has the faculty; I have not; I reasoned that partnership in prose would not affect any chances he may have to attain distinction—of the real kind—in verse. It seemed to me that a man capable of the higher form could not care much for the lower. These considerations encouraged me in my idea. It never entered my head I could be dangerous to Hueffer in the way you point out. . . .[2]

The letter concludes with assertions that Conrad would be careful and scrupulous in his dealings with Ford. 'I shall not go mad and bite him,' he says, 'at least not without fair warning,' and he promises not to sink 'Hueffer's boat.'

That two men of such different temperaments should have joined forces may at first seem surprising, but there were tangible reasons for the experiment. The Henley letter provides a good summary of Conrad's motives: what he needed first of all was the opportunity of working closely with another man on a book about which he would care relatively little. Two years before, Wells had told Conrad that he had 'everything for the making of a splendid novelist except dexterity, and that is attainable by drill'.[3] In Conrad's mind, this drill, or practice in expression could best be exercised on a work about which he could feel relatively objective, and free from the personal involvement in the theme of the story that so often tended to spoil his work. There was, moreover, a definite need for money, and Conrad believed that with the combined efforts of two men a popular book could be produced in fairly short order which would go a long way towards relieving his impecunious situation. Indeed, he borrowed considerable sums from Ford with a view of being able to repay them as soon as their first book was published.

Ford's motives for entering into the agreement were also varied. Doubtless the opportunity of working with a man he admired personally and who belonged to the new school of writers Ford not only approved of but wished to join, was important to him. Moreover, he was a naturally generous man, especially where artistic matters were concerned and, in keeping with his grandfather's injunction, he felt it a matter of simple duty to help Conrad in his work. A further reason for his willingness to enter into collaboration with Conrad is hinted at in Conrad's letter to Henley, and that is the difficulty Ford had experienced in finding publishers for his own work. Coming after his easy successes as a boy of eighteen or nineteen, this failure was a matter of some chagrin to Ford who in his early twenties had written in addition to his poems and the biography of his grandfather, at least two novels which he had been unable to place. Thus he presumably hoped that working with Conrad would help his own career as a novelist.

What made the collaboration practicable was largely the intellectual and artistic agreement that united the two men. In their first long talk together, during which each was obviously sounding out the other, they found they had similar literary tastes. Both admired Turgenev, both agreed on the importance of the novel and on the necessity of finding a new form for it. 'But,' Ford writes, 'what really brought us together was a devotion to Flaubert and Maupassant. We discovered that we both had *Félicité*, *St. Julien L'Hospitalier*, immense passages of *Une Vie* by heart. Or so nearly by heart that, what the one faltered over the other could take up.'[4]

The two writers were also alike in other ways. Because of his international upbringing and German forebears, Ford could naturally sympathize with Conrad's position as a foreigner in England. One night, for example, they went together to a London music hall.

> On that night at the Empire there were at least one clergyman with a number of women: ladies is meant. . . . And, during applause by the audience of some *too* middle-class joke one of us leaned over towards the other and said: 'Doesn't one feel lonely in this beastly country!'. . . Which of us it was that spoke neither remembered after: the other had been at that moment thinking so exactly the same thing.[5]

Thus the two men came together naturally and, as soon as Ford's lease of his Limpsfield house had expired, he returned to Kent where he took a cottage in Aldington, only a few miles away from Conrad. From the first the arrangement contained exotic elements, of which the most obvious was Conrad himself. Forty-one years old when the collaboration began, Conrad, at least in the eyes of H. G. Wells, 'was the strangest of creatures. He was rather short and round-shouldered with his head as it were sunken into his body.

He had a dark retreating face with a very carefully trimmed and pointed beard, a trouble-wrinkled forehead and very troubled dark eyes, and the gestures of his hands and arms were from the shoulders and very Oriental indeed . . . He spoke English strangely. Not badly altogether; he would supplement his vocabulary—especially if he were discussing cultural or political matters—with French words; but with certain oddities. . . . He would say, "*Wat* shall we do with *thesa* things?" and he was always incalculable about the use of "shall" and "will".[6]

A few years before he had married Jessie George, the daughter of a warehouseman and a woman of little formal education. She was an efficient housekeeper, however, and her calm manner in contrast to that of her fiery husband was doubtless essential in the upbringing of her children, Borys and John.

In contrast, the Hueffer household could hardly have been more different. Ford, at twenty-four, was still 'the longish, leanish, fairish young Englishman' whom Henry James characterized as Densher in *The Wings of the Dove*. He was, like Densher, 'one of the generally sound and generally pleasant; . . . he looked vague without looking weak—idle without looking empty. . . . He suggested above all, however, that wondrous state of youth in which the elements, the metals more or less precious, are so in fusion and fermentation that the question of the final stamp, the pressure that fixes the value, must wait for comparative coolness.'[7]

Soon the two men began to prepare for their collaboration. Ford had already read Conrad's work, and he sent his only published novel to Conrad, who after reading it, reported his criticisms.

I have read the *Shifting of the Fire*. I have read it several times looking for your 'inside' in that book; the first impression being that there is a considerable 'inside' in you. The book is delightfully young. Mind I say delightfully instead of drearily or morally or any of these things which politeness would have induced me to paraphrase. The movement, the imagination, the conviction of it are delightful (in the literary sense too).

Felicitous phrasing is plentiful and with that the writing is wonderfully level. There is certainly crudeness in the presentation of the idea. The facts, the emotions, the sensations are painted somewhat as the scenery for the stage is painted, but Youth does not make for fineness—except in inexpressible ideals, in acted dreams, in the spoiling or making of a life. Never in writing about it. More could have been made out of the situation by a more spiritual method. The analysis is however not crafty, is true and every fact is significant. That's indubitable. Nevertheless it is apparent only on reflection.

And that's *the* fault, why exactly it is so I am of course unable to say. This is a matter of fact to me only so far as it is a matter of feeling. I feel that the effects are partly lost. . . . No doubt the general cause is (O! happy man) youth—inexperience. How it worked I can't say. . . .

What is mostly obvious is the talent of the writer and that I have the sense to recognize. I need not say that I am in accord with the idea—in complete accord. Have you written far Serafina (or Seraphina?). . . .[8]

Shortly afterwards, Conrad wrote to bring the collaboration closer to actuality. They had agreed that *Seraphina*, the novel which Ford was then writing, was to be the book on which collaboration would take place and Conrad was anxious to see it:

> Come when you like. . . . You will always find me here. I would be very pleased to hear Serafina *read*. I would *afterwards* read it myself. Consult your own convenience and (especially) your own whim. It's the only thing worth deferring to.[9]

Ford made the appointment and after lunch at the Pent, he started to read *Seraphina* or *Romance* as it was later to be called. As the hours wore by, Conrad who had at first sat hunched in a chair, silent, brooding and depressed, began to groan, but Ford kept on with his account of the adventures of John Kemp. Eventually, however, the groans changed to ejaculation: 'O! O! . . . O God, my dear Hueffer . . .' 'O God, my dear *faller*, how is it possible . . .'[10] And so the collaboration began.

At the beginning, their work on *Romance* was sporadic and disjointed. Both men were writing their own books separately and only occasionally would they work together on *Romance*. After a year and a half, this sort of collaboration proved to be fruitless, so they gave the book up. In the meantime Conrad had been involved with *Lord Jim* and Ford had been writing the book that was to result in *The Inheritors*. Towards the end of 1899, Conrad asked to see this 'extravagant' novel with the suggestion that it might be suitable for collaboration.[11] What he wrote after having read it indicates the sort of difficulty they had encountered earlier with *Romance*, but it also shows their point of juncture.

> What you have written now is infinitely nearer to life, to reality than anything (in prose) you have written before. It is nearer 'Creation' than the *Shifting of the Fire*. That much for the substance. I do not want to

repeat here how highly I think of the purely literary side of your work. You know my opinion. But beautiful lines do not make a drawing—nor splashes of beautiful colour a picture. Out of discussion there may come conception however. For discussion I am ready, willing and even anxious. If I had influence enough with the publishers I would make them publish the book in your name alone—because the *work* is all yours. I have shared only a little of your worry.

Heinemann (and McClure* too I fancy) are waiting for our joint book and I am not going to draw back if you will truly consent to sweat long enough. I am not going to make any sort of difficulty about it. I shall take the money if you make a point of that. I am not going to stick at that trifle. Do come when you like. Bring only one (or at most two) Chapters at a time and we shall have it out over each separately. Don't you good people think hardly of me. I've been—I am animated by the best intentions. I shall always be.[12]

For the next few months the two men laboured hard together. In a letter to a friend, Ford commented that he was working like 'a galley-slave,'[13] and Conrad also realized how arduous and discouraging the work had been: 'What will be the end of this I can't imagine or rather I imagine only too well,' he writes. 'I don't wonder you are not disposed to write. You had some anxiety and bother—hadn't you? Would it do you good to come and talk over the last Chaps. again? I am ready for that now. The MS is in Heinemann's hands.'[14]

The acceptance of the manuscript cheered them up, however, and Conrad wired his congratulations, saying that he would make it plain to the publishers that the work was mostly Ford's.[15] When the book was published in 1901, it first received such favourable reviews that Conrad wrote to say he felt 'more and more like a thief' of Ford's cleverness,[16] adding that Galsworthy had also read the book and 'sung the praises of your art.'[17] But the period of rejoicing was short-lived: later reviews were hostile and the sales were negligible. Ford certainly was disappointed, and soon both men returned to their customary state of gloom.

The hard work in collaboration and the strain resulting from constant association frequently brought moments of despair and anger. Both partners were susceptible to the irritations and doubts that come with artistic temperaments. Conrad revealed his own feelings

* S. S. McClure, the American publisher.

in a bitter-sweet letter to Edward Garnett written shortly after *The Inheritors* was accepted for publication:

> I consider the accept: of the *Inh'ors* a distinct bit of luck. Jove! What a lark!
> I set myself to look upon the thing as a sort of skit upon the sort of political (?!) novel, fools of the N.S. sort do write. This in my heart of hearts. And poor *H.* was in dead earnest! Oh Lord. How he worked! There is not a chapter I haven't made him write twice—most of them three times over. This is collaboration if you like! Joking apart the expense of nervous fluid was immense. There were moments I cursed the day I was born and dared not look up at the light of day I had to live through with this thing on my mind. H. has been as patient as no angel has ever been. I've been fiendish. I've been rude to him; if I've not called him names I've *implied* in my remarks and the course of our discussions the most opprobrious epithets. He wouldn't recognize them. 'Pon my word it was touching. And there's no doubt that in the course of that agony I have been ready to weep more than once. Yet not for him. Not for him.
> You'll have to burn this letter—but I shall say no more. Some day we shall meet and then. . . !¹⁸*

The strain of the collaboration also told on the domestic arrangements between the two families. For her part, Elsie Hueffer began to feel that Ford was wasting his time in what was proving to be an unprofitable association.¹⁹ Jessie Conrad, on the other hand, seems always to have resented the presence of the Hueffers under her roof. This arrangement was complicated by her dislike of Ford and her feeling of social and intellectual inferiority to Mrs. Hueffer. Conrad himself seems to have been conscious of the difference between the two women, and he addressed Mrs. Hueffer as 'Dearest Señora' or 'Cara Illustrisima Padrona',²⁰ whereas his wife was always plain Jess. At any rate, to judge from Mrs. Conrad's account, the work of the collaborators was an upsetting influence in her house.

> Sometimes the two would elect to start work as we, Mrs. Hueffer and I, were retiring for the night. For hours after I had gone to bed the voices would reach me through the floor. Sometimes the tones would appear to mingle in pleasant accord, their ideas flowing easily, amused laughs and chuckles. At others sounds of wordy strife and disagreement pene-

---

* It is worth noting that Conrad must have realized the impropriety of the revelation he was making about his collaborator, since he asked that the letter be burned. Garnett did not burn the letter but published it.

trated to my ears, and raised voices came distinctly into my room. Then F.M.H., who was a very tall man, would relieve his feelings by thumping the oaken beam that crossed the ceiling below and my small son would stir in his sleep and mutter sleepily: 'Mama, dear, moo-cows down there.'[21]

In the summer of 1899, in an effort to combine work with rest, the two families decided to go to Belgium for a joint holiday. Ford and his wife and child arrived first and were joined in mid-summer by the Conrads and their small son, Borys. Together they moved on to a seaside resort called Knocke, and almost immediately Borys became desperately ill from dysentery. With the necessity of sitting up all night with the child and with the worry over his illness, little was accomplished, either by way of work or rest.

This instance of ill-luck was but one of many that dogged the two families during the years of collaboration, for virtually every member of each family was at one time or other seriously ill. At the beginning of the joint enterprise, Ford was troubled by his eyes, whilst almost for the whole time Conrad suffered from gout, an ailment which increased his irritability. Both wives also suffered from back ailments and in addition to the usual mumps and measles, the children seemed unusually prone to exotic and dangerous illnesses.

In the spring following their Belgian trip, Mrs. Hueffer gave birth to their second daughter, Katherine. Her arrival in April of 1900 necessitated a move to a larger house, and so the Hueffers rented a cottage in Winchelsea in order to be near Mrs. Hueffer's parents, the Martindales. This cottage, made of wide clapboards, similar in style to those used in the Colonial houses of New England, was on the edge of the village and provided from its back windows a fine view over the sea. As it was only a cottage, and therefore somewhat cramped for room, Ford added a large drawing-room in the rear, thus relieving the pressure on the other rooms.

This removal to Winchelsea increased the difficulty of communication between Conrad and Ford, but with the publication of *The Inheritors*, the two men decided to resume their work on *Romance*. Because the sales for the first novel were small, the second was written in an atmosphere of near-hysteria. The financial strain was especially hard on Conrad, who was in debt to Ford, and was constantly aware of his poverty: 'Don't think evil of me,' he writes. 'I am doing my damndest. I have been interrupted; I have been upset too: and generally I am not allowed to forget how impossible my position is daily becoming.'[22] Nevertheless he persevered, and their work went on:

> Anyhow, I have worked as hard as I know how. I think I'll finish my 'Castaway' tomorrow; at any rate I intend if at all possible and you will have me to come up to you for a couple of days on Monday and work there on 'Serafina'. Then Jess would come up for a night and take me home again. I think that is the best scheme for getting forward. Only pray beg Elsie not to make preparations and not to treat me as a guest— if I am permitted to come. Or are you going to London just then? Do not let me *interfere* with your *plans*. I can work here too; and shall work. Never fear. Ah! For three days peace of mind. If I had that I would move mountains. Three days only![23]

> I think I shall run down in two—in three days—and then fetch wife and boy for three weeks. Something must be done. I am finishing Falk story but with me such a statement may mean anything. You two are excellent worthy people deserving of testimonials in jewelled caskets and your own portraits in gold frames.[24]

The writing of *Romance* continued until the summer of 1902, but illness and other distractions kept it from being published until October, 1903. The reviews and sales were better than those of *The Inheritors*, and in a letter to Galsworthy Conrad mentioned that his publishers had told him that the first edition had been sold out after only one month. 'That', he adds, 'is better than anything of mine has ever done. *Et voila!* What a romance!'[25] The book was never, however, a real financial success and certainly did not live up to Ford's and Conrad's expectations.

During all the years of collaboration neither of the participants lived, as Conrad commented 'on a bed of roses.'[26] On the other hand, their life together was by no means wholly unpleasant, despite the evidence of many gloomy letters and Mrs. Conrad's reminiscences. The two men had much in common and, in addition to their joint work, they would go off on little tours of the countryside and travel up to London together. They planned elaborate joint birthday parties for their children, and always spent their Christmases together. For the amusement of their children, Ford built a little wooden water wheel manned by brightly-painted puppets that seemed to be pumping the stream that ran through his garden. While at Aldington, he also continued to play the rôle of country farmer even as he had done at Limpsfield. There he had kept ducks which to their indignation he named after the female members of the Garnett family. 'Lucy is so very greedy,' he would say, 'she always manages to eat some of Connie's share.' 'Katie was such a clumsy thing, she broke one of my tomato frames. Really I could *not* feel fond of her, so we had her roast on Sunday. Rather tough.'[27]

Thus despite the tensions that undoubtedly existed, the Hueffer and Conrad families lived together in peace. When the one writer had house guests, he would automatically bring them for a meal or tea to the house of the other, and on the whole their relationship was decent and friendly. Had it not been so, it would surely never have lasted as long as it did.

II

When Conrad first read the book that was to become *The Inheritors*, he found it attractive—'trés chic,' as he put it.[28] Its subject was political, and therefore was bound to be of interest to the man who was to write *The Secret Agent* and *Under Western Eyes*. Today, the novel seems somewhat trivial; to begin with, it is dated and, since it is a *roman à clef*, much of its interest depends on the identity of the politicians and public figures on whom the characters were based. Because it was written during the Boer War, it reflects Ford's dislike for men like Leopold of the Belgians and Joseph Chamberlain who, he believed, represented an unscrupulous new force that was anxious to sweep away the remains of traditional civilization in order to replace it by a heartless, materialistic code, by means of which they, in a word, would become the inheritors of the earth. So far as it had a moral purpose at all, the novel was directed, as Conrad later explained, 'at the self-seeking, at the falsehood that had been (to quote the book) "hiding under the words that for ages had spurred men to noble deeds, to self-sacrifice and to heroism".'[29]

What is important, however, is not the novel itself, but what it did for the two writers who created it. In later years neither men liked the book, which is understandable, but each was willing to comment on it. From the inscriptions Conrad wrote on its fly-leaves it would appear that Ford was responsible for the idea and for most of the actual writing. 'Discussion there has been in plenty,' Conrad noted.[30] 'My share of actual writing is very small in this book. No passages can be pointed out as written by me. My contribution to the whole is thoroughly mixed with F.M.H.'s prose.'[31]

Many years later, after he had himself become an experienced novelist, Ford looked back on this early book and commented on the difference between his own and Conrad's method, explaining what exactly Conrad's contribution to the book had been. He and Conrad had both tried in their dialogues to represent the indefiniteness that characterizes almost all English conversations. Ford himself had noticed that ordinary conversation in England consists of little more than allusive reference to things understood but never uttered: 'A. says: "What sort of a fellow is . . . *you* know!" B. replies: "Oh, he's a sort of a . . ." and A. exclaims: "Ah, I always thought so . . .".' In his own writing, Ford had tried to reproduce as exactly as possible this style of 'communicating by means of words.' The result, as far as *The Inheritors* was concerned was that its first draft 'consisted of a series of vague scenes in which nothing definite was ever said.' Ford said that his hope was to gain 'an effect of a sort of silverpoint: a delicacy. No doubt he succeeded. But the strain of reading him must have been intolerable.'

Thus Conrad's function 'was to give to each scene a final tap; these in a great many cases, brought the whole meaning of the scene to the reader's mind.' Rereading the book in later years, Ford said he found innumerable passages which he remembered as having been completed and made definite by Conrad. Citing a specific example, he presents the original version as he had written it, of a scene between the 'quite unbearably vague' hero and the Royal financier, and then the way in which the passage was corrected by Conrad:

‘ "You don't understand . . . She . . . She will . . ."

'He said: "Ah! Ah!" in an intolerable tone of royal badinage.

'I said again: "You don't understand. . . . Even for your own sake . . ."

'He swayed a little on his feet and said: "Bravo . . . Bravissimo . . . You propose to frighten . . ."

'I looked at his great bulk of a body . . . People began to pass, muffled up, on their way out of the place.'

The scene died away in that tone. In the book as it stands it runs, with Conrad's additions in italics:

‘ "*If you do not*," (cease persecuting her had been implied several speeches before), *I said, "I shall forbid you to see her*. And I shall . . ."

‘ "Oh, oh!" he interjected, with the intonation of a reveller at a farce. 'We are at that—we are the excellent brother—" *He paused and then added: "Well, go the the devil, you and your forbidding." He spoke with the greatest good humour.*

‘ "I am in earnest," I said, "very much in earnest. *The thing has gone too far.* And even for your own sake you had better . . ."

'He said: "Ah, ah!" in the tone of his "Oh, oh!"

' *"She is no friend to you,"* I struggled on, *"she is playing with you for her own purposes;* you will . . ."

'He swayed a little on his feet and said: *"Bravo . . . Bravissimo. If we can't forbid him we will frighten him. Go on my good fellow . . ."* and then, *"Come, go on."*

'I looked at his great bulk of a body. . . .

' *"You absolutely refuse to pay any attention?"* I said.

' *"Oh, absolutely,"* he answered.'[32]

This analysis reveals that one value of the book was that it imposed practical limits on experimentation. The reading aloud of the manuscript during the various stages of collaboration, for example, doubtless made the two men conscious of writing for an audience and therefore made them aware that what they wrote had to make sense to the ordinary reader. All along Conrad had felt that the book was 'emphatically an experiment in collaboration.' He was conscious, he added, 'that his scruples in the matter of treatment, however sincere in themselves, may have stood in the way of a very individual talent deferring to him more out of friendship, perhaps, than from conviction; that they may have robbed the book of much freshness and of many flashes of that "private vision" (as one critic calls them) which would have made the story more actual and more convincing.'[33] Yet in fact the experiment may have been more helpful to Ford than to Conrad. Doubtless the exercise of working over a work of no great intellectual importance helped Conrad become more flexible and fluent, but Ford learned the difference between a loose first draft and a publishable book.

More important to both men, however, was the many months' work they devoted to *Romance*. After preliminary readings of Ford's *Seraphina*, they drew up a synopsis for the new book; then in practice they changed whatever was necessary in order to produce a finished novel.

The synopsis opens:

The story begins in a farmhouse in Kent, goes on in Jamaica, then on the Cuban coast and ends in England.

The narrator, John Kemp, driven out of his house by his mother's severity, walks down to Hythe; falls in with some smugglers; joins them recklessly in a 'tub-raising' expedition during which the boat sinks, and is rescued by an outward bound ship.[34]

This straightforward plan underwent many changes under collaboration. As it stood, it relied heavily on chance: it was accidental

47

that Kemp fell in with the smugglers, accidental that he was rescued by a passing ship. What Conrad and Ford did to this section then was to 'thicken' it—to provide in the first place more credible reasons than his mother's tyranny for Kemp's desire to leave the house, to provide connexions in Jamaica to whom Kemp could go, to fill in the background of smuggling on the Kentish coast and to have Kemp mistakenly revealed to the British police as a smuggler himself so that he is required to leave England as a refugee rather than as an adventurer. Such changes were also required in order that every action in the early sections would have a tangible result towards the end. 'Before everything,' wrote Ford, 'a story must convey a sense of inevitability: that which happens in it must seem to be the only thing that could have happened.'[35] In addition, every detail had to be absolutely correct. With his greater experience, Conrad appears to have been more conscious of these matters than Ford, and his scrupulosity is revealed in a letter he wrote regarding the first section:

> Pray note and consider this: on page 32 Kemp *overhears* Carlos and Castro talking. I have corrected the conversation which per se is perfectly good and proper to our purpose; but in what language are they talking? Surely not in English. And how comes Kemp to understand Spanish at this stage in his adventures. Mira Vd.?
> My opinion is that the thing may pass and will pass with the general reader, but what about some private reader?[36]

Further changes were made in the synopsis that tidied up the plot and enlivened interest in the story. In the first version, Kemp's relations with the Jamaicans failed to carry the story ahead: they were, in fact, digressions, for in the synopsis these people never reappear. Thus as the two men worked together on this section, they came to realize 'that every word set on paper—*every* word set on paper—must carry the story forward and, that as the story progressed, the story must be carried forward faster and faster and with more and more intensity. That is called *progression d'effet*, words for which there is no English equivalent.'[37]

It therefore followed that one of Conrad's principal concerns in the third and fourth sections, for which he was largely responsible, was to increase the pace of the work. When he had read Ford's original version of the first of these sections he made the following comments:

48

I've studied P. III as a whole very earnestly. It is most important and it wants doing over. It must be given hard *reality*. The treatment as it stands is too much in the air—in places. I don't want to bother you now by going into the argument. I shall do the thing myself, but of course I would want to talk to you about it.[38]

In general what Conrad did was to simplify the somewhat tangled narrative of this portion of the novel. The published version is more straightforward and clear than the original, as are both the characters and their relationships with one another. As Ford had written it, the novel contained ambiguities, and the characters were not so clear and blunt as they emerged from under Conrad's pen. What is lost, then, is a certain subtlety, but the lucidity and suspense that is gained is certainly more important in this sort of novel.

The final section has been described by Conrad as being 'certainly three quarters MS. F.M.H. with here and there a par. by me.'[39] Conrad had intended to do all of it himself, but because of other commitments had to give it up. 'Vous comprenez,' he wrote Ford: 'now is your time to back me up.'[40] Again it is quite different from the original. In the synopsis, Kemp's trial at the Old Bailey was to occupy only a small portion of the narrative, but in the final version it occupies nearly the whole section and the novel ends with the conclusion of the trial. The reason for this change is not difficult to find, for since a court scene, especially one so remarkable as that of *Romance*, is important and gripping, it provides a strong note upon which to end the novel, whereas the addition of further material would be anti-climactic. Over this portion the two men worked especially closely. When he saw Ford's first draft, Conrad replied that he was 'quite struck. There are excellencies there.' But, he continued, 'it will want correcting here and there, and in places "il y a des longueurs".'[41] Later, when the proofs were ready Conrad again wrote his comments:

Here's the end of *Romance*. I beg to recommend to you earnestly the alterations and additions suggested in my set of proofs. From about half of p. 460 I have written on embodying my conception of the end, which, you'll see, is exactly yours with some alterations.

Jack [Galsworthy] (who leaves tonight) has read with enthusiasm the whole (uncorrected) part. He absolutely admires the whole of the prison scenes and especially the trial. I am of his opinion. He has said several quite intelligent things in appreciation.

I won't bother you with my reasons for what I've done; I have done nothing hastily—and the intention is obvious in every case. Jessie suggested that the reunion with S. should be made plain and (as for the temper of average readers) her opinion may be allowed some weight. As she has volunteered it I must suppose that she had felt the necessity very strongly. Upon the whole I urge upon you to accept my version or rather some version to that effect.

Jack begs that the opening of parph. '*It was rather tremendous*' should be eliminated. His very words are: that the Judge's speech *per se*, coming at the end of the admirable trial scene, has a tremendousness which is diminished by being pointed out. I propose, in case you would consider that change, that the par: should begin straight away with . . . '*My dignity*', etc. However, that is not an important point. I don't know quite how I feel. I am sure your feeling will be right. Be careful. The thing is too emphatically good to be pulled to pieces casually.

I repeat: I've only written the final scene because it would not have been quite fair simply to write you that something had to be done. This is a suggestion—the shadow of a suggestion. *You* must do the thing yourself.

My love to you all.

P.S. Be assured that I've done nothing casually. I've kept this two days. There's no use delaying any longer. I am sure you will not think that I've been wantonly interfering with quite a remarkable piece of work. Quite remarkable in execution, in conception, and still more distinguished in its suggestiveness. I congratulate you.[42]

In later years Ford wrote an analysis of this final passage which shows how Conrad's paragraphs summarize and bring together the events of the tale as a whole: they are like the formal conclusion of an essay. In other words, Conrad was repeating his function in *The Inheritors*: with his definite statement, he was giving the book as a whole 'a final tap'. Thus the collaboration was, as Ford later said, 'a continual attempt on the part of the one collaborator to key up and of the other to key down.'[43] Conrad's concept of the novel as a dramatic rendering of life was the real occasion for most of the changes and simplifications made in *Romance*, and since this novel is primarily an adventure story, his instincts were certainly right.

Yet that Conrad was sensitive to Ford's attempt at artistic rendering is borne out by his recognition that a passage by Ford contained 'the only immortal line in *Romance*.'[44]

This line occurs in a section where the judge of the Spanish court in Havana is questioning a witness from a small village:

'Where do you come from?'
'The town of Rio Medio, Excellency.'
'Of what occupation?'
'Excellency—a few goats . . .'
'Why are you here?'
'My daughter, Excellency, married Pepe of the posada in the Calle . . .'[45]

The 'famous sentence', as Conrad characterized it, 'at which we both exclaimed: "This is Genius!"'[46] is, as anyone with an eye for literary effects will see, 'Excellency—a few goats. . . .' These four words of dialogue succeed in summarizing the whole character of the villager, so that neither his physical appearance nor his manner of speaking need be described.

III

Except for a slight piece, *The Nature of a Crime*, *Romance* was the last real collaboration between the two men. This is not a cause for surprise, since the experience had taught them both what it could, and neither had much to gain from further joint work. Yet the years of close collaboration and companionship were not easily forgotten. During their work together Conrad had noted: 'It is a fact I work better in your house in touch with your sympathy.'[47] And after *Romance* went to the publishers, he wrote: 'I miss collaboration in a most ridiculous manner. I hope you don't intend dropping me altogether.'[48] Even as late as 1905 he wrote to H. G. Wells that Ford was 'a sort of life-long habit . . . of which I am not ashamed. . . .'[49]

In fact, so close had their association become that the work of the one was always before the eyes of the other. Almost until the first World War they frequently consulted each other on various literary matters, great and small. One of the services Ford was able to perform for Conrad was to supply him with ideas for stories and novels. Thus, for example, an anecdote recorded in Ford's *The Cinque Ports* was the basis for Conrad's story, 'Amy Foster'.[50] Ford himself felt that perhaps his greatest usefulness for Conrad was his ability to supply plots that appealed to him, and amongst these may be numbered the story that lies at the core of *The Secret Agent*. In addition, he urged Conrad to write *The Mirror of the Sea*, and even transcribed it from dictation. The second book of reminiscences, *A Personal Record*, was also the result of Ford's suggestion and encouragement.[51]

All through the years of their collaboration and for sometime afterwards each man made himself available to the other. Thus when a part of the manuscript of 'The End of the Tether' was accidentally set on fire at the Pent, Conrad wrote in despair: 'I need your presence if for no more than 24 hours. Il me faut mettre au coeur au ventre. You have a distressful friend. . . .'[52] And so the Conrads went to stay in Winchelsea, and through the night Ford and Conrad worked together so that the instalment of the story could be sent in time to *Blackwood's Magazine*. On another occasion, during one of Conrad's black fits of depression, Ford wrote the necessary portion of *Nostromo*, so that the novel could continue to be serialized.[53] For his part, Conrad also took an active interest in Ford's work and tried to be helpful to him on a number of later occasions. Perhaps the best illustration of the closeness of their relationship is the following letter which Conrad addressed to Ford:

> By the same post with your letter comes the enclosed. [A note from the 'Northern Newspaper Syndicate', Kendal, Westmoreland, asking Conrad for an early story that had not been published serially at 'a modest sum'.] I was going to fling it into the paper basket. Still—if you have something that you do *not* care for *in the least* send it on. I'll put in a few of my jargon phrases and send it on. As I remarked—nothing matters—and we are intimate to say anything to each other. You may as well have this modest cheque. If the thing shocks you tear the sweet note up.[54]

In the course of time the two men drew apart, and after 1909 they saw relatively little of each other. Certain individuals have tried to read much into this 'estrangement' but, as shall be seen in subsequent chapters, their separation was quite natural. What is important in the present discussion is the effect the collaboration had on each writer. In his memorial book on Conrad, Ford himself tried to assess the collaboration as a whole. He denied the claim that he had taught Conrad English, and said instead: 'When I am disposed to rate my interferences with his work at a minimum I think that I merely acted for him as a sort of Thesaurus—a handy dictionary of synonyms.'[55] Ford's function, then, in addition to supplying subjects that appealed to Conrad, was to help him towards a more easy use of the vernacular. H. G. Wells has summarized this rôle neatly: 'I think Conrad owed a very great deal to their early association; Hueffer helped greatly to "English" him and his idiom, threw remarkable lights on the English literary world for him, collaborated with him on two occasions, and conversed interminably with him about the precise word and about perfection in writing.'[56]

Conrad's attitude towards the result of the collaboration seems to have varied. While still at work with Ford he wrote to Edward Garnett that 'strangely enough it is yet my share of *Romance* (collab'on stuff with Ford) that fills me with least dismay.'[57] In later years, however, he tended to disparage the book, considering it of no real importance and claiming that it had been written merely in order to make money. On the other hand, he always defended the writing itself: 'Avouez que c'est bien écrit,' he challenged a Polish correspondent.[58] Thus the experimental nature of the enterprise seems to have proved successful for it will be recalled that Conrad had originally proposed the collaboration in order to gain fluency and that he believed he could accomplish this end only while working on a book about which he would care relatively little. In the end, he became more involved than he probably assumed he would, but this did not lessen the effectiveness of the experiment.

For his part, Ford acknowledged that Conrad had helped him in his own work by advising him to pay attention to cadences,[59] and in general he believed the writing of *Romance* to have been worth the labour expended upon it. 'I at least,' he said, 'learned the greater part of what I know of the technical side of writing during the process . . .'[60] In a letter which must be taken *cum grano salis* he also wrote: 'I learned all I know of Literature from Conrad—and England has learned all it knows of Literature from me—I do not mean to say that Conrad did not learn a great deal from me when we got going; I dare say he learned more actual stuff of me than I of him. . . . But, but for him, I should have been a continuation of DANTE GABRIEL ROSSETTI—and think of the loss that would have been for you young things . . . and think what English Literature would be without Conrad and James. . . . There would be nothing.'[61]

But these comparisons are invidious and foreign to the spirit of their association. Like most literary arrangements, the collaboration was not without strife and difficulty, and Ford's final analysis of their work together seems as just a one as can be found, since it both acknowledges the difficulties and comes from one of the participants. This is what he writes in his book on Conrad:

But in spite of these rubs of the game—and what a game for rubs it was!—our friendship remained unbroken and only interrupted by the exigencies of time, space and public events.* It is in the end better if the public will believe that version—for nearly ideal literary friendships are rare, and the literary world is ennobled by them. It was that that Conrad meant when, looking up from the play of *King John* at which he had been glancing for a little, he quoted to me, who was writing and had to turn my head over my shoulder to listen:

> '*Oh, two such silver currents when they join*
> *Do glorify the banks that bound them in*—'

and he added: '*C'est pas mal, ça : pour qualifier nous deux !*'

And by that he meant not that we were producers of great books but writers without envy, jealousy, or any of the petty feelings that writers not unusually cherish, the one towards the other.[62]

* Ford here is obviously referring to the World War. It is worth noting that at this time the two men agreed that if one of them were to die the other would act as literary executor. Happily both survived the war, and when Conrad died, his former collaborator was living in Paris and therefore was not in a position to do more than write a memorial volume, which he did.

Through all the jam, I think we must have Ford Madox Hueffer, wandering to and fro up and down the corridor, with distraught blue eyes, laying his hands on heads and shoulders, the Only Uncle of the Gifted Young, talking in a languid, plangent tenor, now boasting about trivialities, and making familiar criticisms (which are invariably ill-received), and quite absent-mindedly producing splendid poetry. . . .

H. G. WELLS—*Boon*

Chapter Four

—————《◆》《◆》—————

ESTABLISHED IN LONDON

————— 《◆》《◆》—————

T HE years spent in collaboration with Conrad ended Ford's life as a literary dilettante and turned him into a writer with professional standards. This change did not come about easily, however, and it was only after years of illness, disappointment and depression that he was able to regain an even keel. In his *Autobiography* H. G. Wells characterized Ford as 'a long blond with a drawling manner, the very spit of his brother Oliver, and oddly resembling George Moore the novelist in pose and person. What he is really or if he is really, nobody knows now and he least of all. . . .'[1] What is suggested here in jocular tones was really, however, a serious problem for Ford and one complicated by numerous distressing symptoms.

After his artistic childhood, and his escape to agriculture, the association with Conrad must first have appeared as a solution to his difficulties. With Conrad, he could be established as one of a group of new writers who were changing the whole tone of English letters. It was not too much to expect that as the movement caught on, he could become a successful and independent writer. This, however, was not to be, and except for the collaborations with Conrad, he was able to publish only three books in the eight years between 1896 and 1904, and all of these were relatively minor works. All during these years, however, Ford had been writing a good deal. His novel, *The Benefactor*, and *The Soul of London*, which was the first of his trilogy on life in England, were both written at this time, but the manuscripts sat for months on end in the desk of J. B. Pinker, the agent, and it was not until 1905 that they were published. Even when, towards the end of this period, he secured a publisher for a new book of poems called *The Face of the Night*, his sales were extraordinarily small. In a letter to Wells he observed that after three months of publication, his book had only received five reviews, three of them in provincial papers, and that as far as he could determine, only four copies had been sold.[2]

In the face of such disappointments it was difficult for Ford to know what to do. His uncle, William Rossetti, was later to drop the hint that Ford might be well advised 'to try to get into some regular *groove* of writing, apart from pursuing a wholly speculative career of authorship. . . .'[3] The suggestion arose from Ford's shortage of funds, and the difficult position in which he was placed as a householder and father of two children. Psychologically, his position was very trying: and he imagined that he was counting for little in the eyes of his distinguished relatives. Moreover, the comparative success of friends like Galsworthy and Wells must have reinforced his own sense of failure.

Perhaps, had other circumstances been favourable, Ford might have been able to come out of his gloom, but in addition to his sense of failure as an artist, he was constantly worried by his own and his family's illnesses. Of them all, Mrs. Hueffer probably suffered most from a seemingly malicious ill-health. On one occasion she had a bad fall down a flight of stone steps by the Winchelsea town gate which laid her up for many months and on another suffered from a dangerous abscess under her tongue. During these periods Ford had to cope with the children and meals in addition to his own writing. In the midst of these difficulties, Elsie Hueffer's father, Dr. Martindale, became desperately ill, so that Ford and his wife had to go up to London where they stayed in a hotel awaiting his end. Conrad, ever sympathetic, was 'staggered' by their troubles: 'to think of you hung up in that hotel, waiting under the burden of that God-forsaken errand was too awful,' he wrote. 'Indeed,' he said, 'unless one is perfectly heartless Death is no time for words. The touch of it gives a vision of the world in which words have no place; it unlocks feelings—it sets free thoughts unsuspected in form and substance—and nothing outside matters much. . . .'[4]

Conrad's words were unintentionally prophetic, for the effect of these events soon began to tell on Ford himself. In an effort to seek diversion in London, the Hueffers moved to Airlie Gardens on

Campden Hill, close by John Galsworthy's house. There the two men would meet frequently, often for breakfast. They read each other's works, and Ford submitted the ideas he intended to incorporate in his books on English life to Galsworthy's scrutiny in an attempt to test his own opinions by the 'moderate and easy views,' as he termed them, of a typical product of the English 'establishment'. Mostly, however, their meetings gave Ford the 'mental relaxation' he so needed.[5] For on the other side, there were problems of continued ill-health and problems concerning Conrad. At this time, during the early months of 1904, Conrad's *Nostromo* was appearing serially in *T.P.'s Weekly*, although the novel as a whole was not completed. Conrad therefore moved up to London where he took lodgings near Ford and for days on end he would come to Ford's house for meals and for assistance and comfort in his writing. The strain of these meetings on Ford was considerable, for Conrad was extremely gloomy during this period and convinced that he too was a failure. To encourage and distract him, Ford urged Conrad to write his reminiscences. These, which were later to appear as *The Mirror of the Sea*, Ford took down from Conrad's dictation, often at sessions very late at night so that occasionally the two men would not finish their work until 1 a.m. or so.

Despite the energy expended in these labours, life in London probably could have been borne, but at this point the 'murderous house' began to exert its malign influence.[6] A large, inefficiently designed place, it was full of drafts and thus aggravated the various attacks of influenza that one by one felled the inhabitants of the house until Ford alone remained to look after the children, do the marketing and cook, not only for Conrad but for the whole family. At length, he too succumbed and until the disease had run its course, the situation was very serious.

Ultimately, at the recommendation of W. H. Hudson, Ford and his wife went to stay in the New Forest. Ford had hoped that the stay at Stoke, a village near Salisbury, would restore his own and his wife's health. By late August, however, Ford became even more seriously ill than he had been. His mother came to look after him, but soon decided that a complete change was necessary. Consequently Ford went to Germany for some months, staying partly with relatives and partly at one of the German spas of the sort he later used as a setting for *The Good Soldier*. No one seemed to know what was wrong with him except that it was obvious he was run down and suffering from a severe case of neurasthenia. He was subjected to numerous treatments, but all that happened was that he lost weight. In the meantime, his friends in England wrote him letters of encouragement, Conrad, for example suggesting that he write him letters on Germany which he could then put into publishable shape. 'Directly I get something,' he wrote, 'I shall make a sort of expedition—A Crusade.'[7]

Ford did not follow this suggestion, but instead went to Basel in Switzerland in order to write a life of Holbein. He made little progress, however, and at the end of the year, after a series of rather aimless trips in and about Germany, his mother came over to fetch him home. He went back down to Winchelsea, but soon found the winter loneliness of the place intolerable. 'It's difficult,' he wrote to his friend, Walter Jerrold, asking him to come to stay, 'for me to find a congenial companion—tho' I'd very willingly pay expenses and so on. If you cd. manage it, it wd. be delightful for me: if you couldn't, do you know of anyone—that one could *talk* to—who could? It would be an extreme service.'[8]

Finally, in desperation, he called on Conrad's family doctor, Tebb, only to have this gloomy individual tell him that he had only a month to live. This pronouncement was of course the last straw, but instead of giving up, Ford decided to refute the mournful doctor, with the result that he soon became much better. Later he learned that Tebb had intended his pronouncement to have a tonic effect and he learned too that the cause of his physical ailment was a chronic weak heart.

But what most contributed to his return to health was the abrupt change in Ford's fortunes as a writer, for by the spring of 1905, he suddenly found himself published and well known. What happened has been described by Edward Garnett:

By the way you will be interested to hear that Hueffer has at last been boomed, boomed furiously! And has come into his own. I am so very, very glad. I think that this success may go a long way to putting him definitely on his feet.

A young enterprising firm took up his London book and brought it out with the title: *The Soul of London*. The manager happened to strike on Harmsworth accidentally—and H. read the book for 10 minutes, and said 'We'll give it a column'. The manager, most astutely, went to the *Chronicle* and *Daily News*, etc., and said 'H. is going to give this a col., what'll *you* give?' *They* said a col. and a half! etc. etc. So the boom

came off all on one day, and the glorious Press was filled with trumpet-
ings of *The Soul of London*.

It *is* very good, you know; the best thing he's done. And I hope and
trust it will definitely pick him up, for if ever a man wanted recognition,
poor Ford does.[9]

Ford himself was naturally excited by his good fortune and wrote
to Jerrold: 'The rather overpowering reception of the work over-
excited me a little and has knocked me over a little. . . .'[10]* His
health was not yet secure, but the success of his book encouraged
him, and he quickly regained the frame of mind necessary for
further work. In 1905 and 1906 he published six books including the
monograph he completed on Holbein the Younger, a sequel to the
London book and the first of a trilogy of historical novels based on
the life of Katherine Howard, the fifth of Henry VIII's queens. His
new publisher was Alston Rivers, a young firm whose manager,
René Byles, Ford had first met at the National Liberal Club. Byles,
whose energy and business imagination Ford much admired, became a close friend, and Ford noted that 'But for him it is almost
certain that I should have given up writing.'[11] The point is worth
noting, however, that it was not merely his business skills that were
important to Ford, but his enthusiasm for Ford's writing. 'He almost
made me believe in myself,' Ford later commented.[12] All of Ford's
other friends and relatives—Conrad, Wells, Galsworthy, his Uncle
William and perhaps even his wife—were all too busy with their
own work to take much interst in Ford's.

One of the first tangible results of Byles's interest was his arrangement, in 1906, for Ford to embark on a lecture tour in the United
States. The Hueffers sailed in style on the crack German liner,
Kaiserin Augusta Victoria, and soon after their arrival in New York
they were enveloped into the literary and social swim. In 1906, the
heart of Manhattan was Fourteenth Street, and Washington Square
and Gramercy Park were the most fashionable sections of town. The
city had then a certain homogeneity and intimacy that it has since
lost, and as a result, Ford as a distinguished visitor was generously
fêted. Of the many literary figures he met, the most important for
the moment was Samuel McClure, who at the time was one of the

* 'Hurrah for *The Soul of London*!' wrote Conrad from Capri. 'Brute as I am by nature
and training, I was touched by the sight of those pages so familiar in a way and so strange
now, when far away from you I went off following your thought from page to page.'
Joseph Conrad to Ford Madox Hueffer. Letter, 9 May 1905. G. Jean-Aubry, *Joseph
Conrad, Life and Letters*, Vol. II, p. 19.

leading publishers in the United States. McClure had already published *The Inheritors* and *Romance*, and it was Byles's idea that Ford should induce him to bring out American editions of others of Ford's books. In this he succeeded in part, for the year following his visit, Ford's three books on London and the English countryside were published by McClure in a one-volume edition called *England and the English*. In addition to accomplishing this mission, Ford met in the offices of S. S. McClure two people who were soon to develop into good friends. The first was the American novelist, Willa Cather, and the second was William Aspinwall Bradley, a man who in the 1920's established one of the most important and influential literary agencies in Paris and whose friendship for Ford was to prove beneficial later on.

During the time Ford spent in the United States he also visited Philadelphia, Newport and Boston. These trips were arranged for the purpose of lecturing, but along the way Ford made a number of acquaintances. In Boston, he already knew Ferris Greenslet who for many years was an important publisher and literary figure there, but he also met James Brendan Connolly, who was then famous as an athlete, soldier, sailor, war correspondent and novelist.

Of all these places, however, Ford much preferred New York and doubtless the memories of this first trip were to influence his decision to spend so many months there in the later years of his life. It was pleasant for him in a way that London was not. Boston he had found a pale replica of Hampstead, but New York was new and different without being at all impersonal. He was made much of and he had a good time. 'It isn't then to be wondered at,' Ford later noted, 'that I liked New York. I found there new health and a new hold on life.'[13]

The life of a tourist is expensive, however, and soon the Hueffers were forced to return to England. They booked passage on a more humble ship than the *Kaiserin Augusta Victoria* and were back home by the beginning of 1907. With the return of his spirits and health, however, life in the cottage at Winchelsea began to seem confining. A few years previously, the occasional tea-parties with Henry James at Lamb House and the week-ends with the Wellses at Sandgate had provided enough variety and entertainment, but now Ford began to feel strongly the limitations of country living. In *The Heart of the Country*, which was the sequel to the London book, he had remarked that the great benefit of the country was that it provided solace from

61

city living. But to live exclusively in the country was a different matter. Therefore, soon after his trip to America, Ford began to spend more and more time in London. By the summer of 1907 he took a small flat in Holland Park Avenue, which was later to serve as the premises of *The English Review*. Here the Hueffers could entertain their London friends, and with the convenience of a London *pied-à-terre* Ford could easily attend meetings with other writers. He soon began to be a frequent attendant at a luncheon group that met every Friday at the Mont Blanc restaurant in Gerrard Street, Soho. This informal club was founded by Edward Thomas and Edward Garnett and included among its members W. H. Hudson, W. H. Davies, Stephen Reynolds, Galsworthy and Conrad. Ford was also introduced by Edgar Jepson to another literary society called The Square Club where men like Belloc, Chesterton and Maurice Baring dined once a month.

In short order, then, Ford found himself at least a junior member of London's literary 'establishment'. Since at the outset of his career he had particularly avoided entangling himself with literary society, this change of habit indicates a change within Ford himself. The collaboration had been the first stage of his real apprenticeship as a writer, and his companionship with Conrad had made him conscious of literature as a career. The London experience confirmed this impression. Not content with a mere extension of sociability, however, Ford soon began to think of combining in London, as they had not previously been combined in England, the idea of writing as *métier* and the idea of writing as a movement in the arts.

Of the young English writers, Ford was one of the few who were seriously interested in the mechanics of style. Not even Conrad, with whom Ford spent hours discussing *le mot juste*, was the enthusiast Ford was on this subject. For his part H. G. Wells, who was often exposed to these discussions, was content to say, after the controversy with Henry James that arose from the publication of his parody, *Boon*, that he would rather be called a journalist than a novelist.

But Ford's whole literary experience led him to look upon technique as all-important. He knew the French novelists of the nineteenth century had been careful and self-conscious stylists and, as a naturally facile writer himself, he had learned in the collaboration with Conrad, that facility or native talent was not enough. Gradually, therefore, he began to think of writing as the French think of *métier*. He did not believe in art for art's sake; he merely disavowed ulterior purpose in art and became convinced that the function of art is merely to render life. But to give a true picture of life is a difficult task; it requires mastery of the techniques of writing so that the truth the writer sees will not be falsified by ineptitude or carelessness.

Although it took some years for these notions to mature, Ford was writing letters to his friends as early as 1900 commenting on the technical aspect of their work. One to John Galsworthy about his novel, *Villa Rubein* is typical. After commending Galsworthy for the 'distinction' of his novel, thus using a phrase Conrad might have used, Ford points out that despite this quality, the book does not contain enough inevitability and that the *progression d'effet* is not sure. 'Then again', he continues, 'there is not enough vinegar in your salad. You are too kind, too deferential to your characters; you haven't enough contempt, enough of the *saeva indignatio*. Perhaps you have not enough aloofness from them; have drawn them too much from life. Catholicity is the first necessity of a writer on men; but there must also be room enough for the reaction. Turgenev had plenty, plenty, plenty of human sympathy, but all the time he was putting in his Bazarovs and his young men and old, his maids and matrons, he knew that he, as Creator, was infinitely above them, and at times that peeped out. Let it come out in your work too. You too are miles above any of the characters you create; you must be or you could not create them. Keep that always in your mind; it is one of the defects of your qualities, of your temperament. . . .'[14]

Ford even wrote about technique to H. G. Wells although he knew that his views would irritate him.[15] In one letter concerning Wells's *Mankind in the Making*, the temperamentally old-fashioned Ford chides the super-modern Wells for his nostalgia. Wells had praised the Elizabethans for their literary achievements, and Ford's comment is 'Oh Lord! What single one of them, except Shakespeare, cd. express a clear thought clearly?' He then goes on to tell Wells that what is needed is 'to use our vernacular so skilfully that words, precious or obsolete, will not stick out or impede a reader.' For this purpose, he adds, 'slang is an excellent thing.'[16]

Thus Ford became chief lecturer on technique to his friends. To him, decent clear writing was of more importance than all the Fabian socialists put together. He knew he was almost alone in this concern, but at least he had an audience in his London friends. Soon, however, he became convinced that something more definite and influential than the writing of personal letters should be undertaken to make the English writer and his public aware of the importance of technical competence.

The only criticism Ford had himself published before 1906 were the two monographs on Holbein and Rossetti that had been issued through Duckworth's Popular Library of Art. In these books he concentrated on the techniques employed by these painters, for in art as in writing, Ford was primarily interested in craft. At the time these books were being published, he wrote to Edward Garnett, who was then employed by Duckworth's suggesting that a similar series of monographs should be published on writers:

> The idea keeps booming in my head: Why shouldn't there be a popular Library of Literature on the lines of yr. Library of Art?—conceived on the broad general idea of making manifest, to the most unintelligent, how great writers *get their effects*. As distinct from the general line of tub-thumping about moral purposes, the number of feet in a verse, or the amiable and noble ideas entertained, by said Great Writers, of Elevating and of making the world a better place.
>
> The idea, I say, keeps booming in my head—why couldn't one make some sort of nucleus, just some little attempt at forming a small heap on which people could stand and get a point of view with their hands a few inches above the moral atmosphere of these Islands. You obviously are out of sympathy with the whole drift. But wouldn't it be worthwhile just trying?
>
> I ask you, because there *is* the P.L. of A.—a sort of machinery, and there is *yrself*, a sort of centre. It's after all, the thing I've most at heart in a dismal world of falling leaves—and, if it doesn't appeal to you, I shall—I feel it really!—make a desperate attempt; of yes, a (very) forlorn hope, in other quarters.[17]

Garnett was not, as Ford suspected, interested in the scheme, so that it was not until late in 1908, when Ford founded *The English Review* that the ideas expressed in this letter were to be broadcast publicly. In the meantime, however, there was the connexion with *The Daily Mail*, which was then Lord Northcliffe's main London paper. During the Times Book Club struggle Harmsworth began publishing a literary paper to rival *The Times Literary Supplement*. He hired Edmund Gosse as editor of 'Books', as the journal was called, but after six months, Gosse resigned and Archibald Marshall, the former assistant editor, was promoted to the editorial chair. Marshall, who was also a director of Alston Rivers, then asked Ford to contribute a weekly column to the paper. Here at last was Ford's opportunity and, as he later wrote to R. A. Scott-James, 'because I have the itch to discuss Literary Topics, I had also devised for the Supplement several sets of leaders and correspondences of kinds that appeared to me to be popular and also Refined—such topics as "The Novel versus the Serious Book"; "How the Stage influences Literature"; "The Relative Importance of Technique and Inspiration" with carefully devised contributions from such distinguished authors as myself, Conrad, Galsworthy, Wells and others of my intimates.'[18]

In fact, Ford contributed some fourteen 'Literary Portraits' to this review, in which he presented both biographical and critical comments on writers like Wells, Belloc, Shaw and Mark Twain. Since the Supplement did not pay, Northcliffe decided to abandon it, and Ford was discharged. He was able to continue his weekly series, however, in another journal, *The Tribune*, for which he wrote nearly thirty articles on Continental and English writers. Although these journalistic experiences occupied less than nine months of 1907, they undoubtedly proved useful to Ford in his later endeavour, *The English Review*.

For Ford, the years 1903 to 1908 may justly be called, then, a period of consolidation, both of his opinions and of his position as a man of letters. After the terrible despair of 1904, he had slowly regained an interest in life, and step by step, his confidence in himself was restored. He had also come to realize that since his career was to be that of a serious artist, he would have to encourage others to take a serious attitude towards art, and help other writers gain recognition.

What made it possible for Ford to assume this attitude was the relative success of his own books. In the three years after 1905, Ford published books of all types—novels of contemporary life, historical novels, poems, art criticism, fairy-stories and books of travel. Among these were two trilogies—the three novels on Katherine Howard and the three books on England. For the modern reader this second trilogy has the disadvantage of seeming somewhat old-fashioned without having attained the stature of social history. Yet all three— *The Soul of London, The Heart of the Country* and *The Spirit of the People*—are still interesting and readable. In his preface to the first book, Ford indicated the method for the trilogy as a whole: 'I have tried to make it anything rather than encyclopaedic, topographical or archaeological. To use a phrase of literary slang I have tried to "get the atmosphere" of modern London. . . .'[19] Thus the trilogy is largely an impressionistic work. Lacking ulterior motive, it was not written with a moral purpose or even to extol the picturesque. The last of the three books, *The Spirit of the People*, does indeed contain generalizations that arise from the observations made in the earlier volumes. But Ford makes it plain that his views are purely personal. 'They are matters to promote argument; they are views, not statements of fact, spoken with any *ex cathedra* weight. They are intended to arouse discussion, not to instruct; they are part of a scheme according to which one thinker arranges his ideas.'[20]

In spite of the time he gave to these books and to his little studies in art criticism, Ford was primarily a novelist. By the time he was thirty-five years old, he had written no fewer than eight novels, half of which were historical. Of these eight, only three—the Katherine Howard trilogy—are of much interest today. These books, *The Fifth Queen*, *Privy Seal* and *The Fifth Queen Crowned* have a curious history. While preparing his books on London and the English countryside, Ford had become interested in the private correspondence of Henry VIII which had just been published. As the founder of English Protestantism, Henry was, for Ford, an important figure in the development of the British character and therefore by implication important for a novelist of contemporary life. He had already done considerable research into Tudor times with the intention of writing a life of Henry VIII when he discovered that someone else had already started a biography. Ford therefore decided to turn his researches in the period into a series of novels.

The historical novel presented an interesting challenge. Ford later wrote that after he had read all the facts he could find about Henry VIII in the British Museum, he suddenly realized he knew nothing whatever about Henry: 'Should I have found him affable, or terrifying, or seductive, or royal, or courageous? There are so many contradictory facts; there are so many reported interviews, each contradicting the other, so that all *I know* about this king could be reported in the words of Maupassant in introducing one of his characters . . . that he was a gentleman with red whiskers who always went first through a door.'[21]

Twenty years after he concluded the Katherine series, Ford wrote another historical novel on the hundred days of Napoleon, and at that time he considered the limitation and function of the historical novelist. That the historical novelist was not so important as a writer on contemporary life he made clear in his preface to *The Good Soldier*, but he had a certain usefulness:

> The business of all novelists is to trick you into believing you have taken part in the scenes that they render. But the historical novelist is on the horns of a dilemma: he must either present you with a superficial view of history given by the serious and scientific Historian than whom no one is more misleading, or, driving deeper, he must present you with the mendacities in which mankind perforce indulges when treating of contemporary events or its immediate fellows. For who are we to know the truth? . . . He [the Novelist] may, nevertheless, convey a sense of the truth truer than that reached by the industrious compilings of the serious—and so portentous!—Chronicler! For I bet that your sense—not your details—of medieval life came to you from Scott and your mental coloration of seventeenth century France from *The Three Musketeers*. . . . For the worst historical novelist is better for giving you a vicarious sense of existence than the most industrious of compilers of scientific evidence. And the novelist is there to give you a sense of vicarious experience. What, without him, would you know?[22]

In the characters of his principal subjects, Henry and Katherine Howard, Ford recognized two of the forces he had frequently observed in his studies of the English type. He thought of Henry as an old-fashioned Chamberlain or Northcliffe who was quite willing to sacrifice principles, including the religion of his fathers, for private gratification. Katherine, on the other hand, represented the sort of innocence and essential goodness he had found in country characters like Meary Walker. Historically, these long-suffering angels seem to be trod under by the iron heel of new ages, but somehow, memorialized in the arts and in men's memories, they survive to become the heroes and heroines of later generations and finally gain revenge over those who had defeated them.

Katherine, then, is one of the immensely 'good' characters who appear in many of Ford's novels. The rôle of the good man in modern life—how he always suffers, always is misunderstood and usually in the end hated and despised by his fellows, as Christ was hated and despised by his contemporaries—was one which especially interested Ford. Indeed all of Ford's novels up to the writing of *The Good Soldier* are variations on this theme, although none of them, except possibly *A Call* and *The Young Lovell*, treats it with much profundity or conviction. A point not to be forgotten, however, is that the *Fifth Queen* trilogy, like *Romance*, *Ladies Whose Bright Eyes* and *The 'Half Moon'*, were planned not so much as novels but as romances, tales of adventure and heroism. Conrad considered 'the whole cycle' of the Katherine books 'a noble conception—the swan song of Historical Romance . . .'[23] and that was largely its function and purpose. But even behind his romances there lay a serious intellectual concept. To Ford romance was not merely adventure and excitement. Rather it was the living of a life according to a code of morality that was ideal rather than real. This dichotomy was eventually to emerge as Ford's central concern as a novelist. While naturally sympathetic to the ideal, he realized that it was often humanly unattainable. Thus in *The 'Half Moon'*, another historical romance of the period, he attributes entirely to sexual jealousy the weird incantations of the English witch of Rye, Anne Jeal, which eventually cause the death of the hero of the novel who had inadvertently neglected to return her love. This situation, which is crudely presented in *The 'Half Moon'*, is still illustrative of Ford's central attitude. Thus his novels cut both ways: they criticize society for hypocritically ignoring its ideals, and at the same time they suggest that the ideals have too little relationship to the human situation. In the Katherine Howard novels, this theme is presented with frequently harrowing insights and, in so far as the situation concerns one of the most central figures in English history, Ford seems in these early books to have been anxious to explore the very essence of British nationality and character. Thus these novels constitute a natural sequel to the trilogy on London and the English countryside and foreshadow his Tietjens tetralogy.

Although Ford's work as a novelist shows a progression in skill his early novels vary immensely in quality. It is tempting to say that some were merely written as pot boilers, but the real reason for the signs of haste many of them reveal may be found in his relations with publishers.

That fourteen different publishers brought out his first twenty-eight books indicates the difficulty Ford had in placing his work and in obtaining good sales. In 1909 his agent, J. B. Pinker, noted that the average sale for Ford's novels was only 2,000 copies.*[24] Thanks to Pinker, Ford was able to receive decent advances on royalties, but as his books usually failed to pay for these advances, Ford found

---

* By the end of his life, Ford's average English sales had fallen to 1,500 copies, and in general, the sales were twenty per cent below the number of copies printed. Ford's average English royalties were £100 per book.

it increasingly difficult to obtain adequate remuneration for his labour.[25] As late as 1923, with forty-seven books to his name, he still had trouble in placing his work.[26] That Ford himself was fully aware of the vicious circle in which he was caught is revealed in an outburst to his agent Pinker, written in 1914:

> I have worked damned hard for many years to establish my name as a good will and that's all there is to it—conceit or no conceit. I don't need money and, unless I can get a good price, I won't sell my immortal soul to any of your blooming devils.
>
> I want also stability; I can't think it to be either good or gracious to go jumping about from publisher to publisher as I have done in the past.[27]

Unfortunately, there were many times when Ford really did need money, and the financial worry which then beset him clearly had a deleterious effect on his work. Even more trying were the demands made by publishers that novels be turned out according to certain formulae. The Pinker correspondence shows that the book trade considered literature as so much merchandise. Contracts were signed demanding a novel a year with specific deadlines,[28] and one publisher refused Ford's *A Call* because it was only 50,000 words long instead of 70,000. He pointed out that six shilling novels were always between seventy and eighty thousand words in length, and he suggested that Ford's novel be 'brought up' to the required length.[29] The tyranny of the Victorian 'three-decker' had merely been replaced by the despotism of the Edwardian six-shilling novel. Faced then with a market whose principles were roughly those of Hollywood today, any artist dependent upon writing for his income would be forced from time to time to 'produce' slovenly or hasty work. Certainly Ford did, and so did Conrad and many other writers. Thus it was inevitable, as Ezra Pound commented, that much of Ford's 'best prose was probably lost, as isolated chapters in unachieved and too-quickly issued novels,'[30] and it became impossible to 'weigh the vision' that created 'one of the finest chapters in English' against the 'weariness or confusion' that made the novel as a whole 'claptrap'.[31]

What made Ford's situation worse was that he refused to write according to a saleable formula. Interested principally in using the novel as a vehicle for experimental writing, he paid little attention to commercial considerations. His natural facility with words made it possible for him to conduct his experiments in the form of novels that would 'get by', but he was really only interested in the experiments themselves. For this reason, as Violet Hunt noticed, Ford usually lost interest long before he came to the end of a book. As an artist, however, he 'knew perfectly well the place, as it were, where they broke their backs, where he lost touch with his idea or went off at a tangent and began to hurry up because he was so tired of it. He always wanted to tear them up when they were done.'[32]

Because by nature these experiments often failed, and because they resulted in an emotional weariness, Ford, in Pound's words, 'wasted 40 novels' in which there are 'excellent parts merely buried in writing done at his second best.'[33] The ordinary reader therefore rarely found what he was looking for in Ford's novels, and Ford never became a popular success.

The novels of contemporary life which Ford wrote prior to 1910 have much the same theme as the *Fifth Queen* trilogy, but concentrate on the nature of power. *The Benefactor*, written during the collaboration but not published until 1905, serves as a model for most of the others. Conceived of as an 'extension' of the character of Ford's father-in-law, Dr. Martindale, this novel presents an immensely kind and good man who, unlike the mild and passive Katherine Howard, plays an active part in society and uses his means and position to help others. His *raison d'être* is explicitly stated: 'Seeing always, clearly enough, the ends and aims of others; never having had any very conscious goal of his own, he had always been content to step out of the way, and to supply the immense incentive of applause.'[34] Originally entitled *The Altruist*, the book is an examination of altruism in the modern world, and shows that kindness begets not gratitude but hatred. All those whom the hero, George Moffat, has helped turn, in the end, against him and, to the great joy of his townspeople, he is ruined.

A more sinister result is the ruination that encompasses all who are touched by Moffat's generosity. Madness, vile public success, self-ruin and sexual frustration come from his helping hand, for those who receive his benefactions do not understand his motives; they assume them to be as selfish as their own and react accordingly. But Ford is writing more than a philippic against modern society: he is also attacking the Protestant ethic as it is popularly understood in England. For the trouble with Moffat is that he is what Ford calls a 'Christist' rather than a Christian. Literally following the teachings of Christ, Moffat has ideals which can only be realized in an ideal world. He is too good for the actual world and, since his altruism is unrealistic, it ruins his own peace and happiness as well as that of everyone else. He is like the early Christopher Tietjens of the war novels, and his code causes so much sexual frustration and hatred that the only other decent character in the book is driven to chide him for his exquisite virtue and says: 'Self-sacrifice: doesn't that ever end?'

The Benefactor is a more serious book than its successor, *Mr. Apollo*, but in this later novel, published in 1908, Ford increases the power of his central character by actually making him a god. In a somewhat outrageous manner, Ford takes up the argument of a Dostoievsky's Grand Inquisitor and shows that even a god would be incapable of coping in a world whose basis has become so twisted and hypocritical. Although the novel is facetious in tone and imperfectly conceived, it contains the serious idea that any man who tries to act like a god, who is, as it were, a Christist, is presuming too much and is courting disaster. One of the functions of sex is to remind man that he is, after all, human, not divine.

An English Girl, the other novel of this period, combines some of the features of these two earlier novels and adds yet a third dimension, a comparative analysis of the United States and Great Britain. The contrast is limited to the alluring and comfortable upper-class social life represented by the English heroine, and the less refined but more responsible life of the young heir to an American fortune, Don Kelleg. In his American hero, Ford incorporated several of the features he had used in previous characters: Kelleg is young, immensely rich and powerful; yet as a representative of the younger generation, he is not omniscient. Unlike Moffat, who always remained on the outskirts of public activity, Kelleg is deeply thrust into the actualities of life. In common with many of Henry James's American characters, he is fascinated by the sophistication of European manners, but his delight is spoiled by a growing feeling of responsibility towards the world which had provided his fortune. His wealth is not his own creation, but he knows he cannot escape its implications. Like Hamlet with Ophelia, he would have preferred the pleasures of a quiet life with the English girl, but, since he goes 'down town' in a way the heroes of James's novels rarely do, he realizes that an English life would be incompatible with what he knows he must do.

The publication of this novel in 1907 indicated that Ford had

71

come a long way since his first writings. Despite certain lapses, *An English Girl* has a breadth of conception and seriousness of purpose that none of his earlier books possessed. The characters are more human and real than the divine Mr. Apollo or the historically remote Katherine Howard and, although technically inferior to the *Fifth Queen* series, the novel is more sustained than anything he had hitherto written. In short, *An English Girl*, which Conrad thought in many ways 'magnificent',[35] is Ford's first serious novel of contemporary life.

Its publication was alone sufficient to suggest that Ford's days as an apprentice novelist were over. His achievement as a writer together with his new position in London were gradually bringing him to the forefront of Edwardian letters. The few years that were to follow marked the culmination of this progression.

A Sunday Morning Tragedy

I bore a daughter flower-fair,
In Pydel Vale, alas for me;
I joyed to mother one so rare,
But dead and gone I now would be.

Men looked and loved her as she grew,
And she was won, alas for me;
She told me nothing, but I knew,
And saw that sorrow was to be.

I knew that one had made her thrall,
A thrall to him, alas for me;
And then, at last, she told me all,
And wondered what her end would be.

She owned that she had loved too well,
Had loved too well, unhappy she,
And bore a secret time would tell,
Though in her shroud she'd rather be. . . .

Opening stanzas of a poem by Thomas Hardy. *The English Review* was
reputedly founded in order that this poem might be published.

Chapter Five

————⟨⟨•⟩⟩⟨⟨•⟩⟩————

THE ENGLISH REVIEW

————⟨⟨•⟩⟩⟨⟨•⟩⟩————

I

THE longer Ford stayed in London, the more aware he became of the precarious condition of English letters. The situation of 1907 was probably no worse than it has been subsequently, but the general tone of literary life was certainly lower than it had been twenty years earlier. As the publishing houses increasingly stressed commercial values, literature began to be treated merely as a marketable commodity. This development in turn affected standards of literary judgement, so that criticism became largely a matter of advertisement. Almost every book that seemed likely to sell was hailed as a work of genius, and epithets of praise were indiscriminately applied to books of widely varying quality.* Thus the best writers, like Conrad or James, finding themselves considered as one with such literary lights as Dorothea Gerard and Marmaduke Pickthall, encountered a very real difficulty in supporting themselves by what they wrote.

For the novelist or poet, the situation was particularly trying since

---

* Some examples: 'There is no other American novelist doing better work. . . .' This statement applies not to Henry James or Mark Twain or Frank Norris, but to Alice Brown. 'She has won a secure place in the minds of serious students of American fiction. . . .' Again, not Ellen Glasgow or Mrs. Wharton, but Mary S. Watts. Perhaps the best illustration of the profundity of literary criticism at the time is a statement from a review in the Chicago *Herald*: 'Here is a book that must be read to be properly appreciated.' These statements appear in the endpapers of Macmillan's (of New York) edition of George Moore's *Brook Kerith*, as advertisements of their current novels. It may safely be added that London journals were as absurd as the American ones here quoted, if perhaps not quite so funny.

even the few journals that had literary pretensions tended to ignore fiction and poetry, concentrating instead on books of travel, biography and philosophy. The younger writers suffered most of all. The inhospitable reception given them by *The Athenaeum*, *The Times Literary Supplement* and *The Quarterly Review* not only discouraged them but hurt their sales. The hostility of these and other magazines was due in part to the distrust of art that had risen in Great Britain after the aesthetic movement of the 1890's and Oscar Wilde's trial, but it also existed because there were no journals with true literary standards capable of exerting a corrective influence. The entrenched interests never reform themselves of their own accord. At the turn of the century, W. E. Henley's *New Review* had provided an intelligent and sympathetic forum for the best writers of that period, but Henley had died in 1903, and no one had come forward to take his place. The times, however, were by no means unpropitious for the establishment of a new literary magazine: contributors were available in sufficient numbers and, thanks to the writings of Kipling, Stevenson and Henley himself, the general public had to a large measure got over its distrust of the arts.

As Ford learned more of the inner workings of literary London, he became convinced of the necessity of taking some action which would at once ensure a regular income for those of his talented contemporaries who were in some need, and provide a centre for the revival of English letters as a whole. Perhaps because of his Pre-Raphaelite background, which had taught him the value of joint effort, Ford was particularly conscious of the results that could be obtained through coöperation. Having recognized the talent of such seemingly diverse writers as Cunninghame Graham, James and Wells, he had also expressed, both in private correspondence and in the articles he wrote for Northcliffe's book review, his concern for a conscious literary attitude and movement. But he was now anxious to bring these writers together in a tangible manner, for their mutual benefit and for the benefit of literature generally.

Not alone in this concern, Ford had already, by January of 1908, discussed with H. G. Wells the possibility of starting a magazine which would, amongst other things, publish Wells's new novel, *Tono-Bungay*.[1] The original idea was that Ford and Wells would be joint proprietors and editors and that the first number would be published in February of 1908. Ford was full of high hopes, but for his part Wells asked for delays and procrastinated over his rôle in the enterprise. Finally, when he realized that he could not depend on Wells, Ford approached a friend of his from Winchelsea, a man by the name of Arthur Marwood who came from an old Yorkshire family and who had read mathematics at Cambridge. He was also interested in the arts and in worthy projects, however, and was therefore sympathetic towards the proposed review. According to Ford, this general interest was converted into action when one day Marwood came to his house with the news that every review in London had rejected a new poem by Thomas Hardy called 'A Sunday Morning Tragedy'. This fact so shocked him, apparently, that he was determined then and there to start a review so that this poem and others like it might be published. While perhaps apocryphal, the story is symbolically true, for soon afterwards the two men pooled their resources and undertook the proprietorship of a new literary magazine.

From the beginning, Ford wanted the review to serve as a rostrum for a new literary movement: he continually consulted friends like Wells and Galsworthy, and the whole first number of the magazine was put together one night at Conrad's house in the country. 'I shall never forget the cold of that night,' Conrad later recalled, 'the black grates, the guttering candles, the dimmed lamps—and the desperate stillness of that house, where women and children were innocently sleeping, when you sought me out at 2 a.m. in my dismal study to make me concentrate suddenly on a two page notice of the *Ile des Pingouins*. A marvellously successful instance of editorial tyranny!'[2] To provide offices for the review, Ford converted his flat in Holland Park Avenue, and there, over a fishmonger's shop, he lived and managed the review's business. He contrived to give an aura of tradition to the place by lining the stairs with Pre-Raphaelite engravings by Madox Brown and Rossetti and with drawings of Conrad and others by Rothenstein, and by the door he placed a gilt plaque which read 'English Review, Ltd.' Despite its strange location and the frequency with which it was assailed by beggars, thieves and refugees from the Czarist secret police, it soon became one of the literary salons of London, as much at home to Thomas Hardy and Arnold Bennett as to Ezra Pound and W. B. Yeats.

The first thick number of the review, bound with heavy blue covers, was published in December of 1908 and sold for half a crown. Unlike many magazines which after an exciting opening number tend to peter out in subsequent issues, *The English Review* published in its first issue a selection of writing that was to be typical of its entire first year. Its table of contents is therefore worth quoting in its entirety. The review opened with Hardy's poem, 'A Sunday Morning Tragedy', and this was followed by Henry James's story, 'A Jolly Corner'. Then came the first portion of Joseph Conrad's *Some Reminiscences*, Galsworthy's short story, 'A Fisher of Men', a travel article on Stonehenge by W. H. Hudson, a translation by Constance Garnett of Tolstoi's 'The Raid' and the opening chapters of Wells's *Tono-Bungay*. The remaining section of the magazine included a critical essay on Henry James, articles on social questions by Cunninghame Graham, W. H. Davies, Arthur Marwood, H. W. Nevinson and a few reviews, including one by Conrad of Anatole France's *Ile des Pingouins*.

Later numbers maintained this high standard. Number three, for example, contained contributions by Gerhart Hauptmann, W. B. Yeats, Walter de la Mare, R. H. Mottram, John Galsworthy, Norman Douglas, Granville Barker, Joseph Conrad, Vernon Lee, H. G. Wells, the Ali Khan, R. A. Scott-James and F. E. Green; while Number Seven included Galsworthy, Gerald Gould, Eden Philpotts, Ezra Pound, Ella D'Arcy, Wyndham Lewis, Conrad, H. M. Tomlinson, Stephen Reynolds, Hilaire Belloc and Edward Thomas.

So long as Ford remained in complete control of the magazine, imaginative literature occupied most of its pages, and only a small number were devoted to reviews, criticism and general articles. Later on, under new proprietors, Ford was forced to enlarge the section containing 'serious literature', but his first policy was clear: since there were already plenty of heavy quarterlies full of articles on economics and politics, *The English Review* was to be a truly literary magazine. Each issue of the review normally opened with a section of verse by two or three different poets because, as Ford later explained, 'we acknowledged that verse writing was the Senior Service'.[3] These poems would be followed by an essay or travel article, which in turn would be followed by a short story and a portion of the serial then being run: in the first numbers it was Conrad's *Some Reminiscences*. Ford realized that nobody liked serials but thought the publicity the author received made up for the disability. The magazine would then close with more short stories, perhaps another serialized book like Wells's *Tono-Bungay*, and a few short articles. This method of alternating types seems deceptively simple, but in his letters to Edward Garnett and Arnold Bennett, Ford showed that he had a carefully worked-out plan, whose purpose was to introduce a slight shock to the reader's interest so that he would approach each piece in a fresh frame of mind.

Ezra Pound has written that one reason for the success of *The English Review* was the existence of a group of writers of high quality upon whom Ford could depend to maintain his standards. More important, however, was the editor's instinctive eye for good writing. In her book of memoirs, Violet Hunt recalls the first time she brought a sheaf of her manuscripts to the editorial office. Ford sat with them, opening and shutting them and glancing at a page here and there, without reading any of them straight through. Then he suddenly made his selection. At other times he would go with his sub-editor, Douglas Goldring, to the nearby Empire Theatre where, during the duller turns, he would make his choices from the manuscripts Goldring had brought along. While such methods of editing seem haphazard and irresponsible, Ford has explained his peculiar ability to choose quickly. In an article on D. H. Lawrence, he describes how he chose the short story *Odour of Chrysanthemums*. If, he writes, the first few sentences show that the author's subject is to be a clear and careful projection of life as it is, and if the opening words set the tone of the story and give enough information, then you needn't read further. 'You can pitch the story straight away into your wicker tray with the few accepted manuscripts. . . . Because this man knows. He knows how to open a story with a sentence of the right cadence for holding the attention. He knows how to construct a paragraph. He knows the life he is writing about in a landscape just sufficiently constructed with a casual word here and there. You can trust him for the rest.'[4]

This method might not work for other editors, but it certainly worked for Ford and *The English Review* since, in terms of literary history, the magazine is probably most famous for the 'discoveries' it made. Of the hitherto unknown writers whose first work was published in *The English Review*, the appearance of D. H. Lawrence was probably the most important while that of Wyndham Lewis was the most spectacular.

In 1909 Lawrence was an assistant-master at a board school in Croydon. He had submitted some of his poems to the Nottingham University *Magazine*, but when they were rejected, Mrs. Lawrence sent them to the new *English Review*. When the poems arrived at

Holland Park Avenue, they caused a great stir. Asked by his secretary, 'You've got another genius'? Ford replied, 'It's a big one this time."[5] According to Violet Hunt, Ford was 'beside himself with pleasure at his discovery,' and the poems, written very close and in pencil, went in 'in chunks,' appearing as the first item in the November 1909 issue.[6] Although Lawrence and Ford were never particularly friendly, Lawrence recorded his debt to Ford by thanking him for printing his first work and describing him as the first man he had ever met 'who had a real and true feeling for literature.'[7]

Norman Douglas was introduced to the review by Joseph Conrad, and his contributions were enthusiastically received by Ford who even, in later years, described Douglas' short piece 'Sirens' as 'the most beautiful thing we printed.'[8] Eventually Douglas became sub-editor of the review and acknowledged that its reputation was wholly due to Ford, crediting it to his 'infectious enthusiasm and flair for literature. . . .'[9]

Another of the 'discoveries' appeared in an extremely mysterious manner. One day in the spring of 1909, while Ford and Marwood sat together despairing over the quality of the May number, to their consternation a weirdly-clad figure entered the office. He was dressed in a long black coat and was bundled up with scarves. Ford took him to be a Russian anarchist and exclaimed that the review was not interested in publishing accounts of the secret police. But the visitor said nothing and merely drew from his voluminous pockets several bundles of manuscripts. These he presented to the editor and silently withdrew.

When he had recovered from his surprise, Ford began to look at the manuscripts and then with joy realized that the success of the May number was assured. Thus Wyndham Lewis was introduced to the world with the publication of his short piece, 'The Pole'. In later years Lewis, who was never one to praise without reason, wrote that he thought Ford 'as good an editor as could be found for an English literary review. He had by birth artistic associations and could write himself much better than most editors.'[10]

Another writer whose first work was published in *The English Review* was H. M. Tomlinson who, like a number of other young men, 'les Jeunes' as Ford used to call them, had seen the new magazine and, immediately recognizing its quality, sent his manuscripts to it and contributed to making it a success.[11] Naturally Ford balanced his support of the young by securing contributions from such 'world figures' as he termed them as President Taft and Anatole France, and he also printed the poetical 'remains' of Swinburne and Rossetti. Yet his real interest was with the young—so much so that, with Lawrence and Pound and Lewis and Cannan, *The English Review* really became the centre of a revival in English letters. While consolidating and confirming the reputations of older writers, it also inspired new movements among the younger writers and was ultimately responsible for Imagism and Vorticism.

But despite its literary success, the review was an economic failure. Part of the fault must be attributed to Ford who badly neglected the business aspect of his enterprise. Although admittedly inexperienced in financial matters, he tried to look after circulation and advertising himself. Then realizing after some months that he hadn't the time to devote to them, he tried to find a business manager, but instead of securing an expert, he engaged another writer, Stephen Reynolds, whose actual occupation was that of fisherman. As Violet Hunt said of the editor, 'He seemed like an infant in charge of a motor-car. . . .'[12] Ford had realized that his plan to run the magazine on a profit-sharing basis would cause quarrels and recriminations but, as he wrote to Edward Garnett, 'in some things I am an idealist and my ideal is to run the "English Review" as far as possible as a socialistic undertaking. The kicks I shall get will be the price I shall pay for indulging my idealism and these I trust to bear with equanimity.'[13] Soon enough Ford become involved in wrangles with his contributors. He quarrelled with Arnold Bennett, for example, because Bennett had submitted his 'Matador of the Five Towns' through an agent, an action Ford considered insulting to his personal friendship with Bennett. These rows made for bad blood and acted as a tremendous nervous strain on Ford.

By August of 1909, his idealism had taken its toll: the £5,000 put up by Marwood and himself was exhausted, and Ford decided to suspend operations.* At this juncture, his brother-in-law, David Soskice, undertook to form a syndicate that promised to continue the review without interfering with the editorial policy, and at the same time to pay Ford a salary as editor. To these arrangements Ford naturally agreed, because he still hoped the magazine would be able to provide space for distinguished writing. Soon, however, the arrangement became unsatisfactory. Ford discovered he was to be paid nothing for his services and once, after returning from a brief

*Ford's share was £2,800; Marwood's £2,200.

journey to France, he found Galsworthy installed in his editorial chair. Galsworthy left, and there was no ill-feeling between the two men, but Ford soon realized that the syndicate wished to use the review almost entirely for political purposes, and he was forced to turn over space that had formerly been given to imaginative literature to articles of propaganda for the Liberal Party.

In a desperate attempt to save the magazine, Ford tried to find a buyer who would continue to publish the review along its original lines. Amongst those approached was S. S. McClure of New York, but even Willa Cather's support of the scheme failed to convince him. Finally Violet Hunt persuaded Lady Mond, the wife of the munitions magnate, to buy it. The inner story of this manipulation is complex and involves highly personal matters, but the upshot was that the Monds bought the magazine and then, contrary to Miss Hunt's intention, discharged Ford and installed Austin Harrison as editor. For a while, thanks to Ford's decency in helping the new editor, the review maintained respectable standards, but soon it began to deteriorate. By 1912, according to Sir Compton Mackenzie, it had sunk to 'the bottom of mediocrity'[14] and by 1913, D. H. Lawrence sadly noted how 'piffling' it had become.[15]

However convenient it would be to blame the collapse of Ford's review on financial mismanagement, it would be an over-simplification of London literary life to do so. What happened was that many of the old guard, finding their positions under attack by the young, adopted a hostile attitude towards the review, while the incompetents clubbed together to cry it down. For when *The English Review* first appeared it was clear that it had standards and as a result it made a definite impression. In his book on the Georgians, Frank Swinnerton described the excitement with which it was read.[16] For the first time in many years, he wrote, English literature was treated as something that was as important and exciting as politics and sports. The review was therefore a threat to the established journals and, to save themselves, their proprietors reacted as expected.* With characteristic vigour, Ezra Pound summed up the situation by comparing Ford with T. E. Hulme. 'Hulme wasn't

---

* An examination of the files of *The Spectator* which commented on the review over the months illustrates their point of view. Such adjectives and phrases as 'remarkable only for its offensiveness', 'meaningless except for its profanity', 'squalid writing' and 'strange medley' are found frequently in its reports. At least *The Spectator* had the gumption to comment; other journals like *The Times Literary Supplement* and *The Athenaeum* pretended *The English Review* did not exist.

hated and loathed by the ole bastards,' he wrote, 'because they didn't know he was there. The man who did the *work* for English writing was Ford Madox Hueffer (now Ford). The old crusted lice and advocates of corpse language knew that *The English Review* existed.'[17]

What did they do? Some of the older men who were not asked to write for the review were so insulted that they slated the review and attacked Ford's character in private. The younger critics, on the other hand, submitted their manuscripts with the expectation that they would be printed. At this point they encountered Ford's standards which were, as Wyndham Lewis said, '. . . too exacting for latter-day England.'[18] The consequences, here described by Edgar Jepson, were inevitable:

> Ford demanded a quality of writing in that review such as no review had demanded before, or has since, and it was by that demand that he so hindered the recognition and advancement of his novels. As editor he rejected the work of so many critics. For the life of me I do not see what else he could have done; there was his standard of writing, and they could not reach it. I felt sorry for them, for they tried so hard to write. But after all it is hardly fair to expect a man, who makes it his business to teach other people to write, to be able to write himself.[19]

Many of these disappointed critics, of whom several were men of power and influence in the literary life of London, took their revenge by denigrating both Ford and his review. Ford himself was soon aware of the hostility and believed that *The Times Literary Supplement* 'had a down on him.'[20]

Yet the collapse of the review cannot wholly be attributed to the revenge of critics, and there is no question that Ford engaged in a number of squabbles. Since many of these were with his closest associates, they were to prove costly to himself and his enterprise. In addition to the relatively unimportant spat with Bennett, Ford quarrelled with both Wells and Conrad. The cause of the first disagreement was the extent of Wells's financial participation in the review, but Ford made matters worse by writing to Mrs. Wells an abusive letter in the course of which he asserted that while Wells was free to rob him personally, he had no right to damage the review. He had come to realize, he added, that he should never have trusted Wells in the first place. The cause of the squabble was Wells's desire to publish *Tono-Bungay* in book form before the serialization of the novel was completed in *The English Review*, and thus Ford had reasons for complaining, but his method of approach was hardly conducive to improving the situation.[21]

The Conrad row, which in its way was more serious and left deeper scars, occurred because of Conrad's failure to supply the portion of *Some Reminiscences* that was due for the July 1909 number. Hearing that Conrad was ill, Ford inserted a note saying that owing to Conrad's 'serious illness' the series would be postponed. Conrad then broke into a fury and complained to Garnett that '*indisposition* was a quite strong enough word for all practical editorial purposes.'[22] On the face of it, this quarrel would not appear a very serious one, but because *Some Reminiscences* was so intimately connected with the very essence of *The English Review* it had lasting consequences. During the years following the publication of *Romance*, Conrad and Ford had continued their collaboration in a sporadic fashion, and their third joint book, *The Nature of a Crime*, was published pseudonymously in *The English Review*. In addition, Ford helped Conrad with several of his own books and considered that one of the real purposes for founding his review was to give Conrad an outlet. For this purpose he urged him to write *Some Reminiscences*, and that book in turn became central to the review itself. In order to get him started, Ford induced Conrad to leave the Pent, where he found it difficult to write, and to come over to Ford's house a few miles away at Aldington, where he could concentrate on his work. At the time, Conrad was convinced that he would never make any money from his writing, but since Ford was paying him more than he had ever received before for his contributions to *The English Review*, Ford did not take Conrad's pessimism seriously.[23] Thus as the 'result of a friendly suggestion, and even of a little friendly pressure,' to use Conrad's own words, the various portions of *Some Reminiscences* came to be written.[24]

Yet writing a book in these circumstances was hardly likely to be a smooth operation, for as Ford later observed, Mrs. Conrad was even more opposed to the idea than Conrad was. Moreover, Conrad was afflicted by gout and thus given to violent explosions of temper. In the end he used Ford's announcement of postponement as an excuse to suspend the serial publication of *Some Reminiscences* altogether. The real reason was, however, that as a Pole he objected to the presence of Ford's brother-in-law, a Russian, as head of the syndicate that owned the review. In his concern for the review and his realization of its increasingly precarious financial situation, Ford then told Conrad that his withdrawal had ruined the chances of S. S. McClure's purchase of the review. This development enraged Conrad who then wrote to Pinker about Ford saying:

> His conduct is *impossible*.... He's a megalomaniac who imagines that he is managing the Universe and that everybody treats him with the blackest ingratitude. A fierce and exasperated vanity is hidden under his calm manner which misleads people ... I do not hesitate to say that there are cases, not quite as bad, under medical treatment. ...
> Generally he is behaving like a spoilt kid—and not a nice kid either.[25]

Regardless of who is to blame for these quarrels, they certainly had a bad effect on *The English Review* and on Ford himself. In the incident noted above, Conrad seems to have been principally at fault, but the growing antagonism that existed between Ford and his associates was due in considerable part to Ford's own personality. Richard Aldington, one of Ford's younger friends at the time, has since observed that:

> Ford had what the old-school-tie people of pre-14 considered an 'offensive manner', and naturally a man who thought literature more important than cricket and money was a bounder. ...
> But—remember—Ford *was* offensive, talking under his breath to try to make people crane to listen, swanking, bragging, maligning—a village blacksmith of scandal. ...[26]

Wyndham Lewis, another young contributor to the review, described Ford as a 'flabby lemon and pink giant, who hung his mouth open as though he were an animal at the zoo inviting buns' and said that he acted like 'one of those military *sahibs* who used to sit on the balcony of a club in Hindustan with two or three other *sahibs*, *stingahs* at their sides ...' who behaved as though they were 'among the more swagger representatives of white empire in Asia.'[27]

Even with giving due allowance to personal animosity, these characterizations do not present Ford in an agreeable light. Nevertheless, it is possible without making an excursion into amateur psychology to see why Ford behaved in the way he evidently did behave. For many years, as we have seen, he was extremely doubtful of his own gifts, and in comparison to his well-known relatives and successful contemporaries, felt that he was a failure. Gradually, however, he had become deeply attached to the literary profession and then, almost overnight, he was a success. At the remarkably early age of thirty-five, he became the heart and centre of the most lively literary movement England had experienced in many years. He was intimate with the great and a figure of consequence in literary circles. He had, in a real sense, arrived. Because of the suddenness of his success he was doubtless very conscious of it and, as one who had long felt inferior, he now gloried in his superiority. Hence his tendency to assume attitudes and engage in gossip.

Contributing to these mannerisms was Ford's eccentricity, a trait he shared with a number of other literary figures of the turn of the century. As H. E. Bates has noted, 'eccentricity in literary men was the vogue,'[28] and Violet Hunt observed that both Conrad and Ford cultivated phobias of one sort or other.[29] Thus the pattern of eccentricity that Mr. Bates particularizes:

> To be devastatingly witty, unconventional and abominably rude; to pretend not to understand a name, a simple remark or a line of argument simply in order to twist it round and make a conversational conceit of it; to lambast the conventionalities, the proprieties and the bourgeois habits of the day; to make of oneself an outsize in character, as Dr. Johnson and Byron and Wilde and so many others did in the days before young writers shot each other down from thirty thousand feet or blew each other to pieces in rat-filled trenches; to compensate oneself for a lack of creative genius by exploiting a tremendous gift of the gab. . . .[30]

While these generalities do not exactly fit Ford, there is little doubt that as a young and successful editor, he was given to at least some of these mannerisms. That he was vain was likely and, according to Wyndham Lewis, necessary, but he never used the review for his own benefit and never even had his name as editor printed in the review. To that extent he really was, as Henry James had called him, 'un jeune homme modeste'. Nevertheless, he was pleased to be able to assemble in his tiny flat above *The English Review* offices most of the distinguished literary names in England, and he enjoyed giving dinner parties for Henry James or Arnold Bennett, Thomas Hardy or W. H. Hudson. David Garnett, a young man at the time, attended one party at which all 'who were invited were poets who had to compete for a crown of bay-leaves by writing *bout-rimés*. I did not know by any means all of the celebrated figures present at this contest, but they certainly included Ezra Pound, who had just appeared in literary London, wearing one earring, which was considered very scandalous by certain ladies. Dollie Radford won the first prize and looked very much like an Italian painting in the crown of bay-leaves;

Hilaire Belloc won the second prize and Mrs. Gordon Woodhouse afterwards played the harpsichord.

'There were many others present, more distinguished, for it was Ford's greatest period, when he could get hold of anybody.' Altogether, Mr. Garnett has remembered Ford as 'an outstanding figure in literary London; he was arrayed in a magnificent fur coat; wore a glossy topper; drove about in hired carriages; and his fresh features, the colour of raw veal, his prominent blue eyes and rabbit teeth smiled benevolently and patronizingly upon all gatherings of literary lions.'[31]

Underneath, of course, there were grave doubts, and Violet Hunt has told of how, after all the guests had departed, 'the editor was left with a few broken sandwiches and half cups of tea, with which nothing could be done till morning, sitting by his dying fire and an empty coal scuttle that he was too lazy to go out and replenish, or thumping his piano and shouting, "Madam, will you walk?" for his own dreary amusement and company. Mrs. Chandler, in her room below, who pitied him, has often told me this.'[32] David Garnett has recounted a similar episode when, after the two had had a cheerful tea together, Ford became melancholy and began to sing a few sad songs, including an old Westmorland song about the old horse who is neglected and spurned in his old age. Upon finishing it, Ford turned to Garnett and said: 'I am that poor old horse, David. I am old, and I am cold, David. And I am no longer fit for anything. They do not pity me, David, but throw me aside. . . .'[33]

Extremes of temperament are natural to most writers, but because of his unusually vivid imagination, Ford suffered from them more than most do. He was very sensitive about his position, and adverse criticism touched him deeply. H. G. Wells must have been aware of this aspect of Ford's character when he wrote to G. K. Chesterton: 'I hate these attacks on rather miserable exceptional people like Hueffer and Masterman. I know they aren't perfect men but their defects make quite sufficient hells for them without these public peltings.'*[34] Because, to use Ford's own phrase, 'the heart of

* The attack referred to was a review in the *New Witness* of Ford's and Violet Hunt's *Zeppelin Nights*, by J. K. Prothero, the pseudonym for Ada Elizabeth Jones, who later married Cecil Chesterton. Amongst her more offensive observations was this statement: 'It is generally supposed that Mr. Hueffer is not exactly of pure European extraction, and this book seems certainly to confirm such impression . . . the writer's fear of bodily hurt is more accute than one associates with men of our blood.' At the time of this notice —January 1916—Ford was in training with the Welch Regiment.

another is a dark forest,' many of Ford's acquaintances never realized what lay beneath the various personae he adopted or why he often acted in a seemingly irrational and certainly trying manner. Both Stephen Crane and D. H. Lawrence realized his true nature, however, and Crane once answered a complaint about Ford's arrogance by writing: 'You are wrong about Hueffer. I admit he is patronizing. He patronized his family. He patronizes Conrad. He will end up by patronizing God who will have to get used to it and they will be friends. . . .'[35] Lawrence, in turn, wrote to Violet Hunt that although Ford appeared to be tiresome, 'He is really such a lot better fellow than he thinks he ought to be, to belong to this shabby state of things, but he daubs his dove-grey kindliness with a villainous selfish tar, and hops forth a very rook among rooks, but his eyes, after all, remain like the Shulamite's, dove's eyes.'[36]

Despite the complexity of relationships to which Ford's personality certainly contributed, the failure of *The English Review* must in the end, as Richard Aldington says, 'be laid to the stupidity and genuine hatred of culture displayed by our countrymen.'[37] For petty squabbles cannot explain why the circulation of the review hardly ever rose above 1,000 copies a month.[38]

Yet for all its ups and downs, Ford was not—at least in later years —dissatisfied with the result of his editorial labours. 'To some extent that undertaking had justified its existence for me,' he wrote. 'It had got together, at any rate between two covers, a great number—the majority of the distinguished writers of imaginative literature in England of that day and a great many foreign writers of eminence.'[39]

When Ford handed over his review to the new editor, the event was noted by Arnold Bennett who, in praising Ford for his achievement, also summarized what *The English Review* had come to mean:

In fifteen months Mr. Hueffer has managed to publish more genuine literature than was ever, I think, got into fifteen numbers of a monthly review before. . . . Mr. Hueffer's enterprise, audacity, and expertness ought to be recognized in some formal public manner. As a haven for Literature the 'English Review' has been unique, absolutely.[40]

II

Originally, when in the summer of 1907 Ford took the maisonette in Holland Park Avenue, he had intended it not as a bachelor *pied-à-terre* but as a London residence suitable for his wife and children as well. Soon, however, the flat proved too small and cramped for them all, and so Mrs. Hueffer, whose health was precarious and who was by temperament a country-dweller, moved back with the children to Sussex. After a while she sold the Winchelsea house and took another place called Hurst Cottages in Aldington. There Ford would go for visits, but as *The English Review* got under way, he was forced to spend more and more time in London. His bachelor life there might have been supportable had he not been plunged into so many worries connected with the review. But living alone in the office-flat, he naturally became depressed and gloomy when, for all the glamour of the undertaking, it seemed on the point of failing.

It was at one of his lowest moments that Violet Hunt suddenly came to the rescue and embarked Ford and herself on one of the most highly-publicized and unfortunate romances of contemporary English literature. The daughter of Alfred Hunt, a well-known water-colourist, Violet shared the same Pre-Raphaelite background Ford had grown up in, and therefore was sympathetic towards him as few of his contemporaries were able to be. Furthermore she had money of her own and a position in Society. Together with her mother, Mrs. Alfred Hunt, who was herself a female novelist of some reputation, she lived in a house on Campden Hill called South Lodge, and there she regularly entertained all sorts of literary, artistic and social people. But at fifty-one, although still beautiful, she wanted to settle down and become domestic.

Thus, despite the disparity of their ages, these two people met at a crucial moment in both of their lives, and each found in the other what he had been lacking for a long time. As a result, in about six months' time, Ford asked his wife for a divorce. At first Mrs. Hueffer agreed and the papers were served, but then she changed her mind. Her refusal to proceed with the divorce has been attributed to her Roman Catholicism, but since in fact she was an Anglican, it must have been due to her preternaturally high principles. Instead, then, of agreeing to the divorce, Mrs. Hueffer sued for what is technically known as the 'Restitution of Conjugal Rights' and Ford found his name literally plastered over the newspaper hoardings on every London street corner. At the trial consequent to this action, Ford was ordered to pay £3 a week for the support of his wife and children. Since he was already paying £9 a week he quixotically refused to accept a judgement which he felt to be an aspersion of his honour, and instead went to Brixton Gaol for ten days in defiance. In part his hope was that his wife might relent and grant him the divorce. When she declined to do so, Ford was infuriated and for some time considered himself a martyr. The loss of *The English Review* added to his sorrows, and after his release he moved to South Lodge as a paying guest of Mrs. Alfred Hunt, Violet's mother.

During the summer of 1910, for the sake of the diversion, Ford and Violet decided to take a trip to Germany in order to stay with some of Ford's wealthy relations along the Rhine. At Boppard, they visited his Aunt Emma, and from his first cousin, Mimi, he learned of an old German law which gave option to the children of German parentage to assume German nationality, even though the parents had themselves become naturalized in other countries. Aunt Emma, wanted to claim the distinguished author and editor for the Fatherland, and Mimi pointed out that in Germany divorces were far easier to obtain than they were in England. They both suggested that he go to Giessen where there was a clever lawyer and where the local Grand Duke was a sympathetic family friend. The idea was that he should take up residence until he could obtain German nationality and procure a German divorce.

Ford had almost no knowledge of legal matters, and at the time he was emotionally upset, so that what may now seem an incredible adventure, presumably seemed to him a feasible way out of his difficulties. At any rate, he went to Giessen, which is a small university town north of Frankfurt in Hesse, and settled down for the length of time necessary to become a German citizen. He took rooms in lodgings, but soon found them depressing. 'In one,' he wrote, 'is a table, a writing-desk, a sofa, five chairs, and about two hundred and fifty ornaments, ranging from bits of coral like human brains to gilded busts of Lohengrin. In the other room is a bed, a table, a chest of drawers, cupboard, washstand and two hundred and fifty more ornaments.'[41] The purpose of his stay was to represent himself as an eminently respectable burgher. He might have succeeded, but Giessen proved so dull and his surroundings so unattractive, that he wrote to ask his friends to visit him. Violet and her mother came, and tongues began to wag: then came Ezra Pound who dressed in bright green shirts with glass buttons on them, and the town fathers raised their eyebrows even further. More disastrous, however, were the involved legal proceedings into which Ford entered with the supposed help of the German lawyer. It slowly became clear that this functionary's intention was to create as much red tape as possible in order to enlarge his fees.

The weeks and months went by, but apparently without result. Ford grew more bored and irritable and the lawyer more complicated. In the end, Ford apparently assumed he had obtained his nationality and divorce and wired Violet to meet him in France. It is impossible to know whether he was merely so confused by the profusion of legal papers with which he was confronted that he honestly thought he had obtained his divorce, or whether he gave in to wishful thinking. In any event, he had not obtained the divorce.

Shortly after leaving Giessen in September 1911, Ford met Violet at Rheims, and, after a day or so there, they proceeded to a seaside resort in Belgium where they were interviewed by two English publications, the *Daily Mail* and *The Throne*, a magazine published by Ford's friend, René Byles. These two periodicals then published photographs and articles which referred to Violet as 'Mrs. Ford Madox Hueffer'.

When Elsie Hueffer read these reports, she was understandably indignant, since she had in fact never received any divorce papers from Germany and considered herself still married to Ford. She therefore sued the two periodicals. The *Daily Mail* sensibly apologized, but René Byles chose to fight the suit, which then took place without either of the principals, Violet or Ford, being able to make a statement. In the circumstances, it was inevitable that *The Throne* libel case should be decided in favour of Mrs. Elsie Hueffer. The resulting scandal, however, was of little benefit to any of those involved in the case.

There is something of the flavour of an impossibly plotted bad novel in these episodes and there is much that is grotesquely comic. But to Ford and Violet the results were not at all funny. The publicity of the various cases was such that Ford's name became notorious all over England and the enemies he had made while editor of *The English Review* crowed with righteous indignation. Henry James and Cunninghame Graham severed relations; the Garnetts and Conrads sided with Mrs. Elsie Hueffer, and of his earlier acquaintances and friends, only H. G. Wells (who himself had had some experience with marital difficulties) stayed loyal. Harassed on all sides, Ford who was apparently as fond a father as could be imagined, was especially worried that he would be alienated from his children's affections. Then came the various legal expenses which, together with the debts incurred by *The English Review*, forced him into the bankruptcy courts. On top of all else, Ford's German aunt who had promised to leave him a sizeable amount, cut him out of her will when she heard of the divorce scandal; and Violet's own sisters went to court over Violet's executorship of her mother's will, thus tying up the trust for years. As a result, Ford had to sell all of his possessions.

For one who had risen so rapidly to a position of prominence in London, the collapse of both career and marriage must have been nightmarish. And for Ford, who was so sensitive about personal reputation and honour, the events of 1910 and after must have been excruciating. To be sure, he learned an immense amount about people through these experiences, and this knowledge was to be useful for him in *Parade's End* and other novels, but at the time it gave him little solace. What doubtless saved his sanity was his lack of ambition and his devotion to hard work. Conrad had been one of the first to notice how unambitious his collaborator was, and for once in his life it was to have a practical usefulness for Ford. In the late autumn of 1911, he was able to escape briefly to Rome in order to write an article for *Collier's* on the investiture of a number of American Cardinals, but even in London, during days that were otherwise devoted to legal proceedings, Ford continued to devote every morning to his work. His perseverance in writing presumably acted as a safety valve for him. Violet Hunt has recorded how he sat 'in the Futurist room, neatly and with aplomb dictating his daily screed of typewritten pages. He preserved at least his literary balance, the pendulum of his thought ticking backwards and forwards with an even motion. Great man! He could concentrate. His inner commotion was subdued by the superior claims of Literature on its votary.'[42] This habit of daily work was one he had picked up early in his career and was one he maintained until he died. The astonishing thing, however, is that during this agonizing and tumultuous period Ford wrote one of his most controlled and perfect novels, *The Good Soldier*, and published the best poetry he ever wrote.

VATES, THE SOCIAL REFORMER

What shall be said of him, this cock-o'-hoop?
(I'm just a trifle bored, dear God of mine,
Dear unknown God, dear chicken-pox of Heaven,
I'm bored I say.) But still—my social friend—
(One has to be familiar in one's discourse)
While he was puffing out his jet of swit
Over his swollen-bellied pipe, one thinks
One thinks, you know, of quite a lot of things.

(Dear unknown God, dear queer-faced God,
Queer, queer, queer, queer-faced God,
You blanky God, be quiet for half a minute,
And when I've shut up Rates, and sat on Naboth,
I'll tell you half a dozen things or so.)

There goes a flock of starlings—
Now half a dozen years ago,
(Shut up, you blighted God, and let me speak)
I should have hove my sporting air-gun up
And blazed away—and now I let 'em go—
It's odd how one changes;
Yes, that's High Germany.

—RICHARD ALDINGTON

Chapter Six

————《◆》《◆》————

POET AND NOVELIST

————《◆》《◆》————

I

Publishing difficulties, bad sales and frequently hostile reviews notwithstanding, Ford wrote no fewer than sixteen books during the period immediately following the collapse of his marriage and the loss of *The English Review*. Between 1911 and the day on which he joined the British Army in 1915, he published three books of poems, including his collected verse, two volumes of literary criticism, a book of memoirs, two novels in collaboration with Violet Hunt, seven novels of his own and three books of propaganda.

That these years, in spite of their bitternesses and frustrations, should have marked the first real flowering of Ford's talent may seem paradoxical, but the explanation is not hard to find. Up until the establishment of *The English Review*, Ford's life had been relatively quiet and easy. The failure of the collaboration had disappointed him and had even contributed to his temporary breakdown, but Ford still had many friends, a sufficient amount of money and a happy family life. Against this background, the founding of the review seemed to be the culmination of a successful literary career. By 1911, however, Ford's ship had capsized: his reputation was ruined, he had lost his family, his former friends avoided him and he was bankrupt. Thus in his late thirties he was forced to start all over again. Many men in similar circumstances would have turned their faces to the wall and given up; but Ford endured his adversity and kept on writing. The horrific experiences he underwent after

94

1910 made him grow up very rapidly and much of his work during this period reflected this new maturity.

Naturally not all of the books he wrote during these years are 'de profundis'; and a number of them even show signs of haste. Yet on the whole, they are better than anything he had hitherto produced. Of his two books of literary criticism, the first is a collection of essays he had written in large part as editorials for *The English Review*. Representing in essence the literary philosophy of the review, *The Critical Attitude* has as its thesis the necessity of assessing the arts according to intelligible standards. It is not enough, Ford says, to judge literature according to personal perference or by the amount of morally uplifting material it contains: literature, like painting or sculpture, should be judged solely by its artistic achievement. *The Critical Attitude*, is not, however, dedicated to art for art's sake; rather it considers form and substance as inseparable.

In *Henry James, A Critical Study*, Ford continued his disquisition on the state of the English novel. In his oft-quoted prefatory remark, Ford made it clear from the beginning what he thought of James and what he thought of the importance of the arts. 'Mr. James,' he said, 'is the greatest of living writers and in consequence, for me, the greatest of living men.'[1] Having said that, Ford turned to James's work with a frankness that is normally reserved for discussion amongst professional writers. Yet his attitude towards James always seems to have been somewhat ambiguous: he admired immensely the technical skills of 'the Master', but at the same time he found James's aloofness from his subject, though artistically correct, a sign almost of sadistic cruelty. Moreover, although he used James as a model for some of his own work, he was also not above parodying him. The real reason for Ford's ambivalence towards James seems to lie in the frustration he must have encountered in using James's method but not being able to adapt it for his own ends. Ford was to write a number of pseudo-Jamesian novels before he could release himself from the limitations that the use of James as a model imposed on his own subject. At any rate, *Henry James, A Critical Study* does honour to James by taking him so seriously. James for his part was 'vaguely aware' that the book was out, but perhaps because he realized it was outspoken, or perhaps because he was offended at being the subject of a book by a man whose marital conduct distressed him, he said he 'wouldn't touch it with a ten-foot pole.'[2]

95

The organic view of art expressed in his criticism also characterized another of Ford's concerns during this period—the writing of poetry. The years immediately preceding the first World War were distinguished by a poetic revival in England, and through *The English Review*, Ford had helped to encourage it by bringing various poets together for the first time. Afterwards, when he moved to South Lodge, he found himself entertaining a circle of poets that included Ezra Pound, W. B. Yeats, Hilda Doolittle and her husband Richard Aldington, D. H. Lawrence, F. S. Flint and, later on, T. S. Eliot.

Ford's own poetry had been, up to this time, as he admitted in his introductory essay to the *Collected Poems* of 1913, somewhat casually produced. He had written five volumes of verse, but on the whole his poetry took second place to his work in prose. All along he had considered verse-making a somewhat automatic process consisting of a more or less rapid transference of an emotion to paper. The result was that much of his early poetry was derivative of the nineteenth-century nature poets and of the Pre-Raphaelites. Generally facile with here and there a felicitous line, his verse was essentially undeveloped.

By the time he moved to London, however, Ford had begun to take poetry more seriously than he had formerly done. Previously his poetical preferences had been largely the result of temperamental predilections, but his talks with Ezra Pound sharpened his critical attitude and forced him to adopt consistent standards for the judging of poetry. Soon he was able to identify with precision the two qualities he most disliked in the poetic tradition into which he had been born. The first was specialization of subject-matter and the second was formality of verse structure. Thanks largely to Wordsworth, and later on to William Morris and Lord Tennyson, the subjects thought suitable for poetic treatment had become increasingly limited. Wordsworth's dictum that poets should write naturally of natural things gave rise to a school of nature poetry that lasted well into the present century. Victorian industrialism furthered this tradition, for many poets, appalled by the ugly new cities and factories that were rising over the English countryside, found solace and inspiration in what still remained unspoiled, and they looked back to earlier ages where they fancied purer motives controlled life. Thus nature and medievalism became the two principal subjects for poetry. Poems were not to deal with life as it was but with pomegranates and daffodils, open casements and thatched cottages.

While Ford recognized that there was nothing *wrong* in writing about country farmers and medieval knights and ladies, he also saw that it was utterly false to write solely of these things. For the danger inherent in such subjects was that they could easily convert poetry into a literature of escape that could only be of interest to dear old ladies sitting in wicker chairs. If poetry, then, was to remain alive as a literary form, it had to deal, as novels dealt, with contemporary life, with life as it is rather than with life as it might be nice to have it. Since twentieth-century life was principally a life of cities, Ford therefore urged that poems should be written about subways and motor-buses instead of donkey-carts and country-lanes. He summarized his views in a letter written to Mrs. C. F. G. Masterman, who had shown him some of her verses:

... My dear lady, your poems in the future must not be written in that pleasant and sheltered verandah with the grey sea and the grey sky and all the chastened romance of it. That is holiday time. Your poetry should be your workaday life. That is what is the matter with all the verse of today; it is too much practised in temples and too little in motor-buses. ... LITERARY! LITERARY! Now that is the last thing that verse should ever be, for the moment a medium becomes literary it is remote from the life of the people, it is dulled, languishing, moribund and at last dead. ...

Yes, remember that when next you sit down to write. And sit down to write, metaphorically speaking, in a railway waiting room, or in a wet street, or in your kitchen ... where something real is doing and let your language be that of the more serious witnesses in Blue Books. My father once wrote of Rossetti that he set down the mind of Dante in the language of Shakespeare. That was clever of my father, but could there have been a greater condemnation of that magic Amateur ... for what the poet ought to do is to write his own mind in the language of his day.

Forget about Piers Plowman, forget about Shakespeare, Keats, Yeats, Morris, the English Bible and remember only that you live in our terrific, untidy, indifferent, empirical age, where not a single problem is solved and not one single Accepted Idea from the poet has any more magic. ... It is for us to get at the new truths or to give new life to such of the old as will appeal *hominibus bonae voluntatis*. Only to do that we must do it in the clear pure language of our own day and with what is clear and new in our individualities.[3]

97

More distressing even than subject-matter, however, was the manner in which many poems were still being written. The final paragraph of Ford's letter to Mrs. Masterman shows this concern. The language of the Bible and Shakespeare, much of it being the language of great poetry, has echoed down through the centuries in English verse. The reasons for its perseverance are partly conscious and partly unconscious. The unconscious syllogism runs perhaps like this: Shakespeare wrote great poetry. Shakespeare used a particular vocabulary. I wish to write great poetry. I will use Shakespeare's vocabulary. The trouble with this otherwise promising arrangement is that it permits, under the general heading of poetic licence, the perpetuation of an entirely literary language. Archaisms, inversions of phrase for the sake of the rhyme, imprecision of diction, mismatched imagery, the use of a peculiarly 'poetical' vocabulary for the sake of its suggestiveness—all of these were common features of the verse of the latter part of the nineteenth century and were being continued in the work of the more popular magazine poets of the twentieth.*

Ford was explicit in his attitude towards such abuses of poetic licence. 'You see,' he later wrote, 'I hate—and I hated then—inversions of phrase. A line like *A sensitive plant in a garden grew* filled me with hot rage. If the chap wanted to say that a sensitive plant grew in a garden, why didn't he say it—or if he could not find a rhyme for garden, let him for Heaven's sake hold his peace. It seemed to me to be unskilful botching—and it was!'[4]

Verbal incompetence, he continues, will lead directly to falsification of content: 'You will write doth love instead of loves so as to fill up the line; you will look for a rhyme to the word stream and you will find cream and be led away into imagining your lady as a milkmaid—that sort of thing. . . .'[5]

In his early poems, Ford had been guilty of the sort of slovenliness he here criticizes, and he had also confined himself, as was perhaps natural since he was then living in the country, to rural topics. But by 1910 he had begun to change, partly because of his own observations and partly because of his friendship with Ezra Pound. *Songs from London* (1910) and *High Germany* (1912) show signs that Ford was emerging as an original and contemporary poet. Here are the opening lines of 'Finchley Road':

* A glance at D. G. Rossetti's 'The Blessèd Damozel' will illustrate a number of these qualities.

> As we come up to Baker Street
> Where tubes and trains and buses meet
> There's a touch of fog and a touch of sleet;
> And we go on up Hampstead way
> Towards the closing in of day. . . .[6]

By present-day standards there is nothing striking in these lines, but for the first decade of the century their subject-matter was distinctly new. The subjective image of the fifth line contrasts awkwardly with the precision of the other lines, but at least there are no inversions or archaisms: the language used is the colloquial language of the twentieth century.

The opening lines of another poem in *Songs from London* come even closer to the living tongue. The name of the poem is 'Views'.

> Being in Rome I wonder will you go
> Up to the Hill. But I forget the name . . .
> Aventine? Pincio? No: I do not know.
> I was there yesterday and watched. You came.[7]

This new sort of verse was a direct result of Ford's prose instincts. Over the years, both alone and with Conrad, he had developed the method he called 'Impressionism' whose primary purpose was a direct rendering of life as it is in the simplest possible manner. This technique required conciseness and the elimination so far as was possible of adjectives and adverbs. In their place, the writer had to be able to choose the exact noun or verb—*le mot juste.*

In applying this particular prose technique to English verse, Ford was in fact bringing the whole tradition of French nineteenth-century fiction to bear on twentieth-century verse. Along with Ezra Pound, he realized that poetry had to 'catch up' with prose. To help make it do so was Ford's great contribution to contemporary verse. As Pound himself has put it:

Mr. Hueffer believes in an exact rendering of things. He would strip words of all 'association' for the sake of getting a precise meaning. He professes to prefer prose to verse. You will find his origins in Gautier or in Flaubert. He is objective.[8]

No man can write really good verse unless he knows Stendhal and Flaubert. To put it perhaps more strongly, he will learn more about the art of charging words from Flaubert than he will from the floribund sixteenth-century dramatists.[9]

It is he (Ford) who has insisted, in the face of a still Victorian press, upon the importance of good writing as opposed to the opalescent word, the rhetorical tradition. Stendhal had said, and Flaubert, de Maupassant and Turgenev had proved, that 'prose was the higher art'—at least their prose.[10]

The interest in prose naturally led to a consideration of the possibility of new rhythms, especially those deriving from prose. In his early poems, Ford had experimented with loose forms and had written occasional poems in free verse, but in later years he wrote almost exclusively in this form. Symmetrical or rhymed verse he found either 'a cramped and difficult medium—or an easy and uninteresting one.'[11] One reason for his adoption of vers libre came from his belief that just as each age demanded its own rhythm and method, so each person had his own rhythm and way of speaking and writing. In the hands of an amateur, vers libre can be an easy way of side-stepping discipline, and Ford realized that it was not difficult to write bad free verse. Thus he doubtless agreed with T. S. Eliot's comment that 'No vers is libre for the man who wants to do a good job,'[12] but he also realized how extraordinarily difficult it was to write good free verse, for impressionism in poetry required an even more painful self-negation than it demanded in prose. The poet, as he said, 'must observe with exactitude and reverence, and with exactitude and reverence he must render.'[13]

In his own work Ford therefore restrained his rhythmic variations. He either imposed an over-all form from without or maintained an internal rhythmic pattern within a loose framework. His experiments were on the whole independently made and he established his poetical standards by himself. Thus, by the time the Imagist group of poets was established, he was a person of some influence among the younger poets and represented a style of poetry quite distinct from that of William Butler Yeats.

In his early years at least, Yeats was especially concerned with the latent magic that inhered in particular words. For him, the language of the poet had to be musical and above all suggestive. In Yeats's view, the poet used words in a manner quite different from that of the writer of prose. Ford, on the other hand, stood for clarity, for the precise object as against the general idea. His method consisted 'in getting exquisite poetic meaning out of the mere transcription of natural objects, without any comments or ejaculations whatsoever.'[14] He did not mean that objects necessarily had to be symbolic, however. They merely had to be apt and somehow inevitable, just as the tram accident which befalls the deafened Razumov in Conrad's *Under Western Eyes* is an inevitable but not necessarily symbolic occurrence.

Although Yeats was by far the more accomplished poet, Ford's influence was at first the more pervasive. Indeed Ezra Pound and the Imagists may be said to have followed Ford more than Yeats— 'He and Yeats are the two men in London,' said Pound. 'And Yeats is already a sort of great dim figure with its associations in the past.'[15] Pound's comment suggests the degree to which the young poets of London were conscious of themselves as a group and is a natural antecedent to the establishment of the first lively movement English poetry was to experience in the twentieth century.

The beginnings of Imagism seem to have been partly serious and partly frivolous. A good deal has been made by literary historians of the rôle played in its organization by the philosopher, T. E. Hulme, a humorous and libidinous man who happened to be interested in French symbolist poetry and who had written a few poems in a style derivative of their work. In fact, however, the movement seems to have been something of a joke—merely a means of getting some publicity for a group of young poets who up till 1913 had been ignored by the general public. The idea was that if several young poets like F. S. Flint, Hilda Doolittle, Richard Aldington, Ezra Pound and John Gould Fletcher would band together and publish an anthology with a forceful enough 'manifesto' of their aims and desires, their joint effort might pay dividends in the form of increased sales of the work of individual contributors. Ezra Pound and Hulme were the chief instigators of this scheme, and in 1913 they published the first anthology under the provocative title of *Des Imagistes*. As it was a great success, the new 'movement' continued, but after a year or so it was more or less taken over by Amy Lowell, largely as a means of self-advertisement. By 1915 Ezra Pound had pulled out, but D. H. Lawrence was happy to join in for whatever financial profit it might bring him.[16]

However trifling this movement may seem, it had its serious side, and the 'manifesto' published in the 1915 anthology is worth quoting. The aims of the group* were, it said: '1. To use the

* This manifesto was apparently agreed to by all of the contributors: Aldington, H.D., Flint, Fletcher, Lawrence and Amy Lowell. Pound and Hulme were conspicuously absent.

language of common speech, but to employ always the *exact* word, not the merely decorative word. 2. To create new rhythms—as the expression of new moods—and not to copy old rhythms, which merely echo old moods. . . . 3. To allow absolute freedom in the choice of subjects. . . . 4. To present an image (hence the name imagist). We are not a school of painters, but we believe that poetry should render particulars exactly and not deal in vague generalities, however magnificent and sonorous. . . . 5. To produce poetry that is hard and clear, never blurred nor indefinite. 6. Finally, most of us believe that concentration is of the very essence of poetry.'[17]

While the only purely Imagistic poetry that is likely to endure is that of H.D., the movement as a whole had a considerable effect on the course of modern verse. One of the original Imagists, Richard Aldington, has this to say of the importance of the group:

> They dealt a blow at the post-Victorian magazine poets, whose un-appeased shades still clamour for Imagist blood. They made free verse popular. . . . And they tried to attain an exacting if narrow standard of style in poetry. . . . And to a considerable extent T. S. Eliot and his followers have carried on their operations from positions won by the Imagists.[18]

Although Ford himself never joined the Imagists officially, he was attached to the movement in much the same way Ford Madox Brown had been connected with the Pre-Raphaelite Brotherhood. Many of the points made in the Imagist manifesto had been voiced by Ford years before, some as early as 1902.[19] And now, as an older man, he was content to comment on Imagism in his weekly column in *The Outlook* or to contribute a parody to the 1914 anthology.* During the years when Imagism flourished, however, his work changed in accordance with some of the tenets of the movement, and he learned a certain amount from H.D. The tone of the early, somewhat muted 'To Christina at Nightfall' gave way to the more vivid 'To all the Dead' which is included in his book *High Germany*. According to Violet Hunt, this poem was written after Ford had had a vision while sitting in a café at Giessen. Doubtless inspired by his own somewhat ridiculous position as an exile for the purposes of divorce, it is a sardonic comparison between present-day pettiness and vulgarity and the greatness of the past. Like T. S. Eliot's more

---

* Ford himself was parodied by Richard Aldington; see 'Vates, the Social Reformer' at the head of this chapter.

famous song of Prufrock, the poem makes its point through a series of dramatic contrasts. The stylized Chinese queen of antiquity who sits on a lacquered throne is compared to two Chinese chiropodists who are seen from a window overlooking the Rue de la Paix in Paris, while the commonplace man from Sandusky, Ohio, who talks about 'progress' is placed against the brave legends of ancient Germanic heroes. In his *Ancient Lights*, written at about the same time, Ford had noted that as we became more civilized—living in streets named after Peace—we became less conscious of dignity and truth: 'We don't care enough about anything to risk hurting each other's feelings. As a man I find this delightful, and it is the only position that, in a democracy, mankind can take up if it is to live. . . . We are a practical people, but it is impossible to be practical in the things both of Heaven and of earth. There is no way to do it.' Thus it follows, as he says a little later, that 'Life is very good nowadays; but art is very bitter.'[20]

Ford's best-known poem is 'On Heaven' which was written just before the war in response to Violet Hunt's request that he write down heaven for her. 'I want no beauty,' she said, 'I want no damned optimism; I just want a plain, workaday heaven that I can go to some day and enjoy it when I'm there. . . .'[21] In response to the prescription, Ford put his heaven in Provence and placed his hero at a café table in the *place* of an old town, waiting for his love to come:

> The *Place* is small and shaded by great planes,
> Over a rather human monument
> Set up to *Louis Dixhuit* in the year
> Eighteen fourteen; a funny thing with dolphins
> About a pyramid of green-dripped, sordid stone.
> But the enormous, monumental planes
> Shade it all in, and in the flecks of sun
> Sit market women. There's a paper shop
> Painted all blue, a shipping agency,
> Three or four cafés; dank, dark colonnades
> Of an eighteen-forty *Mairie*.[22]

God is pictured as an immensely good man and kindly host, and the main quality of heaven is that it is free from doctrines and theorizings: all the cares and worries of this world are absent, while all the best parts of human life are retained.

> And, thank God, we had nothing any more to think of,
> And, thank God, we had nothing any more to talk of;

103

Unless, as it chanced, the flashing silver stalk of the pampas
Growing down to the brink of the Rhône,
On the lawn of a little château, giving onto the river.
And we were alone, alone, alone . . .
At last alone . . . [23]

That Ford's heaven is so human may appear to be an indication
of his naïveté, but in fact his emphasis on the earthly pleasures of
heaven suggests not that he was blasphemous but merely that he did
not subscribe to the systematized solutions offered by official reli-
gions and reformers. For at heart, 'On Heaven' is not so much a
vision of another world as a description of the good life in this
world. Since, in the words of the poem, 'God is our father and loves
all good lovers . . .' and 'has a kindly smile for many a poor sinner,'[24]
he provides in his heaven the things people who are nervously
exhausted really most yearn for—a quiet café with an orchestra, a
drive through a beautiful countryside and a nice view in the cool
of the evening. One reason for Ford's insistence on these particulars
as against vague visions of eternal, harp-playing bliss, is revealed in
his statement that 'Most poets fail, and the art of poetry has become
discredited, usually because poets will try to convey to the world
the idea that they are more refined or more romantic than they
really are, or that their eyes are not upon and their minds not occupied with the world in which they live. So the world suspects them—
and warrantably—of insincerity and want of knowledge; the world
therefore prefers to read the *Daily Mail*—which does not know anything but which to the measure of the light vouchsafed it, has a
certain sincerity. And the world is quite right.'[25] Thus, although
Ford's statement of what he meant by heaven may not be theologic-
ally respectable, it is psychologically true and is refreshingly free of
cant and hypocrisy. Doubtless it was partly for these qualities that
Ezra Pound once called it 'The best longish poem yet written in the
"twentieth-century fashion".'[26]

For 'On Heaven' Ford employed a strongly rhythmical free verse,
the rhythms varying from section to section. These rhythms are
regular enough, however, to prevent the poem from being diffuse
and disorganized, and sufficiently free to keep the lines from becoming tedious. Ford's verse is a compromise between the stiff and the
formless and is well suited to a narrative poem. As Conrad Aiken
put it: 'Mr. Hueffer very often employs a rhythm which is almost as
dispersed as that of prose; but the point to be emphatically remarked

is that he does so only by way of variation on the given norm of movement, which is essentially and predominantly rhythmic. Variation of this sort is no more or less than good artistry. . . .'[27] Pound even went so far as to find parallels with Homer: 'Apart from narrative sense and the main constructive, there is this to be said of Homer, that never can you read half a page without finding melodic invention, still fresh, and that you can hear the actual voices, as of the old men speaking in the course of the phrases.

'It is for this latter quality that Ford's poetry is of high importance both in itself and for its effect on all the best subsequent work of his time. Let no young snob forget this.'[28]

A more Imagistic poem than 'On Heaven' is 'Antwerp' which was written after the invasion of Belgium by the Germans in 1914. At the time, T. S. Eliot called it the 'only good poem I have met with on the subject of the war.'[29] First produced as a pamphlet by Harold Monro's Poetry Bookshop with a violent cover design by Wyndham Lewis, it opens with these lines:

> Gloom!
> An October like November;
> August a hundred thousand hours,
> And all September,
> A hundred, dragging sunlit days,
> And half October like a thousand years . . .
> And doom!
> That then was Antwerp. . . .[30]

The poem is about the effect of war on the helpless civilian population. There are sections devoted to courage and pain in the mud-soaked Belgian trenches, but most of the poem has to do with non-combatants. The final section depicts the scene in the railway station at Charing Cross where the mothers are waiting to see whether their sons are amongst the returning wounded: this coda is impressionistic and the staccato lines are an understatement of the anguish of the scene.

> This is Charing Cross:
> It is midnight;
> There is a great crowd
> And no light.
> A great crowd, all black that hardly whispers aloud.
> Surely, that is a dead woman—a dead mother!

She has a dead face;
She is dressed all in black;
She wanders to the bookstall and back,
At the back of the crowd;
And back again and again back,
She sways and wanders.

This is Charing Cross;
It is one o'clock.
There is still a great cloud, and very little light;
Immense shafts of shadows over the black crowd
That hardly whispers aloud . . .
And now! . . . That is another dead mother,
And there is another and another and another . . .
And little children, all in black,
All with dead faces, waiting in all the waiting-places,
Wandering from the doors of the waiting-room
In the dim gloom.
These are the women of Flanders.
They await the lost.
They await the lost that shall never leave the dock;
They await the lost that shall never again come by the train
To the embraces of all these women with dead faces;
They await the lost who lie in trench and barrier and foss,
In the dark of the night.
This is Charing Cross; it is past one of the clock;
There is very little light.[31]

In many ways the best of Ford's early poems, 'Antwerp' unfortunately concludes with lines that diminish its effectiveness. These final lines also show where Ford differed from what was to become the predominant poetical method of the century. For instead of relying simply on the 'objective correlative' he had created impressionistically, he felt the need of emphasizing his personal involvement in the scene by adding the line—

'There is so much pain'.

and concluding with the inartistic *cri de coeur*

'Oh poor dears!'[32]

II

Between 1910 and 1915, in addition to his books of poetry and criticism, Ford published nine novels. Of these, only four are of interest today. Two of the minor novels, written under the *nom de guerre* of 'Daniel Chaucer', are skits—the first, *The Simple Life Limited*, pokes fun at the socialists while the second, *The New Humpty-Dumpty*, set in London and a modern Ruritania, satirizes contemporary international politics and finance. *The Panel*, published under his own name, is a parody of Henry James, while *The Portrait* is an historical romance with the usual self-sacrificing Fordian hero. More important than any of these is a novel placed in Arthurian England called *Ladies Whose Bright Eyes*, which is renowned mostly for emphasizing those elements of the medieval world that Morris and Tennyson carefully excluded from their idyllic portraits of the Middle Ages. Using the method employed by Mark Twain in the *Connecticut Yankee*, Ford sends his modern hero, Sorrell, back into the thirteenth century by means of a train wreck. There, expecting the ladies he meets to be romantic heroines languishing helplessly at jousts, he is both surprised and delighted to find them not only sexually alive but accomplished as politicians. They are, in short, as the title indicates, 'Ladies whose bright eyes/ Rain influence, and judge the prize.'[33] For their part, the men are far from being paragons of chivalry: instead they are, as they probably have always been, *hommes moyens sensuels*. A delightful romp, *Ladies Whose Bright Eyes* for once and all takes medievalism off of its pedestal.

Of the four remaining novels of the period, *The Young Lovell* is the only historical novel and is also placed, like *Ladies Whose Bright Eyes*, in medieval England. Having already in the earlier novel dealt with the concept of historical reality, Ford here emphasizes the strange power of the sexual instinct over men who are otherwise wholly rational. His own experiences from 1909-1912 had shown him the power of sexual jealousy, but the value to fiction of these harrowing pre-war years lies in Ford's astonishing ability to be objective while at the same time humanly sympathetic. It was easy enough for him to see, that is to say, that the sexual instincts more often than not ran counter to the professed codes of morality and social responsibility; at the same time he refused to believe that the only solution was a ruthless suppression of those instincts. Thus *The Young Lovell*, which is a variation on the Venusberg legend, is simply a parable of what happens when a young man is powerfully and ineradicably smitten by the goddess of love. The situation is presented through a young knight, Sir Paris Lovell, a man of probity and honour who while embodying all the chivalrous virtues, suddenly and apparently without thought, abandons all of his standards and runs away with a beautiful and sensuous maiden. The reactions to this event are as varied as there are types of humanity, and the hero undergoes a great deal of difficulty before any solution is reached. Too much of a human being to make a moral judgement, Ford concludes his story of the knight who broke the pledge by uniting half of him with his charmer in a mystical Elysian field, while the other half remains below in the rôle of a religious penitent. What Ford seems to be suggesting is that those who are fortunate or unfortunate to be struck by a really devastating love can only hope to survive if they forfeit all worldly influence and, in the worldly realm, pay the penance required. Ford here merely recognizes the dichotomy long ago admitted by the Church of Rome which, in Blake's phrase, provides the bricks from which brothels are made.

Thus in *The Young Lovell* Ford treats sex with a psychological honesty that is rare in English literature. Love for him is not an impulse that can be turned on and off at the individual's convenience so that he can get on with his everyday affairs; rather it is at once a blessed and a cursed affliction. Implicitly criticizing the whole tradition of English fiction which presents love as either a romantic idyll filled with tender phrases and casement yearnings or, conversely, as the result, by way of wedding bells, of an industrious career in worldly strife, Ford stresses that the impulses of love are neither controllable nor rational. All that is certain is that you cannot have the best of both worlds. Thus for Ford, Fielding's *Tom Jones*, in so far as it rewarded a lecherous young man of the world with an innocent and beautiful Sophia Western was both an immoral and an inaccurate book.

By contrast, *Mr. Fleight*, his next novel, is a political story and continues an interest first expressed in the collaborated novel, *The Inheritors*. The function of the book is to show that, owing to the moral degeneracy that has seeped into public affairs, the only sure way to political success and power is through money. Ford focuses his attention on his elderly and omniscient central character, Mr. Blood, a man who in former times might have been interested in public affairs, but who is now cynically withdrawn because he knows how corrupt the power world has become. Blood is usually remote, but for his own amusement and to prove his thesis that money will buy anything, he quite outrageously agrees to help the rich, basically decent, but quite unqualified Jew, Mr. Fleight, to become a Member of Parliament. Through the progress of Mr. Blood's plans for Mr. Fleight, Ford reveals the complete corruption that has overtaken English political, social, literary and journalistic life. In the end, however, after a good deal of damage has been done, Mr. Fleight, like Mr. Blood before him, grows disgusted with the corruption he has encountered and withdraws from public life. Ford's point is concise: even the 'dirty Jew' will not corrupt himself to the extent the public school gentleman will—which leaves little to be said for the 'backbone' of England. Thus the novel presents a picture of contemporary life that is as unsavoury as anything later produced by Wyndham Lewis. Yet instead of moralizing, Ford merely shows that no one is free of blame or guilt. In Yeats's phrase: 'The best lack all conviction, while the worst/ Are full of passionate intensity.'[34] Ford's is a bitter-sweet picture of a rotting corpse, the fag end of the Edwardian era that tottered to its close on the fourth of August, 1914.

Wholly different in tone is *A Call*, which is an allusive and sophisticated treatment of upper-class London society. The characters and setting are Jamesian and so, in part, is the method, but the subject is more daring than most of those taken up by 'the Master'. It is the tale of a decent, scrupulous and intelligent young man, Robert Grimshaw, who has the misfortune of being in love with two women at once. Essentially an examination of the nature of love (complete with a psychologist, surely one of his earliest appearances in English fiction), the book takes up the theme of *The Young Lovell*, thickens it and places it in a plausible contemporary setting. The general result is misery caused by failures of communication and the inability of established moral codes to deal with actuality. Once again, no one is entirely blameless. A psychological rather than a moral or ethical novel, its primary note is one of pity for the human lot, pity that so much misunderstanding should develop between people because of social scruples and the inability to recognize the true nature of passion, when for all of them life should have been peaceful and agreeable. In a sense it could be said that Ford wrote 'On Heaven' for the people of this novel and for others like them caught up in similar situations.

Altogether then, the sixteen novels Ford wrote prior to the World War show a wide range of interest; yet at the same time he was really dealing in all of these novels with two general concepts. The first was the decay of public morality with its attendant distrust of the good man. This idea, made individualistic through Ford's distinction between the Christian and the Christist, naturally led to a consideration of the nature of man himself, with special emphasis on his most vital and most guarded quality—his sexual life. Whether set in the palace at Richmond or in a Mayfair drawing-room, not to mention the first-class saloon of a transatlantic liner, these same concerns were continually reasserted. Yet for all his range and his interest in what William James called 'live options', none of these sixteen novels was wholly successful. In later years, Ford himself looked back on them, acknowledging that he had written 'rather desultorily' a great number of books, and admitting that they had all been, as he said, 'in the nature of *pastiches* or pieces of rather precious writing, or of *tours de force*.' Thus it was not until his fortieth birthday that he really tried to put into one novel all the things he had learned in writing the others. On that day, he said, 'I sat down to show what I could do—and *The Good Soldier* resulted.'[35]

The problem that presented itself was simply how to combine the various concepts which interested him in a coherent contemporary situation. Hitherto, most of Ford's novels dealing with life in modern London had a certain air of unreality. Either they contained too many elements falsely combined so that the total effect was jumbled, or they were too thinly conceived and overly dependent on social ephemera. Most of these difficulties seem to have been due to his reliance on the Jamesian method which carried with it certain elements of James's personality that were essentially different from Ford's. To overcome this debility, Ford apparently decided, as Virginia Woolf did some years afterwards in *To the Lighthouse*, to present his characters in an isolated situation, so that he could concentrate on them without being distracted by the necessity of filling in the background of an English social milieu. Ford's own Continental experiences came to his aid at this point, for in choosing a German spa as his locale, he selected a type of place with which he had long been familiar. Moreover, he had met in these watering-places precisely the types of people he wished to deal with. There were, to begin with, the Misses Hurlbird, 'two adorably old-maidish maiden ladies from Stamford, Conn.'[36] whom he had met in 1904 at a Rhenish spa. With their pre-Revolutionary sympathies and the portraits of Cornwallis and General Braddock that still hung in the drawing-room of their Connecticut house, they were to provide many useful details for the portrayal of two of the characters of

The Good Soldier. More important, perhaps, was the meeting in 1911 in the Belgian town of Spa with a former Army officer who seems in many ways to have stood as model for Captain Ashburnham in the novel. This individual was 'a queer, heavy, retired English Lancer captain called Campbell. He was not otherwise distinguished by any great appearance of intelligence. But he deserves to be remembered and honoured along with St. Francis of the Birds and when the cattle at midnight on Christmas Eve talk from stall to stall and in the byres, surely they remember his name. He was the apostle of the four-footed dumb beasts.' Almost single-handed Campbell had convinced the butchers of Belgium to adopt humane methods in their slaughter-houses. That he succeeded was nearly miraculous for, as Ford notes, 'He had no French, no Flemish, no signs. He was more inarticulate than you would believe possible, even in his own tongue.' Yet he was inwardly driven to his task: 'His extraordinary passion burning through a heavy and slow body was something hardly to be believed in.'[37] If elements of Captain Campbell appear in Ashburnham, Nancy Rufford, the innocent young girl who is caught up in the politely murderous relations of the two couples of *The Good Soldier*, has been identified by Violet Hunt as Maleine, a fair-haired girl who worked as Ford's secretary and towards whom he had a chastely romantic attraction.

Given this material which he presumably considered as representative of the human lot, Ford proceeded with his situation. For the purposes of his novel he chose two gracious and genteel couples, one English, the other American who, year after year, meet for the cure at the German spa town of Nauheim. Both are from 'good families' and to all appearances live in a graciously civilized manner. The English husband is Captain Ashburnham, a tall, manly former Army officer who embodies many elements of the Fordian 'good man' hero by being generous, chivalrous and publicly righteous. He is married to Leonora, an Irish woman who has all the virtues (and vices) of a frugal French housewife. Unlike her husband, she is rational and materialistic and is a Roman Catholic. The American couple consists of John Dowell, a somewhat faint and indeterminate individual from Philadelphia, and his wife, Florence, the product of a respectable and 'nice' Connecticut family. So far, so good: on the surface the Dowells and Ashburnhams appear simply as two upper-class families who out of esteem for each other arrange to meet for their annual cure at Bad Nauheim, a town half way between Frankfurt and Ford's least favourite German town, Giessen. Yet underneath, the most appalling things happen with such persistence that it is difficult for Dowell, who relates the story, to tell what is more real—the elegant façade they present to the world, or what lies behind it. For it soon emerges that Dowell's wife, Florence, though she refuses him intercourse by feigning a heart ailment, in fact sleeps secretly with anyone attractive enough who comes along. At Nauheim, making use of her husband's ignorance of her true nature, she determines to have an affair with Edward Ashburnham. In a sense, her instinct in selecting him is justified, for in his turn, despite appearance of dog-like fidelity, Ashburnham is in fact a libertine. He is also, however, a sentimentalist, so that instead of being attracted to Florence, he forms a romantic attachment to a young girl called Nancy Rufford.

Originally the novel was to have been called *The Saddest Story*, and that is an accurate description of it at least from the point of view of Dowell who can see no sense in the horrors that soon begin to accumulate upon the heads of the participants. For him it is sad rather than tragic since he can find no tragic inevitability in the situation in which the Ashburnhams and Dowells have become involved. They are merely two couples who have met through the years at Nauheim. In a sense, of course, Dowell is right. At first he had assumed that the superficial politeness of all of them betokened an internal serenity, but before long he realized the true situation:

> No, by God it is false! It wasn't a minuet that we stepped; it was a prison—a prison full of screaming hysterics, tied down so that they might not outsound the rolling of our carriage wheels as we went along the shaded avenues of the Taunus Wald.[38]

What has made the story horrible is the gradual revelation of the uncontrollable passion that exists in people who ordinarily follow the generally rational conventions of society. For each of the characters, when faced with the really searing problem of human intercourse, especially in its sexual aspect, has nothing to rely on but some ready-made system of absolutes. The result is that each of them signally fails to come to grips with the true nature of this society in miniature. The sentimental Ashburnham, normally honourable and humane, has relied on his public virtue and good form to counterbalance his private weakness. His wife, on the other hand, is a logician at every level and sees his hypocrisy. Unfortunately, however, she is herself blind to the very idealism that motivates

Ashburnham in both sin and virtue. From this sort of situation there is no solution except suicide and that in fact is the course both Edward and Florence choose. In his quaintly mannered prose Dowell describes the denouement in these words:

> Well, it is all over. Not one of us has got what he really wanted. Leonora wanted Edward, and she got Rodney Bayham, a pleasant enough sort of sheep. Florence wanted Branshaw [the Ashburnham country house], and it is I who have bought it from Leonora. I didn't really want it; what I wanted mostly was to cease being a nurse-attendant. Well, I am a nurse-attendant. Edward wanted Nancy Rufford and I have got her. Only she is mad. It is a queer and fantastic world. Why can't people have what they want? The things were all there to content everybody; yet everybody has the wrong thing. Perhaps you can made head or tail of it; it is beyond me.[39]

The continual irony that Ford has introduced into the book with, as Mark Schorer has pointed out, often comical effects, comes from the failure of Dowell, the narrator, wholly to understand the tale he is telling. Fancying himself more acted upon than acting, he never considers what his own behaviour means to others. He continuously understates and forgets the most important events of his story, only mentioning them casually and long after they are over. The problem the novel presents cannot, however, be solved merely by dismissing Dowell as a simpleton. Soon enough one realizes that he does not realize the implications of his own passivity and that he misinterprets the actions of others. Yet he is not wholly a fool. Throughout the novel Dowell is made to say, 'I don't know; it's beyond me.' The reader's immediate reaction is that Dowell is merely the imperceptive narrator; yet since he is so obviously concerned with telling the truth and since he apparently has no private axe to grind, the reader is finally forced to take his protestations to heart. For what, after all, is the truth? It is true, as Dowell suggests, that Ashburnham is a sentimentalist; it is equally true that Dowell himself is one, though he does not know it. Yet with this information the reader is no nearer the truth of the relationships portrayed than he was before. Dowell's ignorance, in other words, cannot be entirely responsible for all the horrors of the novel.

By adopting the Conradian device of a narrator, Ford made the psychological implications of *The Good Soldier* considerably more subtle than they were in any of his earlier novels. In essence the situation is the same: the publicly good man finds himself entangled in a love affair with such horrific developments that his essential decency has to give way to his passion. But what the addition of a narrator provides is a focus on the essential nature of the good man that was hitherto lacking in Ford's novels. Virtually all of the central characters of the earlier novels—Moffat in *The Benefactor*, Don Kelleg in *An English Girl* and the Young Lovell himself—appear as 'heroes'; that is, they set the standards of behaviour in the novels in which they appear and are relatively free from critical appraisal. They are all idealized, albeit from the Pre-Raphaelite 'failure cult' point of view. But by having Ashburnham viewed by Dowell, an obtuse but well-meaning individual, Ford is able to stress both the nobility of Ashburnham and his fatally unrealistic view of the world. Thus, though seen at one remove, he emerges vividly as a plausible and coherent character.

The epigraph of the novel is 'Beati Immaculati', and certainly Ashburnham is pure of heart. That he is not pure of deed is merely Ford's way of saying that the Sermon on the Mount, as a 'Christist' as against a Christian document, is, at least in the pre-war years of 1913–14, an ideal rather than a real guide for human behaviour. That is not so much a criticism of anything as a statement of actuality; yet what Dowell's continual praise of Ashburnham stresses is Ford's wishful desire that this standard could be employed amongst human beings. Thus Captain Ashburnham is Ford's first wholly modern hero—an averagely sensual man placed in the absurd position of at once recognizing the benefits of an ideal code but humanly incapable of living up to it. What makes the portrayal of Ashburnham moving is his awareness of the hopelessness of his situation; the other characters for the most part are only out for a 'good time'.

As a social document, *The Good Soldier* presents a number of attitudes, none of them capable of coping with the fullness of the situation presented. Ashburnham's altruism is ultimately as useless as Leonora's hard-boiled practicality; Dowell's vague chivalry is as ineffective as Florence's clever duplicity, and the only really innocent figure of the book, Nancy Rufford (she is the true object of the epigraph) is the sacrificial victim loved by or at least honoured by all four of them and killed by them all. Thus, in the particular situation of this novel, whose characters are so similar to the expatriates of Eliot's *The Waste Land* who sit in the Hofgarten, reading 'much of the night' and going 'south in the winter', the point is that *The Good*

Soldier offers no solution. It merely presents a situation in which people have lost the ability to communicate with one another. Why this should be is not an easy question to answer, so that the apparently obtuse Dowell's reiterated 'I don't know' seems ironically to be the only proper comment to make.

In so far as it depicts the inability of human beings to deal with actual human relationships, *The Good Soldier* is the Edwardian novel *par excellence*. Anticipating Yeats's 'The Second Coming' and Eliot's *The Waste Land* by about ten years, Ford presented the essential conundrum of pre-war English civilization. The result is essentially one of stasis: it is 'the saddest story' because of its insoluble frustration. Given life as it was during the few years preceding the outbreak of the World War, there simply was no viable solution. It took a world-wide holocaust to reassert live moral values—strangely enough through a generation known popularly as 'the lost generation'. Ford's Tietjens tetralogy was to be his own vehicle for rehabilitating his Ashburnham type and giving him a solution to the problems raised by *The Good Soldier*. Seen in actual terms, Ford was later to note that in pre-war England Captain Campbell had been unable to secure legislation for his passionately held belief in humane slaughter. Yet by 1919 Captain Tietjens, like Captain Ford, his creator, was to find a means of reconciling his public actions with his private beliefs.

But if *The Good Soldier* is to survive in English literature it will have to depend on being more than an historical document: it will have to be recognized as containing matter applicable to all times. That it seems likely to succeed in this respect may be gathered from Graham Greene's characterization of it along with the Tietjens tetralogy as being 'almost the only adult novels dealing with the sexual life that have been written in English.'[40] For the impressive thing about *The Good Soldier* is not merely that it succeeds in capturing an era but that it presents a perennial human situation within the framework of a masterly literary performance. This achievement depends largely on Ford's use of the apparently unperceptive narrator, a device which posed a number of problems. Of these, the conception of Dowell was the most important, for he had to appear both obtuse and capable of revealing the implications of a particular scene. Ford's solution was to make Dowell's observations effective on three levels. At the lowest he appears a snob incapable of understanding either his own importance or the subtleties of his friends' relationships; at the second level he draws apparently valid conclusions according to his own concept of the relativity of truth. Yet at the highest level, which ironically is not far removed from the lowest, he is forced to the inevitable conclusion of real ignorance about the whole affair. Although not entirely successful in playing this subtle game, Ford at least avoided making Dowell an outrageous or sinister character like the narrator of Camus' *The Fall*. Thus the reader both sympathizes with Dowell and is irritated with him. This ambivalence of attitude is in itself an instance of psychological honesty.

In his preface to *The Good Soldier* Ford wrote that what he had wanted to do for English literature was what Maupassant's *Fort Comme la Mort* had done for French. Superficially, the two stories are similar in so far as the pursuit of Annette de Guilleroy by Olivier Bertin is something like the growing love Edward Ashburnham feels for Nancy Rufford, his young ward. Both novels present a psychological war of attrition and deal with the interplay of contradictory scruples. But Ford's remark about Maupassant refers not so much to subject-matter as to technique. For many years prior to 1913 Ford had considered himself in the tradition of the French novel of the nineteenth century rather than in the tradition of Fielding and Thackeray. This heritage, so important to both Conrad and himself, presupposes a conscious awareness of technique so that the subject could be put across in the most interesting and economical way possible.

The first task of an artist is to try to impose some sort of form on life. As Ford himself put it, 'Life meanders, jumps backwards and forwards, draws netted patterns like those on the musk melon. It seems the most formless of things.'[41] But as the artist's gift is his power to see the pattern, so his duty is to make it plain to the reader. To do so he must work consciously to make sure that nothing interferes with or distorts his ultimate purpose. Once Ford likened form in a novel to the playing of bridge, explaining that the function of each was to take the last trick and thus the game.[42] The artistic conscience therefore above all requires discipline. Every part of the novel must remain subsidiary to the whole; big scenes and characters larger than life must be eliminated if they detract from the view of life that the book as a whole portrays.

The temptation to introduce fabulous characters is of course great, as Dickens knew. But Ford always restrained himself in order to preserve the artistic integrity of the entire work. In a letter written in answer to some criticism by Edward Garnett of a much earlier book, *Mr. Apollo*, he specifically stated that he had refused to create a gigantic character, representing Lord Northcliffe, who would dominate the book. In fact, he cut three whole chapters devoted to this figure in order to create a balanced work of art.[43]

In this book as in *The Good Soldier*, every dramatic moment was therefore keyed down so that it would not blur the importance of less dramatic moments. Given the need for scrupulosity in conception, there still remain the problems of method. Ford believed that the pace of a novel should gradually increase and that every word should contribute to the final effect. He also realized that the complexities of situation and character are best revealed not by narrative but by the use of the time-shift, a device not original with him but one which he used skilfully to make past events as lively as those of the present. The special problem of narrative tone was raised in *The Good Soldier* by the selection of one character to act as narrator.*

In general, the choice of narrative style is of the greatest importance, and there are two distinct methods that have been used in England. The first assumes that part of the function of prose writing is to call attention to stylistic charms and to the personality of the author. The reader is to be made aware of the novelist's presence both through his choice of words and through the personal comments he makes from time to time about his own characters and their story. This method, used by Fielding, Dickens and Thackeray, has long been popular in England, but Ford believed that too often it was sloppy and that the obtruded comments were merely an attempt to cover up technical incompetence. The other method, which Flaubert, James and Ford himself employed, never permitted the intrusion of comments; its purpose was to present the story in such an impersonal manner that the reader would be unaware that he was reading a novel: instead, he would be vicariously living it.

In *The Good Soldier*, Ford solved the problem of narrative tone by making Dowell use a language not much different from that ordinarily used by an omniscient observer. Yet since Dowell is one of the characters, his personality has to be preserved. The compromise solution therefore was to let Dowell comment occasionally on his own narration, but on the whole to maintain a quietness and

* *The Good Soldier* is the only one of Ford's novels that uses this technique, except for *The Inheritors*, written in collaboration with Conrad.

unobtrusiveness of tone so that the book might sound like a long monologue spoken to a friend across the hearth. In the words of the novel: 'I shall just imagine myself for a fortnight or so at one side of the fireplace of a country cottage, with a sympathetic soul opposite me. And I shall go on talking, in a low voice while the sea sounds in the distance and overhead the great black flood polishes the bright stars.'[44] Later on in the novel he noted that 'real stories are probably told best in the way a person telling a story would tell them. They will then seem most real.'[45]

Since the cornerstone of style is vocabulary, Ford was particular in his choice of language. He was especially opposed to the use of 'literary' language; a writer must not copy the style of his predecessors, he said, but write according to his own personality. What makes this task so difficult, however, is the basic lack of clarity of the English language. Not only have many English words multiple meanings, but there are two separate languages, the spoken and the written. Such richness makes possible the glories of English poetry, but is ruinous to clear prose. In the Latin languages, especially French, this problem does not arise, for the written and spoken languages are one. In a long letter to Anthony Bertram, Ford suggested several ways to overcome the difficulties of the English language:

You try—literally!—talking as you write for a month or so and, after that, try writing as you find you talk. I believe you would then find words have quite another savour. Reading French—the best French— is nearly as good if you try here and there to translate as you go along. Nearly as good but not quite, though it does not make you so unpopular as if you try to talk like a book to your intimates. Best of all is to combine the two processes. I am really quite serious in writing that.

What is wrong with your style is that you combine two vocabularies, our spoken language with English-literary jargon and the introduction of one type of word into a passage of another type *blurs* the effect tremendously. And, if you intend to go on writing stories with, for basis, metaphysical ideas you cannot afford a blur anywhere. You may be as chary, as delicate, as you like in the amount of matter you vouchsafe, but what you do give must be extravagantly clear. And that clearness dies the moment there is in the reader's mind the least hesitation about a word. For, remember! If a narrator is telling a story—and particularly if the story be a narrative of personal adventure—the words he uses will be enormously powerful sidelights thrown on his character. They can be used to illuminate a man's history, his tastes, his sensitiveness to his surroundings—innumerable things. Supposing a man of whom you knew nothing and who knew nothing of you said to you suddenly, at a tea-fight: 'This room is more like a J.C.R. than a lady's drawing room!' You might work out a great deal about his character, tastes and past.[46]

The *mot juste* of the French tradition is not of itself sufficient, however, for as Ford and Conrad both agreed, the first function of style was to make the subject interesting.[47] It was therefore necessary to 'use words so that they shall seem alive because of their juxtaposition with other words.'*[48] First, the writer must have a feeling for words, and he must realize that a special or mannered vocabulary deadens the reader's interest in the subject. Early in his career Ford had lectured Wells on the virtues of slang, and in the last book he wrote he repeated his belief in the use of the spoken language:

A really good style, in whatever language, must be founded on the vernacular; the nearer it can come to the common speech of the day without having a shocking, comic, or gross effect, the better the style will be. Grossness, indeed, is preferable to over-delicacy for the writer who wishes his work to go down in posterity. For tomorrow very often accepts words and phrases that the writer's own day will shudder over as being neologisms. . . .[49]

Most of the devices Ford used in *The Good Soldier* are part of what he termed Impressionism. This method of writing, which derives from France, is so widely used today that it hardly needs comment: it aims to show rather than tell the reader what is happening; it is rendering as against description. Instead of chronological narration, it is a series of pictures or impressions juxtaposed by means of the time-shift. This method induces the notion of a continuous present tense and thus a sense of reality. Running through an impressionistic novel of this sort is an invisible thread which at the end can be pulled so as to reveal, as Ford puts it, 'the pattern of the carpet as a whole.' So that this pattern will be clear, nothing irrelevant can be included. Poe's phrase for this sort of writing was 'unity of effect', but the word *form* implies the same thing. Because Ford was able to master these techniques in this novel, *The Good Soldier* really is, as John Rodker said half in jest, 'the finest French novel in the English language.'[50]

* The phrase quoted above—'The great black flood polishes the bright stars'—is an instance of Ford's success in presenting an unusual image in a vocabulary that is at once vivid and ordinary.

Altogether, *The Good Soldier* can stand on equal footing with almost any novel written during the first quarter of this century. Its achievement is not obvious, but when, after a little while, the effect is felt, it is devastating. Ford himself jokingly commented on this quality when he wrote of the man in his regiment in France who had come back from leave looking extremely sick. Ford asked him what the trouble was and he replied: 'Well, the day before yesterday I got engaged to be married and today I have been reading *The Good Soldier*.'[51]

Beneath the sagging roof
The stylist has taken shelter,
Unpaid, uncelebrated,
At last from the world's welter

Nature receives him;
With a placid and uneducated mistress
He exercises his talents
And the soil meets his distress.

The haven from sophistications and contentions
Leaks through its thatch;
He offers succulent cooking;
The door has a creaking latch.

—EZRA POUND

Chapter Seven

———⟪•⟫⟪•⟫———

THE WAR AND AFTER

———⟪•⟫⟪•⟫———

THE years immediately preceding World War I must, in retrospect, have seemed faintly unreal to those who lived through them. Although George V was on the throne, the spirit of Victoria still exercised a strong influence on the manners of the country. The more intelligent members of the British populace were doubtless conscious that Armageddon was round the corner, but the people at large seemed unaware that an era was ending. Underneath this calm surface, however, artistic life was in ferment, and the few years prior to 1914 were characterized by some of the most interesting literary and artistic movements England has experienced during this century.

While Virginia Woolf was undoubtedly exaggerating for effect when she said that human nature changed in 1910, she was certainly correct in using the first Post-Impressionist exhibition as a symbol for an entirely new way of looking at things. For at about this same time, English literature was also beginning to show signs of a rebellion similar to that wrought in painting by the French and Spanish cubists. The literary propagandizing of Ezra Pound and the Imagists has already been noted, but perhaps the most vociferous of all, in both writing and painting was Wyndham Lewis, the founder of Vorticism. Essentially what Lewis and others of 'Les Jeunes' wanted was to move beyond the Impressionism that had been established by James, Conrad and other older writers in *The English Review*. Ford summarized their programme in these words: 'The Cubists, Vorticists and the others proclaimed that the plastic arts must be non-representational; the Imagists, Symbolistes, who joined up, I think, with Vorticism, proclaimed the immense importance of the "live" word—the word that should strike you as the end of a live wire will, if you touch it.'[1] Or, as Lewis himself put it: 'You think at once of a whirlpool. At the heart of the whirlpool is a great silent place where all the energy is concentrated. And there, at the point of concentration is The Vorticist.'[2]

Dedicated to direct statement and the reassertion of individualism, the Vorticists naturally attacked the carefully impersonal works of the Impressionists who always suppressed themselves in favour of the stories they had to tell or the scenes they were to paint. As a result, Vorticism and the movements on its periphery were individualistic, committed and boisterous. Lewis's Rebel Art Centre went to war against the Royal Academy; his magazine *Blast* brazenly attacked all staid and stuffy individuals whose activities interfered with clear thinking and direct statement. In their efforts the Vorticists were so astonishingly successful that, as Ford noted, they 'not only drove the old—oh, the horribly wearisome!—Academics out of the field, the market, and the forum; they created for themselves also a "public" that had never looked at a book otherwise than to be bored with it; or considered that an Art was an interesting, inspiring or amusing appearance.'[3]

The success of such a movement naturally depended on the existence of a cohesive group of individuals who could meet frequently and easily to argue and plot and in general to attract attention to themselves. It was here that Ford was to prove so useful an ally to 'Les Jeunes', for having been the first man in England to recognize them and publish their works in *The English Review*, he was able, in his somewhat godfatherly position to them all, not only to call attention to them through his weekly column in *The Outlook*, but to entertain them frequently and lavishly at South Lodge. That he was out of favour with his more dignified elders because of his marital difficulties in fact helped to endear him to his younger friends, with the result that for a few years prior to the outbreak of war, South Lodge virtually became the centre of these lively and amusing literary and artistic movements. Ford's own sympathies with the young was, of course, the most essential ingredient in this arrangement for, as he later wrote, 'I profess to a certain inherited flair for—a certain sense that it is a duty to forward—the recognition of young men with, to change the idiom, individualities, practising one or other of the arts.'[4]

Soon, then, the garden parties and dinner parties began, with a guest list that sounds like a catalogue of contemporary literature: Pound and Lewis of course, but also Yeats and D. H. Lawrence, Richard Aldington, F. S. Flint, the Compton Mackenzies, T. S. Eliot and Robert Frost, Amy Lowell, Rebecca West, W. L. George and Jacob Epstein. Violet's contribution to publicity was to include at the parties social leaders like Lady St. Helier and Lady Mond who could be counted on to make the new movements fashionable. The house itself soon also gained a physical notoriety, for Wyndham Lewis painted the drawing-room a bright red, converting it into a Vorticist salon, while in the front garden stood a bust of Ezra Pound carved by Henri Gaudier-Brjeska, looking for all the world like a phallic symbol.*

In all this activity Ford played the rôle of a genial and somewhat avuncular host. Nicknamed 'Forty Mad-dogs Hoofer' by Ezra Pound,[5] he presided over Violet's entertainments and when not so occupied, attended Yeats's Monday evenings or went along with the Imagists to poetry readings at the 'Golden Calf', a night club run by Madame Strindberg. Typical of the many reminiscences of Ford at the time is an aperçu of his daily life given Douglas Goldring by one of Ford's friends: 'There is a nostalgic flavour about those days,' he writes. 'I was very lonely in London and going to South Lodge was always something to look forward to. I used to play tennis in the garden opposite with Ford and Ezra in his green shirt which, after the game, Violet would have liked covered up by a coat, when in the drawing room! . . . Ford took me to that Sloane Square Theatre [the Royal Court] once when the Irish players were there and introduced me to Lady Gregory. . . . After that Ford and I had supper in some little restaurant with another poet, W. B. Yeats. . . .'[6]

Faith Compton Mackenzie has also described the Christmas holidays of 1912 which she spent with Ford and Violet:

I once spent Christmas with the Hueffers at a cottage near Burnham Beeches. My contribution to the household was a Sudbury ham, which was fallen upon with greedy enthusiasm by the other guest, Ezra Pound, who talked without ceasing throughout the festival. On Christmas Day Ford could only be approached through the keyhole of his bedroom, in which he was firmly locked against all comers. The cause

* This statue was later removed to Rapallo and set up in the town square.

of this retirement was not made known, but gave a spice to the party, since Violet was continually running up stairs to entreat him, speculating loudly as to why he was up there at all, and giving a touch of drama to the whole affair, so that the trumpery little cottage (which was only lent) achieved a sort of sublimity as the setting of a scene in history. Meanwhile Ezra's monologue went on without serious interruption. Ford, releasing himself from bondage on St. Stephen's Day, descended upon us with his store of intellectual energy unimpaired by festive excesses, full of benevolence, good cheer and lively conversation; in short, he was himself again. And Violet, her great eyes blazing, carved the turkey and what remained of the ham with more than her usual dexterity, her cheeks flushed at the excitement of his restoration. It was really a notable Christmas, for I was, and have always been, devoted to Ford and Violet.*[7]

Neither Ford nor Violet was limited to literary friendships, however, and Violet in particular enjoyed moving in London society. Her relationship with Ford had estranged a number of people, but in the summer of 1913, she was still able to do very well. Here is her comment on the London season of that year: 'Home, and my yearly garden-party never so well attended. Cabinet Ministers, by Jove! Dinners in the House. *Fêtes champêtres* at the Monds' in Lowndes Square, Henley with the Harmsworths, the Cabaret Club and all the charming artist rabble who were on the top of the vogue, and then to the cottage we rented at Selsey.

'A gorgeous season, I wished my poor old mother had been there to see it.'[8]

The Cabinet Minister referred to was probably C. F. G. Masterman, a junior member of Asquith's cabinet and a brilliant young politician who died before fulfilling his potential. Masterman had met Ford in 1905, proposed him for membership in the National Liberal Club and always remained a staunch ally. The Mastermans were frequent guests at the week-end cottage and, as Ford was a keen golfer at this period, he and Masterman would frequently play at one or other of the golf clubs in West Sussex, often with Lloyd George or another of Masterman's friends. In the summer of 1913, the Mastermans joined Ford and Violet on a trip to Germany, but because the German Government suspected that Masterman was

---

* Ezra Pound's own comment on the holiday week written to his mother is worth quoting for contrast: 'Impossible to get any writing done here. Atmosphere too literary. 3 "Kreators" all in one cottage *is* a bit thick.' D. D. Paige, ed., *Letters of Ezra Pound*, New York, 1950, p. 28.

really Winston Churchill in disguise, the vacationers were subjected both to unusual honours and trying inconveniences.

Through all of this social whirl, Ford had been working very hard, mainly to restore his financial position. After the divorce scandal he adopted the pseudonym of 'Daniel Chaucer' in order to keep his earnings beyond the grasp of his creditors, but by 1913 the need for this *nom de guerre* had passed and, although never a best seller, he was able to pay off his debts, which included the large sum of £440 owed to Arthur Marwood. The regular income he received for his column in *The Outlook* was also particularly beneficial for a man whose earnings were normally irregular.

On the surface, then, the two or three years preceding the war seem to have been both pleasant and profitable for Ford. He had regained a good deal of the status and position he had lost in 1910 and he was intimately associated with the most lively literary and artistic movements of the day. Underneath, however, Ford's life with Violet was beginning to wear thin. Rebecca West was probably right when she said that their liaison was 'doomed' from the start.[9] The unpleasantness that had accompanied its inception had in many ways soured it by revealing to each of the partners aspects of the other's character which might not otherwise have become known, or at the least, would have become known only at a later date, by which time they would have become more accustomed to each other's vagaries. The disparity between their ages also contributed to the collapse of their ménage. Violet was a jealous person and, when Ford's proclivity for the society of beautiful women became known to her she was naturally bitter. A voluble talker, Violet reduced the latter days at South Lodge to a morass of squabbling, and took her troubles outside to anyone who would listen to her.

The break did not actually come, however, until after the war: in 1913 and 1914 their domestic difficulties were only beginning. Considering the amount of writing Ford produced at the time, there was little opportunity for disagreement, for in addition to the novels and poems published during these years, Ford collaborated with Violet on a collection of short stories called *Zeppelin Nights* and also wrote a suffragette pamphlet called *This Monstrous Regiment of Women* which was published by the Women's Freedom League. This was but one of several pieces Ford wrote on behalf of Mrs. Pankhurst and the Women's Suffrage Movement. After the outbreak of war he also wrote two books of propaganda in support of the Allies.

Modern propaganda stems from the first World War, and what is now euphemistically called the British Ministry of Information had its beginnings in a small office that was so secret that it was only referred to as Wellington House. Ford's friend, C. F. G. Masterman was placed in charge of this office by Asquith, and shortly after he took over, he asked Ford to write propaganda for him. He made it plain, however, that anything Ford might write would have to appear without official sanction and that he would receive no credit whatever from the government for his work. Ford nevertheless agreed to write for Masterman, and the result was two books, *When Blood is Their Argument* and *Between St. Dennis and St. George*. The first is a scholarly analysis of the growth of Prussian influence over German education, literature and society, and is a well-documented exposition of the development of a deliberate policy of nationalism and xenophobia. The second book is an outgrowth of Ford's belief in the spiritual union between France and England that has persisted despite years of bickering and a long history of war. Written in the spirit of the 'Entente Cordiale' and designed to overcome the pro-German feeling that over the years had become widespread in England, the book stresses both the simple virtues of frugality and industry which characterize the French peasant and the devotion to clear thought which typifies the French artist, and shows why these are the important ingredients of Western civilization. Although written as propaganda, it is a sincere statement of what France means to the world and is, moreover, an integral part of Ford's social philosophy. In preparing this work, Ford was assisted by researchers: one of these was Richard Aldington; another was Alec Randall, who was then a young diplomat and who later, as Sir Alec, became his country's ambassador in Denmark. Despite their help, Ford had to devote a great deal of work to the book, only to find, as Masterman had predicted, that his reward in England was negligible. In France, on the other hand, a translation called *Entre St. Denis et St. Georges* was widely acclaimed and read.

The outbreak of war in 1914 caught Ford in the midst of his propaganda work, and therefore he did not join the army until a year later. At the age of forty-two, which was over the military age limit, it was hardly necessary for him to sign up for a line regiment when, had he used his influence, he could probably have obtained a 'safe' appointment in a government office. But for years Ford had considered himself a member of the governing class and, as a man who took his ideals seriously, he believed the position demanded certain sacrifices. In the words of one of his later fictional characters: 'Damn it all, haven't I been for forty years or so in the ruling classes of this country, haven't I enjoyed their fat privileges, and shan't I, then, pay the price?'[10] At the same time, he realized that not everybody considered him a member of the governing class: he was not a public school man and did not really belong to 'the establishment'; E. V. Lucas told him he wasn't even properly English since he didn't appreciate *Punch*.[11] Moreover, in the early months of the war, he was publicly questioned by the police while playing golf in Sussex, and because of his German name he was denounced as an enemy agent. In short, he experienced the sort of intrusions into his private life that D. H. Lawrence endured and described so bitterly in *Kangaroo*. Yet the truth was that a number of those who actually belonged to the governing class and who bore names unquestionably English, chose to avoid their responsibilities and wangled for themselves jobs in Whitehall and other places unexposed to danger. Ford's decision to join the army was therefore an act of poetic irony. Partly a means of scoring off those who accused him of disloyalty, it was more importantly a way of satisfying himself that he at least was ready to live up to his ideals and responsibilities when the need arose.

On a more personal level, he was also aware that many of the young friends he had entertained at South Lodge were now at the front. F. S. Flint had gone, and so had Wyndham Lewis and Richard Aldington. But what hit him hardest was the death in the trenches of the young French sulptor, Henri Gaudier-Brjeska. Since he had all along believed that the old rather than the young should fight, on the grounds that the old had already tasted much of life, he signed up almost immediately on hearing of Brjeska's death in 1915.

According to his official service record, Ford was commissioned a Second Lieutenant in the Welch Regiment on the 10th of August. Almost immediately afterwards he wrote to Mrs. Masterman that he felt 'as if the peace of God had descended on me—that sounds absurd—but there it is! Man is a curious animal.'[12] In addition to removing his moral qualms, the decision to join the army was also a means of eliminating the domestic friction that was poisoning the atmosphere of South Lodge. It was also a way of escaping from the trials of public life and, as one who knew Ford during the war recounts, 'He was the only intellectual I had met to whom army discipline provided a conscious relief from the torments and indecisions of a sensitive brain. To obey orders was, for him, a positive holiday, and the pleasure he took in recounting rather bucolic anecdotes of the army was the measure of his need for escape from the intrigues and sophistications of Literary London.'[13] In an article written immediately before joining the army,[14] Ford had also said that since by that time he had been a literary man for twenty-five years, he hoped in future to take up some altogether different occupation, and certainly the war provided him with that opportunity.

After receiving his commission, Ford was sent to Tenby in Wales, and there he was assigned to the 3rd Battalion of his Regiment. From the first he found much to be upset by in Army life. Much older than others of his own rank and more distinguished than most of any rank, Ford found himself out of his element. He never, however, took advantage of his position and instead always behaved with great reticence and quietness. A brother officer has described him as he was in 1916: 'He was, of course, years older than myself and had, I believe, been a subaltern for some time. We all liked him in the mess, and for my own part I always found him most kind and helpful, like an elder brother or senior boy at school. I well remember his initiating me into the onerous duties of Orderly-Officer which, as I was young and inexperienced, was then something of an ordeal. Little did I appreciate the fact that I was then being instructed by so celebrated an author, a fact that he kept to himself. The thing that struck me most perhaps, was the "softness" of his voice. He always spoke very quietly, it seemed. Posted to France again, I lost touch with this good friend, but later I heard he had also followed overseas and was at the Base somewhere, interrogating German prisoners.'[15]

Except for the unfamiliarity of military life, the first portion of Ford's army career was not especially burdensome, however. Stationed at Cardiff Castle, he found amongst his fellow-officers the younger brother of his friend, Charles Masterman. He was also able to take week-end leaves which he usually spent with Violet, either at her own cottage in Selsey or at Rebecca West's place in Leigh-on-Sea. Sometimes they would also go to house parties at the H. G. Wellses, where people like Lily Langtry and Ellen Terry would be in attendance.

Army life also had its amusing moments. Thus one evening a

young lady was found in the barracks and was only apprehended after the sergeants had chased her round and over the men's beds. She was then arrested, quite unjustly, according to Ford, 'on an impossible charge'—presumably for having entered Army premises with immoral intentions. Ford then came to her defence and wrote a long memorandum to Headquarters about the incident. This was returned as being both illegible and illiterate because, as Ford later recorded, 'I had worried the good gentlemen by using the words *proprio motu*—"the charge would not lie because the lady had not come into the Rink *proprio motu*—but had been introduced by Cpl. Plant 5/Welch etc." '[16]

Still, Ford's military life was worrisome: in particular he was bothered by the deterioration of his relationship with Violet. She, it is true, was having a bad time living alone in London. On one occasion she invited a favourite niece, the daughter of a clergyman, to visit her; but the invitation was rejected because of the father's (and the Church's) hostility to Violet's 'immoral' conduct. 'This is what you have brought on me, dear Ford,' Violet wrote, 'and you are happy in Cardiff and leaving me to bear it alone. It is this sort of thing all the time. . . .'[17] Violet must have taken her grievances to others, for on one occasion, in March of 1916, Ford had to answer a letter from Wells who had written him on her behalf. The first part of Ford's letter protests his continued affection and loyalty; nevertheless, he realized, as he said, that it was rather dull for Violet merely to be the wife of an army officer. Still, the whole tenor of European life had been altered by the war, and one could not expect to perpetuate a life of continued excitement as in the old days. In Ford's view, Violet simply had not adjusted to changed conditions.[18]

In his spare time Ford continued to do a certain amount of writing and tried to keep in touch with old friends by correspondence. To one of his letters, Conrad sent words of encouragement: 'You won't be surprised to hear that you have been much in my thoughts of late. It must have been an enormous change in your mental habits; but I know your wonderful intellectual adaptability and your letter, most welcome, is very much what I expected it to be.

'Yes, *mon cher*! Our world of 15 years ago is gone to pieces: what will come in its place, God knows, but I imagine doesn't care.'[19]

By July of 1916, Ford was sent out to France with his men. At first he was sufficiently detached to cope with the new situation and was even able to do some writing. With one of his fellow-officers,

Captain H. C. James, he would engage in *bout-rimé* exercises. James would provide the endings, Ford would write the sonnet in English and then James would translate the poem into Latin. In this way, they passed many of the hours of waiting that occupy a soldier's life. In the late summer he was summoned to Paris to be commended by the 'Minister of Instruction and of Inventions Useful to the War' for his work as author of *Between St. Dennis and St. George* which, in translation, was being widely read in France and which had even been 'communicated' to the Institut de France. The minister urged him to continue his work, and Ford wrote 'Une Partie de Cricket' for a Swiss review. Later reprinted in *No Enemy*, it is a comparison of the attitudes taken towards the war by French and English soldiers. But the best indications of Ford's feelings during the first weeks of service in the B.E.F. are to be found in the letters he wrote to his friends back in England. In July of 1916 he wrote to Mrs. C. F. G. Masterman that he was at the Front, 'right up in the middle of the strafe, but only with the 1st Line transport. We get shelled, two or three times a day, otherwise it is fairly dull—after the first once or twice.'[20] A month later he wrote to Conrad, telling him about the mud and the rain of the trenches, but observing that his previous experience of bad weather while slogging back and forth between his own house and Conrad's in Kent permitted him to put up with the cold and wet better than some of his comrades did. The letter concludes with these remarks:

> I have been for six weeks—with the exception of 24 hours—continuously within reach of German missiles and, although one gets absolutely to ignore them, consciously, I imagine that subconsciously one is suffering. I know that if one of the cooks suddenly opens, with a hammer, a bacon chest close at hand, one jumps in a way one doesn't use when the 'dirt' is coming over fairly heavily.
>
> An R.F.A. man has just come along and explained that the 'rain has put the kybosh on the strafe'—so there my dear, you have the mot juste. But it is fairly sickening all the same.[21]

To judge from his letters to Conrad, Ford kept a balance by thinking about his experiences in literary terms. In three separate letters, he related for Conrad's benefit exactly what certain noises are like in trench warfare. One long letter deals with the sounds heavy artillery makes in different weather conditions. Even by September of 1916, he was still sufficiently uninvolved to be able to look objectively at his emotions. After having seen his first war casualty, he remarks to Conrad: 'These things gave me no *emotion* at all—they seemed *obvious*: rather as it would be.'[22]

Then he goes on about fear: 'This of course is the devil—and worse because it is so very capricious. Yesterday I was buying—or rather not buying—fly papers in a shop under a heap of rubbish. The woman was laughing and saying that all the flies come from England. A shell landed in the chateau into whose wall the shop was built. One Tommie said, "Crump!" Another: "Bugger the flies" and slapped himself. The woman, about thirty, quick and rather jewish, went on laughing. I said: "Mais je vous assure, Madame, qu'il n'y a plus comme ça de mouches chez vous." No interruption, emotion, vexed at getting no fly papers. Subconscious emotion, "Thank God the damn things burst".'[23]

Ford's duties as an officer in the Welch Regiment seem to have been various. Because of his knowledge of Flemish and French, he was ordered to buy supplies for his battalion; then, when attached to the Front Line Transport, he was made billeting officer. Because he did not get on with his Commanding Officer, who in peacetime had been a Town Councillor of Eastbourne, he was generally worked hard by his Adjutant. In September Ford took part in the battle of the Somme and a month later was gassed with the result that for the rest of his life he had a stertorous voice. In the late autumn he was withdrawn from the front line and given the task of looking after wounded prisoners of war. On one occasion, his literary past was revived when, entering a hospital tent, he asked one of the prisoners what he did before the war. The soldier, apparently touched by this concern expressed in German, said: '*Herr Offizier, Geisenhist*', and so, as Ford remarked in a letter to Conrad, there again was the famous phrase, 'Excellency, a few goats!'[24]

But by December Ford was himself hospitalized because, as he told Masterman, his lungs were 'in a devil of a way, with extensions at the bases and solidifications and all sorts of things—partly due to a slight touch of gas I got in the summer and partly to sheer weather.'[25] The hospital in Rouen to which he was sent was normally an old priests' seminary, but it had also been used as a hospital by the Prussians in 1870. There Ford shared a room with a Second Lieutenant of the Black Watch, a shell-shock case who was constantly talking to himself and sharpening his Scottish dagger at night.[26]

The experiences Ford had undergone up to this time, which

included the witnessing of the near-destruction of his battalion by German artillery, began to change his whole attitude towards the war. No longer did he describe the scenery for Conrad's literary benefit; no more was he the aloof observer. In his letter to Masterman, he commented sourly on the political situation at home and on the new government under Lloyd George: 'What a Ministry! Everything one has fought against all one's life! Northcliffism, Georgeism, Mondism, Balliolism! If it weren't for Balfour and Robert Cecil—and I don't suppose *they* cut much ice *dans ces parages*. . . .'[27] Then, in another letter, he told his daughter that he was the only one left out of fourteen officers who had come out with him, and 'I am pretty well a shattered wreck—tho' they say my lungs will get better in time. And I sit in the hut here. wh. is full of Welch officers all going up—and all my best friends—and think that very likely not one of them will be alive in a fortnight. I tell you, my dear, it is rather awful.'[28] To Conrad he was even more outspoken, forcibly expressing his horror at the destruction of human life and the growing rage he felt within him whenever he thought of his dead comrades.[29] At about this time he wrote his highly emotional poem, 'One Day's List' in which he commemorated four of his young fellow-officers who had fallen in one day of futile fighting.

For the worst winter months of 1916–17, Ford was sent south to Menton for further recuperation. But there too the weather was cold and, for the first time in years the ground was covered with snow. After a few weeks, he returned again to Rouen where he was first given command of a casualty battalion and later a company of war prisoners. In April he was sent home to England and was there attached to the King's Liverpool Regiment and promoted Lieutenant. While at home he continued his efforts to secure a staff job by writing to influential friends like Masterman. This request was not made from cowardice but from a realization that the best use was not being made of his talents in the Welch Regiment. Nothing ever came of these petitions, however, despite the assurance of one of his commanding Generals that he had been put in for a staff appointment. In retrospect, it is astonishing that the War Office did not employ Ford in some sensible capacity, if nothing more than as a liaison officer, for there can hardly have been many men in the B.E.F. who knew German, French and Flemish as well as he did.

Instead he was once again sent out to France, only to be wounded a month later in an artillery bombardment. Moved to the rear lines, he continued his work as an interrogator of prisoners. Because of a shortage of officers, he also took charge of the training of a large number of French-Canadian soldiers. In January of 1918, he was promoted Captain and two months later returned to England where he was attached to the Northern Command at York as a lecturer.

In addition to the deprivations Ford suffered as an officer in France he was almost continually inconvenienced by lack of funds. When, in 1917, he had returned to England for convalescence, his poverty became so trying that he believed he could not afford to remain a regimental officer. He therefore wrote to his old friend, Edgar Jepson, to ask whether it would be possible to obtain a loan against his copyrights—not an outright grant—from the Royal Literary Fund. He explained that in the earlier years of the war he had been able to make ends meet by his writing, but that now, having been blown up on the Somme and gassed at Armentières, he only had strength enough to run his company. He said he did not want to resign his commission and enlist, but he pointed out that his pay as an officer on Light Duty was barely enough to cover his mess bill.[30]

So far as is known, Ford received no financial aid from the Royal Literary Fund. He did not resign his commission, however, but remained in York until the end of the war. In March of 1918 he was promoted Acting Brevet Major and in January of 1919 he resigned his commission.

While the facts of Ford's official war record demonstrate that Ford's was a hard war—no more trying than that experienced by many others, but a good deal more difficult than the experience of most of his literary contemporaries—there is little evidence as to how well Ford actually performed his duties as a soldier. All that exists is the official comment of his commanding officer, written in Ford's army small book in the space where the commanding officer 'may if he wishes to do so, state . . . in his own handwriting the fact that an officer has shown aptitude . . . .' Lt. Col. G. R. Powell, the C.O. of the 3rd Battalion of the Welch Regiment, wrote this of Ford:

> Has shown marked aptitude for grasping any intricate subject and possesses great powers of organization. A lecturer of the first water on several military subjects. Conducted the duties of messing officer to the unit (average strength 2,800) with great ability.[31]

The 1914 war was not the first war that deeply affected those who had fought in it, but it probably radically changed more people than

any previous war had done. Marking as it did the end of Victorian-
ism, it made the whole atmosphere of pre-war society incompatible
to those who served in the trenches. The world of Ada Leverson and
James Barrie now seemed so unreal and populated by such unsub-
stantial persons that many returning soldiers decided to live according to their own standards and not those of the late Queen. 'Shell-
shock' was how this reaction was described by the civilian world, but
at heart it was a feeling of distaste and bitterness towards all those
who had remained unaffected by the war.

Ford's state of mind at the conclusion of hostilities is revealed in
his tetralogy of war novels, *Parade's End*, and in his semi-fictional
war reminiscences called *No Enemy*. In general, he shared the views
of most of the returning soldiers. He found that many of those who
had remained behind had grown rich, and he discovered that it was
stylish to debunk the heroism of the troops in France. Justifiable as
a counter to the exaggerated hatred of the Germans that had existed
during the war, this was nevertheless not a point of view with which
he could be sympathetic after his months with the B.E.F. Like every
soldier, Ford had looked forward to returning to London, but once
back he found a hostile civilian population and a government unwill-
ing to fulfil its promises. In one of his books of reminiscence he
speaks of feeling like a stranger in his own city. Hitherto he had
always taken London for granted:

> But as I extended my foot to make that crossing something snapped. It
> was the iron band around my heart that had always made it London's
> own. 'London only! London only! This train London only!' say the
> porters beside the trains in Ashford or Darlington or Exeter. . . . That
> could never again be said of me. When I went to London after that it
> would never be '*back* to London'. I should be visiting a town where I
> had no place and that knew not me! I was perfectly aware of that.[32]

For some time during 1918, thanks to his relatively light duty as a
lecturer at York, Ford had frequent opportunity to visit London on
leave. On most of these occasions, however, he did not stay at South
Lodge because he had come to realize that he and Violet were split
by a basic difference of attitude. He believed, as he told Mrs. Masterman, that Violet was 'absolutely untouched, mentally, by the
war. . . .'[33] and he found her vagaries of behaviour tiresome. He suspected Violet of suppressing some of his war poems for some private
end of her own and he knew that at times he was not welcome at her
house.[34] 'South Lodge does not seem too available,' he noted in a

letter asking Mrs. Masterman to find lodgings for him in her neighbourhood.[35] These squabbles, compounded with their pre-war disagreements made Ford realize that they had grown so far apart that it was impossible for him to consider reuniting with her. For Violet, now in her early sixties, though destined, as it happened, to outlive Ford, this was a cruel blow, and she did not easily accede to Ford's wish.

In the course of these London sojourns, Ford had come to know a number of the young intellectuals who during the war had attached themselves to Ezra Pound and others of the group Ford had so often entertained in 1913 and 1914. Since he had grown antipathetic towards South Lodge, he now began to see more and more of this younger set which included Margaret and G. D. H. Cole, John Rodker, Mary Butts, Phyllis Reid (who later married Aylmer Vallance) and Stella Bowen, a young Australian painter who shared a flat with Phyllis Reid. Most of these young artists, like their counterparts in Bloomsbury, were pacifists. Yet the uniformed Captain Ford was immediately accepted and lionized by them, with the result that he felt happier with them than he did with some of his older friends.

The problem still remained, however, where he was to live after demobilization. At first he had wanted to go to France, but like D. H. Lawrence who had also wanted to leave England immediately upon the conclusion of hostilities, Ford found that his request for a passport was refused. He therefore decided to settle somewhere in the country. This decision was one which he had really taken while fighting with the B.E.F. in France for, like many men in similar circumstances, he had then thought not so much of people but of landscapes. His peacetime life had been clogged with people just as the trenches were with soldiers, so that what he wanted after the war was not more people but a quiet life in the country. The country, moreover, the land, was what he had been really fighting for. An outgrowth of his own earlier experience in Kent, he saw in the landscapes of France the same values he cherished in England. These he apostrophized in his war poem 'Footsloggers':

> It is because our land is beautiful and green and comely,
> Because our farms are quiet and thatched and homely,
> Because the trout stream dimples by the willow,
> Because the water-lilies float upon the ponds,
> And on Eston Hill the delicate, waving fronds

Of the bracken put forth, where the white clouds are flying,
That we shall endure the swift, sharp torture of dying . . .[36]

As a provisions and billeting officer Ford had seen in France the
sufferings of a civilian population which was, except for the accident
of geography, essentially the same as that of Sussex or Kent. And,
observing in the person of Madame Rosalie of Nieppe a tranquil
bravery that had overcome the loss of her entire family and most of
her possessions, he said to himself: 'What the devil! If she can stick
it, I too can!'[37]

Thus, like Christopher Tietjens in the tetralogy, Ford found the
war a hardening experience: he found that he had to discover within
himself the ideals and traditions for which he was suffering, and that
he had to act in a positive and decisive way. Hence the decision to
break with Violet and to move to the country. In the words of the
quasi-fictional central character of *No Enemy*:

I do not desire money, glory, the praise of my kind whom I distrust,
nor yet to dominate humanity, which is a beast that I dislike. I do not
desire friends; I do not desire broad lands. So, thinking about things in
the wash-house of Madame Rosalie, I said: 'I must dig myself in.' I
said, indeed, twice: 'I must dig myself in. . . .'

I must have a dugout, as proof as possible against the shells launched
against me by blind and august destiny; round about it there must be
the strong barbed wire of solitude and, within the entanglements, space
for a kitchen garden.[38]

Thus with this plan in mind, he approached the young Australian
painter, Stella Bowen. 'He began to tell me about himself,' she later
recorded, 'filling me with pride by confiding all his troubles and
weaknesses. The most monumental of authors—the fountain,
apparently, of all wisdom, who appeared already to have lived a
dozen lives, now—amazingly—announced that he wished to place
his person, his fortune, his future in my hands. Revealed himself as
a lonely and very tired person who wanted to dig potatoes and raise
pigs and never write another book. Wanted to start a new home.
Wanted a child.

'I said yes, of course.'[39]

Because of the publicity that had attended his liaison with Violet,
Ford was determined to keep this new arrangement as secret as
possible. The move nevertheless caused him a great deal of trouble,
and a number of people who remained loyal to Violet wrote to

demand an explanation of his conduct. To most of these requests Ford made no reply, for his view was, as he later wrote to Jepson: 'One's friends must accept one's actions and divine the justifications for those actions—or one must do without friends!'[40]

In May of 1919, only a few months after his release from the Army, Ford and Stella Bowen moved to a small village in West Sussex called Hurston. 'We knew we were going to be very poor,' Stella later wrote, 'because Ford had no money beyond what he earned and he had not written a novel since before the war. So when we heard of a farmer who had an empty cottage at five shillings a week, and found it to be very old, charmingly situated, and named Red Ford, we took it immediately. . . . It *looked* all right, and that was the main thing. It looked like home.'[41]

The cottage was tiny and also, to judge from Ezra Pound's poem about the place,* leaky, but Ford was soon hard at work repairing the roof, laying down a wooden floor to cover the mud and fashioning crude furniture from an odd lot of oak boards he purchased from his meagre funds. Soon he and Stella were well established in their humble cottage; they had a cat and a dog, chickens and ducks for eggs and meat, and a garden full of tomatoes, beans and sweet corn. Still, the place was really too small for them, and Ford began to look for another house. In September of 1919 he found what he wanted in nearby Bedham, but was unable to move in immediately because the lease had not expired. In a letter to his new friend Herbert Read, he enthusiastically described the place, adding that his neighbours included such people as Sir Bysshe Shelley and Sir Edward Elgar. Peace and quiet was what Ford wanted, however, and he urged Read not to reveal his address.[42]

As a symbol of his desire to begin a new life after the war he changed his surname by deed poll from Hueffer to Ford. During the war, the possession of a German patronymic had been a disadvantage, and Ford suffered annoyances because of it. He was sufficiently loyal, however, not to change it until June 28, 1919. Ford himself instances various reasons for his new name, amongst them 'to oblige a relative'[43] and the difficulty of pronouncing his former name which, he claimed, made prospective readers shy away from buying his novels in bookshops. Gerald Duckworth put the question succinctly: ' "And how *should* one pronounce your beastly name? Hoo-effer? Hweffer? Heifer, Hyoofer? It's impossible to know." '[44]

* See epigraph for this chapter.

138

A further reason for the change was that it released him from his entanglement with Violet Hunt who always called herself Mrs. Ford Madox Hueffer and thus ran the risk of additional lawsuits instigated by the first Mrs. Hueffer.*

The use of 'Ford' as a surname had its disadvantages, however. Like the adoption of a new name upon elevation to the peerage, the change of a well-known author's name causes confusion and tends to reduce him to the rank of a beginner.†

Ford stayed in Red Ford for almost a year before moving to Bedham. His new house was called Coopers and there, late in 1920, his daughter, Esther Julia, was born. In her reminiscences, Stella Bowen has described the place as 'an extravagantly beautiful and quite inaccessible spot on a great wooded hill about ten miles from Red Ford. There was an immense view, and lovely paths winding through beech woods all over the hillside. Our cottage, white plaster and oak beams with a steep tiled roof, was about three hundred years old and had settled well down into the hillside. There was an orchard full of wild daffodils running up to the hard road at the top of the hill, a small wood full of bluebells lower down behind the cottage, and below that, a big rough field. Ten acres in all, sloping towards the view.'[45]

Since his land was not especially suitable for the growing of vegetables, Ford concentrated on raising pigs and planting potatoes. At first he was full of high hopes, and his letters to friends at the time contain a good deal of agricultural matter. In May of 1921, he wrote to his agent, J. P. Pinker, to offer him some of his farm produce, such as newly hatched ducks at 96/- the dozen. 'My hay crop is singularly well-harvested,' he wrote. 'I could supply your stables at extremely low prices considering the quality of the article.' He then described his pedigree pigs, Anna and Anita, who were registered in the Large Black Pig Society's herd book and promised to take Pinker to a celebration dinner should these pigs win prizes at the Lincoln Show, which he confidently expected them to do.[46]

Soon, however, came the drought. In the beginning it was not too bad, and in a letter to Edgar Jepson he describes his daily life:

We are, but for the drought which is ruinous for my agricultural pursuits, remarkably flourishing, for us in our humble scale—at least, I am

* One such lawsuit took place as late as 1925.
† Ford's publishers at first tried to alleviate this difficulty by printing both names on his books.

enjoying a mild boom-kin in the U.S.A. and thus the New World redresses. . . . Of course, if you yourself would come it would be delightful and I could give you plenty of poker of which I have been playing a good deal with U.S.A. pilgrims to this shrine. They come in small shoals to talk highbrow; and we set them to feed the pigs—of which I have a number—or to carry the hay of which we have successfully harvested a nice little stack. And in the evenings I take their money at poker—and we have sweet corn and pumpkins growing, so they feel homesick. . . .[47]

Then, after a fortnight, disaster overtook the Ford farm as the drought worsened. From dawn till dusk he and Stella would carry water from the well for the animals and for the flower and vegetable gardens.[48] Finally, at the end of the day, they would stop and change for dinner, Ford donning an ancient dinner jacket for the occasion. This transformation sometimes disconcerted his guests, but Ford, had a simple reason for the gesture which he transcribed as an epigraph to one of his books as it had earlier been expressed by Niccolo Macchiavelli: 'But when evening falls I go home and enter my writing room. On the threshold I put off my country habit, filthy with mud and mire and array myself in costly garments; thus worthly attired, and for four hours' space I feel no annoyance, forget all care; poverty cannot frighten me . . . I am carried away.'[49]

Doubtless a number of Ford's friends thought it odd that he should retreat into the heart of the country from cosmopolitan London, and doubtless even more thought his living conditions excessively rude. But as Stella Bowen recounted, neither she nor Ford considered they were slumming. 'His geese were always swans,' she reports, 'and a tumble-down labourer's cottage, once he had made it his home and polished its woodwork and painted its walls, assumed in his eyes the dignity of a gentleman's country residence. The simplicity of heart that made small things seem important, like the earliest salad, or the purchase of an old bit of brass or an effective arrangement of our meagre possessions, made Ford a delightful companion. He was never bored.'[50]

Isolated as they were in winter, they entertained many guests during the summer. From London came young friends like Alec Waugh, David Garnett, A. E. Coppard and Anthony Bertram, while the American visitors included Monroe Wheeler and Glenway Wescott. One American admirer, Professor L. M. Price of the University of California was immediately upon his arrival on a hot

July afternoon, put to work haying, for Ford was never one to stand on ceremony with his guests. In the evenings, as Stella has recorded, 'There would be supper, late as usual, under the apple trees, Chinese lanthorns in the branches, a moon, a sweet-smelling tobacco plant, and nightingales. And all of us very late to bed.'[51]

Most of the talk centred on writing, for Ford was a great raconteur and loved to discourse on technique and style. To those who asked his advice he would write immense letters of encouragement and instruction. He was of course pleased to be approached as an expert by the young, but most of his interest came from sheer love of his art.

Thus he would write to Anthony Bertram, who had enquired about the proper treatment of subject-matter:

> ... I think it's more practical to begin with an action or incident and spin your subject round it than to begin with a 'subject' and work architectonics out of it. Every incident—anecdote—has of necessity subject, atmosphere and the inevitabilities of character behind it. I believe that's really the sound way to elaborate a novel: think of an anecdote: double it: halve it: add three ... and so on as we used to set problems at school. [52]

To Herbert Read he wrote of using the prose masters as models:

> No, not a bit have I grown tired of talk about books—and youth is a golden thing. 'Education Sentimentale' is Stonehenge; but 'What Maisie Knew' is certainly Stratford-on-Avon (Though God forbid that the Old Man should hear me say so!). 'Le Rouge et le Noir' is the perfect thing upon which to model one's style, if one does not model it on 'Coeur Simple'—which is worth a wilderness of apes, monkeys, Times Supplement Reviewers and almost every other thing in the world ... But 'The Real Thing' is nearly as good. Only Henry was just a *little* provincial-pharisaic, whereas Flaubert was so huge, untidy, generous—and such a worker! Still, as someone or other said, 'L'un et l'autre se disent' and if you aren't in the mood for Stonehenge the Birthplace is a very good substitute—and Henri Beyle, perhaps a better still.[53]

Later, however, he issued a warning:

> Of course, I see you aiming at becoming another Henri Beyle: but it is a miserable ambition ... Learn of Stendhal all you can—and there is ... an immense deal to learn in an artistic sense ... But don't model yourself on him ... I can imagine no more terrible being to himself than a Yorkshireman, true to type, and modelling himself on Mr.

Beyle! The end would be the most horribly costive neurastheniac you can imagine, with incredible sex obsessions sedulously concealed, swaddled up to the ears in red flannel for fear of draughts, and with more hypochondrias and phobias than are to be found in all Freud, Jung and the late Marie Bashkirtseff put together . . . And with a yellow, furred tongue, and a morgue britannique beyond belief. . . .[54]

Naturally, literary discussion and farming were not all that occupied Ford's mind at this time, and the little 'boom-kin' he mentioned to Jepson was the result of hard work and a tenacious desire, despite disavowals to the contrary, to establish himself once again as a writer. At one point his financial position was suddenly improved by the arrival of a cheque for the film royalties of *Romance*, but most of his income came from current work. Ford realized, and often admitted, that authorship was 'un métier de chien', but he never really abandoned his craft. In later years, Stella Bowen noted that 'There was something about the sight of his large patient fingers tapping at the keys, that I always found infinitely touching. He was a writer—a complete writer—and nothing but a writer. And he never even felt sure of his gift!'[55]

During the war Ford had only managed to write a few poems, and in 1918 these were assembled and issued under the title of *On Heaven and Other Poems*. This collection included 'Antwerp' as well as several poems Ford had written in France. Then, as the war drew to a close, Ford began to plan the resumption of his peacetime literary career. He wrote a translation of Pierre Loti's propagandistic *Trial of the Barbarians* and soon afterwards, with the help of his agent, J. B. Pinker, he received a number of magazine commissions. Soon he was writing reminiscences of pre-war literary London for *The English Review* and for a short-lived periodical called *The Piccadilly Review*. Pinker also helped him by sending his work to America and he was thus able to reprint his articles in *The Dial* and have other pieces published in *The Yale Review* and *Poetry*.

Then in the summer of 1920, at the request of Alec Waugh, who was then employed as a reader for Chapman and Hall, Ford began to gather together the reminiscences he had written for the *Piccadilly* in order to have them published as a book under the title *Thus to Revisit*. Although ostensibly written for money, these articles also had another purpose which Ford revealed in the first letter he wrote to Waugh: 'As for "Thus to Revisit", I had not thought to turn it into a book—if you will look at the last few pages of the proofs enclosed, you will see that they are rather occasional and more written with a purpose—to boost you young things!—than with the repose that a book should have. . . . However, I could easily turn it into a book and would gladly do it for you—write into it, I mean, and add onto it and make it, possibly a little more serene—and possibly a little more malicious, or at least teasing . . . to the self-important.'⁵⁶ But in addition to giving the young the personal support of an older man of letters, these articles were designed as an attack on certain tendencies which Ford had long considered detrimental to a healthy literary society. In particular, they attacked the 'Typical English Critic', the academic who loses sight of what is vital in literature by burying himself in a wilderness of biographical and philological detail. In addition, these articles struck out at the traditional literary periodical which so studiously avoids truly intellectual concerns in favour of politics and economics, and which gives over its columns to articles on prison reform, the tariff and foreign affairs instead of printing imaginative literature.

Ford's outspokenness evidently bothered his publishers, Chapman and Hall, who were obviously fearful of their own position in the literary establishment Ford was attacking.⁵⁷ In the end, however, they must have been convinced that the book was not libellous, for it was duly published in 1921.

For any writer returning from a war, the problem of subject-matter is more difficult than in normal times. Peacetime conditions seem too unreal and fluctuating for a proper assessment, and the war too recent to be dealt with objectively. Ford's first solution was to write mostly about literature, and to look back on an era sufficiently distant so that he could be impartial about it. In reality, however, he was still living the war. Even after he had returned from the trenches for the last time, he noted in a letter accompanying a copy of *On Heaven* that he sent to his daughter, that 'Most of the poems were written in Albert or just in front of Bailleul where the Germans now are again. It is rather an eerie feeling because having had to pay so much attention to the nature of the ground, I seem to know say Armentières and Plugstreet better than any other place in the world. . . .'⁵⁸

As a result of these preoccupations Ford had started a novel based on his war experiences even before the armistice was signed. Although he finished it by 1920, it was not published until 1929, and then only in the United States under the title *No Enemy*. In view of

Ford's literary position, it is extraordinary that no one in England would publish the book for, as Ford himself noted: 'After all, few poets—no man of letters of my standing—has been twice out to France, actually in service and in the trenches, without wangling any sort of a job on the staff, but just sticking it in the Infantry for the love of the job.'[59] After the failure of *No Enemy*, he wrote another novel called *Mr. Croyd* (or *That Same Poor Man*, its alternative title), but it too met a similar fate and was never published. However disheartening it must have been not to have found publishers for these books, the material was not lost for ever, and much of it reappears in the Tietjens tetralogy. From an artistic point of view, it was probably necessary for Ford to rid himself of his heated emotions in these books so that he could later write *Parade's End* with the 'repose' he realized was necessary for a good book.

The one novel that was published as a result of his work in Sussex, *The Marsden Case*, certainly shows signs of stress. Its subject was not new to Ford, for, as he wrote to Jepson, 'it's the one that has haunted me certainly ever since I was eighteen, on and off. It's the story of Ralston, the first translator of Turgenev—a man I liked very much. At any rate, that suggested it to me.'[60]

This novel is thickly plotted and, like some of Ford's earlier books, is overpopulated with characters. Basically a study in honour, it deals with the attempt of an Anglo-German to establish his good name. He tries to abide by decent means but he soon finds himself plotted against and exposed to the whole gamut of public and private misfortune. The novel has a war-time atmosphere, and everywhere corruption, stupid hatreds and dishonesty are evident. In so far as it illustrates what Ford evidently thought was a definite pattern, it is a complex and interesting book, but on the whole it is too muddy and confused to be really convincing. Furthermore, it reveals too much of Ford's own emotional state of mind at the time, and a certain weariness comes through. Because it has a theme similar to the Tietjens tetralogy, however, it was doubtless a useful exercise in preparation for those novels.

Considered as a whole, Ford's best writing of the period is found in his poetry. One poem in particular called *A House* exudes a philosophical serenity and positiveness that seems to be a direct result of his own happy life in the English countryside. Elsewhere Ford remarked on his own strong feeling 'that houses have, not so much immortal souls, as tempers, queernesses, and the power to be mali-

cious or benevolent,'[61] and in his quiet retreat with the unsophisti-
cated and hardworking Stella, he seems to have found a beneficent
haven from the annoyances of the world. Remarking on the subject
herself, Stella noted that 'There is something inexpressibly touching
and reassuring about a very old cottage set in a gentle English landscape, that has been inhabited for many generations by ordinary
country folk. Something which seems to say: if you come inside here,
you can live your own true life in peace and security and privacy. It
will be safe to relax, safe to be honest, and safe to bring your secret
wishes to the light of day; you will be protected from the world and
if you are but humble and modest enough, you will find sufficient
delight in the practical things which you must do in order to live
here, to fill your life.' What the cottage offers, she concludes, 'is an
escape from money and the monied world—that is its message and
its value. . . . '[62]

This statement is virtually a summary of Ford's poem, *A House*.
An allegorical poem of some 500 lines, it not only personifies all
the barnyard animals but also the barn and the house itself. Through
the night, while the farmer, his wife and child dream their hopes and
fears, these other creatures consider their miniature republic. As an
analysis of life, the poem stresses the worth of simplicity, responsibility and endurance, all of which were becoming more and more
central to Ford's attitude towards life.

The poem was published both in Harold Monro's *Chapbook* series
and in *Poetry Magazine* of Chicago. At the end of 1921, it received
Poetry's prize as the best poem of the year, and this public acknow-
ledgement of his work pleased Ford enormously. He wrote Jepson
that 'It pleases me as the first public recognition I ever received—
except from the Inst. de France. . . .'[63] and told the editor, Harriet
Monroe, that he was 'extremely touched and pleased by the reward
of your prize—I don't know whether more touched or more
pleased.'[64]

The other long poem of the period, *Mister Bosphorus and the
Muses* was, for Ford, a departure from his usual subject-matter and
style. He referred to it as an 'immense poem' that 'should annoy
quite a number of people,'[65] and gave it as a full title 'A Short
History of Poetry in Britain, Variety Entertainment in Four Acts,
Words by Ford Madox Ford, Music by Several Popular Composers,
with Harlequinade, Transformation Scene, Cinematographic Effects,
and Many Other Novelties, as well as Old and Tried Favourites.'

Printed with illustrations by Paul Nash, the poem is inspired by and loosely based on Pope's *Dunciad*.[66] By means of a series of amusing parodies of the English poets whose influence still dominated contemporary verse, Ford directed his shafts against the academies and all who object to whatever is new in literature. Since it is a verse play, it has a loose plot which deals with the attempts of the hero, Mr. Bosphorus, a penniless poet, to write publishable poems. When the critics condemn his originality, he tries to write in a manner they admire. Thus there are parodies of Chaucer, Spenser, Pope, Morris, Coventry Patmore and various other established English poets. At each attempt to please the critics, however, Bosphorus falls asleep, and thus the muse he is pursuing escapes him. In the end, it becomes evident that true poetry cannot be written in England, and Bosphorus forsakes the Northern muse for the Southern. Before leaving, however, he apostrophizes his native land:

> But how is it possible that men hold dear,
> In these lugubrious places,
> This dreary land; the clod-like inglorious races,
> The befogged, gin-sodden faces;
> The lewd, grim prudery; for-ever-protracted chases
> After concealed lechery; hog-like dull embraces
> Under a grey-flannel sky; unaired and damp
> Like poems a-stink of the lamp:
> And the learned bronchitics that vamp
> Hodden-grey thoughts all to stamp,
> Craving tenpence for fourpence
> And more pence and more pence
> And grudging us our pence!
> How is it possible that men hold dear
> Our dreary, dripping valleys,
> Monotonous misty alleys
> Whence dully, drearily sallies
> Song of grey sodden birds?
> In the air of frightening keenness,
> The mists of might-have-been-ness,
> The ceaseless, ceaseless greenness,
> The thought as thick as curds![67]

Although this poem has none of the elevation of 'Antwerp' or 'On Heaven', it has some beautiful sections and is based on a serious idea. Certainly Ford's theme—the decline of English poetry and the

146

miserable life allotted an honest poet in England—was of the greatest importance and seriousness to him.

The lines quoted above also suggest that Ford himself was beginning to grow tired of living in the English countryside. Always a somewhat restless person, he had been used to a good deal of travel, and he knew that the city, for all its faults, had certain things to offer that the country could not match. Early in his writing career Ford had observed that the country was a good place for those who had grown weary of the mixed blessings of urban society: it gave them consolation when at last they became disgusted with the falseness and hollowness of a sophisticated existence.[68] But by 1922, despite frequent visits from London friends, the cottage had done its duty by them and Sussex had begun to pall. 'It was the rain we minded most,' writes Stella. 'There was mud all around the back door, and the path down the orchard from the road was a long perilous slide. The pipe which brought our water from the spring would freeze and burst, the kitchen was damp and draughty and it was always cold upstairs. We had no telephone, and (in 1922) no wireless. We were too poor for a library subscription and we never saw a cinema. Petworth was five miles away and the only means of transport was the high, open dog-cart. These things did not matter particularly, but the rain did. Day after day without any let-up at all. And the darkness mattered too. And the mud.'[69] For an artist such surroundings were unnecessarily gloomy, and for a writer who wanted to portray the essence of his own time, the isolation the country represented was certainly dangerous.

When, therefore, Harold Monro suggested that Ford take his villa in the south of France for the winter months, Ford gladly accepted the offer. Immediate action was forestalled since he hadn't even money for the fare, but at the last moment, *The Marsden Case* was accepted for publication, and Ford and Stella were able to leave. Anna the pig was sold and Ford stored his books and possessions with a young London friend. His original intention was that he should be gone only for the winter, but in fact, when he left England in 1922, he really left it for good and never again, except for brief visits, was he to be a resident of his own country.

O Father O'Ford you've a masterful way with you,
Maid, wife and widow are wild to make hay with you,
Blonde and brunette turn-about run away with you
You've such a way with you, Father O'Ford,
That instant they see the sunshine from your eye
Their hearts flitter flutter, they think and they sigh:
We kiss ground before thee, we madly adore thee
And crave and implore thee to take us, O Lord!

—JAMES JOYCE

Chapter Eight

————⟪◆⟫⟪◆⟫————

PARIS AND *THE TRANSATLANTIC REVIEW*

————⟪◆⟫⟪◆⟫————

IN the late summer, Ford, Stella, their daughter Julie and the maid, Lucy, departed for Paris with the intention of staying there for a number of months before going south to Harold Monro's villa. They took rooms in the rue Vavin on the left bank and, while Ford worked on the final draft of *Mister Bosphorus* and made arrangements for the publication in Paris of another book called *Women and Men*, Stella and the others trotted 'around to museums, parks, parties and so on with great enthusiasm and vigour.'[1] The death of Proust, whose funeral they attended, had cast a gloom all over Paris, but a number of friends like Ezra Pound and James Joyce were there, and Ford was kept so busy that he found the city fatiguing after the quiet of Sussex.

With the arrival of winter, they proceeded south to their villa. In the 1920's Cap Ferrat was still a quiet corner of the Riviera, and Ford and Stella were delighted with the place and its climate. 'I wish I could describe,' she wrote, 'how magical Harold Monro's quite ordinary little villa seemed to us when we got there. You climbed up to it by a rough muletrack, or alternatively by long flights of stone steps of a giddy and exhausting steepness. All our luggage and all our provisions had to be carried up by hand; no wheeled vehicle could reach the place. But this steepness and slowness mattered nothing in comparison with the fact that the path was dry. It had been dry since the dawn of history!' Enthusiastic about this change from the mud of Sussex, they found that the house itself had 'three microscopic rooms in front and two behind. The only

150

provision for cooking was the usual peasants' charcoal contraption, but since there was electric light and the water was laid on, my cup of bliss was quite sufficiently full. The front windows opened wide on to a great luminous sky with a Saracen fortress on the skyline opposite, and the translucent blue-green waters of Villefranche harbour below. Down through the filmy tops of our own olive trees we could see a British man-of-war, floating like a child's toy above the sunny depths, and to our right the little dome of coloured tiles on the church belfry poked itself up amid the flat, huddled roofs of the harbour.'[2]

Ford, who was always made happy by a spectacular view, was from the beginning full of gaiety. He was amused by being surrounded by Rothschilds, Westminsters and Marlboroughs and by being in such close proximity to Monte Carlo. But mainly he loved the view of the sea below and the palm trees along the water's edge.[3]

Although Ford did not belong to the 'international set', he soon found himself in the company of interesting people, a change from the isolation of Sussex. On one occasion, he accompanied Turgenev's granddaughter, Lamartine's great-niece and Gautier's legatee when they called on Flaubert's niece. The combination of such famous names delighted him.[4]

After passing the winter months in Cap Ferrat, working on the first of the Tietjens novels, *Some Do Not*, Ford decided, after Easter, to introduce Stella to Provence, a part of France he loved above all others. Using Tarascon as a base, they took picnics to many of Ford's favourite spots in the neighbourhood, visited Arles and the Pont du Gard and at Nîmes attended a bullfight. With the coming of May, the heat began to rise precipitously, however, and at the suggestion of their landlord, they decided to escape high into the mountains of the Ardèche to a little town called St. Agrève. Unfortunately, it turned out to be a rather grim place, lacking in flowers and comfort, but Ford found the quiet and isolation conducive to work, and there he finished *Some Do Not*.[5] It was typical of Ford that, if his work was going well, he could be marvellously indifferent to his surroundings. Like most good artists, he really lived his art. That he was quite aware of this predilection is evident in a letter written a few months earlier to Edgar Jepson:

I have just come across this To-day's Great Thought in Jules Renard. 'Oui, Homme de lettres! je le serai jusqu'à ma mort ... Et, si par hasard, je suis éternel, je ferai, durant l'éternité, de la Littérature. Et jamais je ne me fatigue d'en faire, et toujours j'en fais; et je m'en f . . . du reste, comme le vigneron qui trépigne dans sa cave.'⁶

Altogether, his stay in France had done a great deal to restore his pre-war vigour. Life was so cheap and agreeable that he began to think of settling in France for good. He was also touched by the French habit of respecting artists. Stella Bowen has recounted that when he once received a note which began 'Cher et illustre Maître', his heart was filled with 'simple pleasure'.

After staying most of the summer at St. Agrève, Ford and Stella decided to return to Paris in September. They had originally intended to go back to England, but when Ford succeeded in letting the house in Sussex for another year, they determined to remain in France.

By the autumn of 1923, Paris had become the world's literary capital. Compared to it, London was intellectually asleep and New York genteel and provincial. As a result, a large number of foreign writers moved to France, and Paris seethed with expatriates. Most of these were Americans, but many also came from England and Ireland. Since amongst them were writers like Joyce, Pound, Gertrude Stein, Hemingway and Ford himself, Paris soon became the centre of the first real post-war revival of the arts.

One of the first people Ford met upon his arrival in Paris was his brother, Oliver Hueffer, who was also a writer and who often published his novels under the curious pseudonym of 'Jane Wardle'.* The Hueffers had a large flat in the Boulevard Arago and, at the time of his brother's arrival, Oliver was just starting a new literary magazine called *The Paris Review*, which was being supported by a group of French businessmen. Shortly afterwards Ford encountered his old friend, Ezra Pound, who when he heard of Oliver's review, showed interest in it and suggested that Ford, as editor of the old *English Review* should himself start a magazine. He even produced a White Russian colonel to act as business manager

---

* Oliver Hueffer's career is worth a brief note. His career started in commerce, as an agent for a Virginia tobacco company, but he soon switched over to literature, and produced his own play, *The Lord of Latimer Street*, in London. He then started the Critical Literary Agency in London and married Zoë Pyne, whose brother was a well-known organist in Manchester. During his lifetime he wrote nearly twenty novels, various plays and books of commentary, including *French France*. Frequently on the move and changing occupations, he was, amongst other things, a war correspondent. His first marriage ended in divorce and he later married Muriel Harris, who survives him. He died from a heart attack in London in 1931.

in hopes that a Czarist press located in the Rue des Gobelins would be made available to the review. At this juncture, Oliver Hueffer decided to return to London. Before leaving, however, he sublet his apartment to Ford and proposed to the French backers of his magazine that Ford succeed him as editor. At a meeting called between the French guarantors and a trio made up of Ford, Pound and the White Russian colonel, Ford unfortunately used the somewhat haughty manner he often reserved for commercial people, and the colonel accused the businessmen of being communist-inspired. After that, the French abruptly closed the meeting.

With the withdrawal of their financial support, it appeared that there would be no new literary magazine in Paris, but Ezra Pound continued his agitation for it and claimed to have a whole supply of talent simply waiting for the opening of the venture. By this time, Ford had himself become seriously attracted to the idea:

> It seemed to me that it would be a good thing if some one would start a centre for the more modern and youthful of the art movements, with which, in 1923, the city, like an immense seething cauldron, bubbled and overflowed. I hadn't thought the task was meant for me. But a dozen times I was stopped on the boulevards and told what was needed was another *English Review*.[7]

At this point John Quinn, a well-to-do American lawyer and bibliophile, who was a friend of Pound's, offered to put up half of the money needed if Ford would raise the rest. Ford accordingly put up the money earned from the recent sale of his house in Sussex, and a limited company was formed for the review, with Ford himself, Quinn and Ezra Pound acting as directors.

As Ford had always believed in the existence of an international 'Republic of Letters', he decided to call the magazine *The Transatlantic Review* and, in a prospectus sent round to possible contributors, he outlined its purpose:

> *The Transatlantic Review* . . . will have only two purposes, the major one, the purely literary, conducing to the minor, the disinterestedly social. The first is that of widening the field in which the younger writers of the day can find publication, the second that of introducing into international politics a note more genial than that which almost universally prevails. The first conduces to the second in that the best ambassadors, the only non-secret diplomatists between nations are the

153

books and the arts of nations. . . . The Conductors and Proprietors of the *Review* selected Paris as its home because there is no other home possible for a periodical which desires to spread comprehension between the three nations [England, France and America]. . . . They are, besides, out principally after young literature: there is no young man, be his convictions what they may, who, if he have saved up his railway fare and sixty centimes, will not fly to Paris and cry: '*Garçon, un bock!*' . . . The point is that . . . you don't from here have to write to Oklahoma for contributions: from all the other proud cities you must. . . .[8]

Like *The English Review*, the new *Transatlantic* was to be devoted almost entirely to imaginative literature. Ford was not interested in what he called 'solemnized and portentous journalism' on such subjects as 'political economy, philology, industrial finance, housing questions, municipal trading, fiscal policy, bibliography or the illegitimate birth-rate, psychotherapeutics or even international football, the cursory perusal of semi-official utterances on such subjects passing for an intellectual occupation. . . .'[9] Instead, his purpose was to 'put before the world a picture of the world's real mental activities which are centred in the world's imaginative arts.'[10]

Despite such high-sounding pronouncements, the physical establishment of the review was not easily accomplished. As Stella Bowen put it: 'The whole thing was run in conditions of the utmost confusion. Everything that possibly could go wrong with regard to the printing, paper, packing, forwarding and distribution, did go wrong.'[11] The arrangements made by the White Russian colonel also fell through, and the review soon had to be re-established in a loft of William Bird's Three Mountains Press on the Ile St. Louis. It was Bird who dropped the capitals from the magazine's name so that the long title would fit on one line, and it was at his press that Ford began to give his tea-parties, turning the place into one of the centres of expatriate literary Paris.*

You should have seen those Thursday tea-parties at the uncapitalled *transatlantic review* offices! The French speak of 'la semaine à deux jeudis' . . . the week with two Thursdays in it. Mine seemed to contain sixty, judging from the noise, lung-power, crashing in, and denuncia-

---

* The omission of capital letters which soon set a vogue followed by *transition* and other magazines was thought by some to have been consciously introduced for artistic reasons but the real reason was merely typographical. (William Bird to the writer. Letter, 7 March 1954.)

tion. They sat on forms—school benches—cramped round Bird's great hand press. They all shouted at me: I did not know how to write, or knew too much to be able to write, or did not know how to edit, or keep accounts, or sing 'Franky and Johnny', or order a dinner. The ceiling was vaulted, the plane-leaves drifted down on the quays outside; the grey Seine flowed softly. . . .[12]

Despite these vicissitudes, the first issue was duly published in January of 1924. It was destined to be the first of only twelve numbers, however, because the review soon encountered financial difficulties. The first six months were guaranteed, but when in the summer of 1924, John Quinn died, it appeared as though the venture would collapse. Strenuous efforts were then made by Ford, Natalie Barney and Gertrude Stein to save the review, and in the end Ernest Hemingway produced a wealthy acquaintance, Krebs Friend, who agreed to back it. Unfortunately this new arrangement only lasted another six months because the division of authority between Ford and Friend was never made clear, and a certain amount of ill-feeling therefore arose between them. In December of 1924, Friend withdrew his support and the review ceased publication.

Much of the financial mismanagement of the magazine must be blamed on Ford who admitted that he was 'worse than hopeless' in business matters.[13] Beyond employing an exceptionally able secretary and several not-so-able part-time assistants, he neglected the financial side of the enterprise. Since in the course of the year he also made two trips away from Paris, one of them for over a month, it was probably inevitable that the review should fail.

Still, for as long as it lasted, the *Transatlantic* made a lively contribution to post-war letters and was intelligently edited. For this literary achievement Ford deserves most of the credit. From the beginning he was enthusiastic, and he devoted many hours of work to the venture. One of his first tasks was to write round to prospective contributors and amongst those he approached were his young friends in London. The letter he wrote to A. E. Coppard provides insights into his methods and ideals as an editor:

Have you a short story—or two, or three—that you could let me have for a Review that I myself am going to edit from this city and to publish in New York and London: as there won't be any doubt as to publication and payment, the latter fairly miserable to begin with, though getting better if the Review paid? So that the real advantage to you—as to others of a struggling world—is simply that there is going to be a periodical in which you can print work that the more popular periodicals won't print and mop up a very little money that you otherwise wouldn't get.

It isn't an exaggeration to say that I've started this review with you in mind as I started the *English Review* to publish stuff of Hardy's that other periodicals wouldn't publish. I've a great admiration for your work and though I hope you can serialize all you write I imagine, this old world being what it is, that you may have some that you can't.

I may say that I *prefer* not to have sexually esoteric, psycho-analytic, mystic or officially ethical matter but don't bar any of them obstinately —and if you hadn't short stories available I'd just as glad of 'essays' or any other form.[14]

Other letters were sent to writers like Yeats and Eliot, who were not resident in Paris, and many of these sent contributions or greetings. One of the early 'conspirators' of the *English Review* days, H. G. Wells, sent this message: 'Good luck to the *Transatlantic Review*. I have always considered you one of the greatest poets and one of the greatest editors alive and it gladdens my heart to think that you are creating a successor to the wonderful *English Review*.'[15]

The first number—dated January, 1924—opened with four poems by E. E. Cummings, one by Coppard and two of Ezra Pound's 'Cantos'. These were followed by the first instalment of *The Nature of a Crime*, a book Ford had written some years before in collaboration with Conrad but which only now received official recognition. Luke Ionides' 'Memories'—an interesting series of reminiscences of Whistler, Wilde and numerous Pre-Raphaelites which ran through most of the life of the review—took the position in the table of contents that Conrad's memoirs had occupied in *The English Review*. To conclude the opening section of the review there was a sketch in French on the Place de la Concorde by Jean Cassou; a short story, 'Elsie', by Robert McAlmon and 'Stocktaking' by 'Daniel Chaucer', the pseudonym adopted by Ford for his literary observations.

In the second section of the magazine came the 'Chroniques' whose purpose was to provide a survey of artistic and literary achievement in Paris, London and New York. After a section containing 'Communications' from well-wishers like T. S. Eliot and Joseph Conrad, the 120-page number closed with the first instalment of Ford's own novel, *Some Do Not*.

In many ways the first issue was untypical. In later numbers the layout underwent certain changes and Ford wrote considerably fewer of the pages. After the second number it also became a monthly custom to publish as a regular feature a supplement on painting, literature or music. A special supplement was occasioned by the death of Joseph Conrad.

Thus a representative number would contain poetry, fiction and belles lettres by such writers as A. E. Coppard, Gertrude Stein and Djuna Barnes, the usual communications and reports from abroad and a literary supplement with contributions by men like Hemingway, Tristan Tzara and James Joyce. Typical of the art supplements is one containing reproductions of new paintings by Picasso, Nina Hamnett and Brancusi along with articles by Juan Gris and Bernard Faÿ.

In the course of the year, *The Transatlantic Review* managed to survey most of the important developments in the various arts and provided space for new writers and artists. Beside those already named, the artists included Braque and Man Ray, the musicians, Eric Satie and George Antheil, and the writers, William Carlos Williams, Lincoln Steffens, H.D., Harold Stearns, Paul Valéry, Ivan Beede, Glenway Wescott, Dorothy Richardson, John Dos Passos, Havelock Ellis and Natalie Barney.

Three writers—Gertrude Stein, James Joyce and Ernest Hemingway—had a most important relationship with the review and were to the *Transatlantic* what Wyndham Lewis, Norman Douglas and D. H. Lawrence had been to *The English Review*. In *The Autobiography of Alice B. Toklas*, Gertrude Stein has recorded her first encounter with the *Review*:

We had heard that Ford was in Paris, but we had not happened to meet. Gertrude Stein had however seen copies of the *Transatlantic* and found it interesting but had thought nothing further about it. Hemingway came in then very excited and said that Ford wanted something of Gertrude Stein's for the next number and he, Hemingway, wanted the Making of Americans to be run in it as a serial and he had to have the first fifty pages at once. Gertrude Stein was of course quite overcome with her excitement at this idea, but there was no copy of the manuscript except the one that we had had bound. That makes no difference, said Hemingway, I will copy it. And he and I between us did copy it and it was printed in the next number of the *Transatlantic*. So for the first time a piece of the monumental work which was the beginning, really the beginning of modern writing, was printed, and we were very happy.[16]

Hemingway has claimed that it was due only to his 'obtaining genius'[17] that the *Transatlantic* published Miss Stein's writing, but Ford was also immensely impressed with it, especially since it had been written some eighteen years earlier. Publication started in the April number but by mid-summer, the magazine had begun to experience such financial difficulty that payment for contributions had ceased and it seemed likely that the review would collapse. At this point Hemingway again entered the scene and wrote to Gertrude Stein that unless the review continued to publish her work he would 'make such a row and blackmail it that it will blow up the show.'[18]

This rough treatment was happily forestalled through the more gentlemanly conduct of the editor who apologized for the *Transatlantic's* financial vagaries and told Miss Stein that although he had heard from Hemingway that Eliot's *Criterion* was offering 'real money' for her work, he still hoped to be able to publish it.

> I should be very sorry to lose you, but I was never the one to stand in a contributor's way: indeed I really exist as a sort of half-way house between the non-publishable youth and real money—a sort of green baize swingdoor that everyone kicks on entering and leaving.[19]

Miss Stein replied briefly: 'I like the magazine and I like your editing. I am sincerely attached to both so suppose we go on as we are going.'[20] Thus *The Making of Americans* continued to appear until the demise of the magazine, and its appearance there helped to secure its publication in book form some years later.

The *Transatlantic* is also important in literary history for having been the first periodical to publish a portion of James Joyce's *Finnegans Wake*. A section of this work appeared in the April number under the title 'Work in Progress', an appellation given it by Ford which was widely used by later editors.

According to Ezra Pound, Ford was not anxious to print serials, but he was forced to do so because he 'was absoLOOTly up a tree and cdnt. get decent stuff enough to fill his space except for nuvvelists who wdnt. write anything else.'[21] Nevertheless, from the beginning, Ford had been anxious to publish Joyce because of his admiration for his work, and had repeatedly asked him for contributions. At length Joyce complied by offering him the 'Mamalujo' episode from *Finnegans Wake*, but by that time, thanks to a sudden spate of activity in H.M. Customs shed in Folkestone, Ford hesitated to publish Joyce's piece because he was afraid of jeopardising the magazine as a whole by having one of its numbers seized by the British customs officials on the grounds that it contained pornography. The trouble *The Little Review* had undergone when it published *Ulysses* was still fresh in his mind, and Ford knew the *Transatlantic* could not afford a legal battle.

Still, he was so determined to publish Joyce that in the end he arranged to have the manuscript shown to the 'most representative official Englishman that we could find,'[22] leaving it to him to decide whether the magazine would be impounded if it contained Joyce's contribution. Sisley Huddleston, the Paris correspondent of *The Times*, was chosen as judge, a meeting was called and Joyce read his manuscript. Here is Huddleston's own report of the occasion:

> Joyce read as only he can read: and I waited in vain for the obscenity and blasphemy which I was warned would be present. They were not apparent to me. If they were they were carefully concealed. I reported to Ford that whatever impropriety there might be would not be visible to the naked eye of a British or American policeman. So, in due course, the pages appeared, and helped to make the *transatlantic review* a success.[23]

Because of the appearance in the review of his piece, Joyce looked upon Ford as the godfather of *Finnegans Wake*, and reciprocated four years later by becoming the godfather of Ford's daughter, Julie.

Ernest Hemingway's rôle in the review was twofold. As one of the young writers first brought to Ford's attention by Pound, he was asked to help in the reading of manuscripts submitted by prospective contributors. These he would take in batches down to the Quai outside the review's office, and there he would sort out those to be rejected. Occasionally he rewrote one or two for his own amusement. During Ford's absence for a month in New York, he also edited one number of the magazine, filling it so full of the work of his compatriots, including Dos Passos, that Ford upon his return observed that it provided 'an unusually large sample of the work of that Young America whose claims we have so insistently—but not with such efficiency—forced upon our readers.'[24]

In addition to his editorial work, Hemingway also contributed a number of stories and articles to the magazine. These were not his first appearance in print, for a book of his short stories had already been published in Paris by Robert McAlmon's Contact Press, but the appearance of his work in the distinguished company that contributed to the review helped to establish his reputation. As one of his biographers put it: 'His year with the *transatlantic* . . . probably helped as much as any of his other serious literary activities to get Hemingway's name and fame into general circulation around Paris. . . . It offered him a focus, a kind of responsibility, and a sounding board such as he had not had up to that time.'*[25]

Since the *Transatlantic* was, in Ford's own words, 'a rag-time affair where a great many letters and things did go astray,'[26] the editor, perched in his narrow gallery above Bird's presses, was subjected to all sorts of pressures a more respectable and staid executive would not have countenanced. Yet the informality of the enterprise was one of its more charming features. The result of Hemingway's editing has already been mentioned; but he was not the only person who tried to force his personal predilections on the review. Chief amongst the others was Ezra Pound who also favoured contributions by Americans. In May of 1924, he wrote a letter to Ford criticizing the contributions printed in preceding numbers. He praised Hemingway, Djuna Barnes and McAlmon, but denounced various British contributors whose work he characterized as 'village idyl stuff' or 'Times Lit. Supp. rubbish'. Concluding his letter, which he had humour enough to sign 'Old Glory' he wrote: 'Will come back and manage you at close range before you bring out any more numbers.'[27]

Ford took his friend's strictures in good part but, as an editor of an international magazine, adopted the only line he could. 'Your criticism of the Review,' he wrote, 'is an admirable bit of personal friendship for selected friends, but you cannot run *anything* on concentrated juice of logs rolled . . . nor catch any bird with a net set in its sight.'[28] On another occasion, however, 'the Village Explainer' as Gertrude Stein called Pound, won his point. Here is Ford's editorial note:

> We have handed the editing of the Musical Supplement of this number of the review over to Mr. Pound. His devotion to that art and contempt for our management of such supplements of this review as have appeared have been so great and so vociferous that we have not been able to see what else to do.[29]

Thus, although the *Transatlantic* bore the imprint of Ford's general direction, it was by no means the smooth affair *The English Review* had been. It was not so well organized, and even the paper

---

* *The Transatlantic Review*, it may be mentioned, was the first periodical to review favourably Hemingway's book, *In Our Time*.

and printing were inferior. Yet the review was typical of its time and place. It was lively and bumptious, irreverent in its attacks on literary propriety and filled with new and unknown names.

The original plan had been to divide the pages of the review evenly between French, English and American contributors but, partly because of the pressures exerted on him by Pound and Hemingway, Ford was not able to maintain an even balance between them. In the year's run there were therefore a total of some ninety American pieces, sixty British and forty French. One reason for this discrepancy was that many more American pieces were submitted than French or English.

In the matter of 'discoveries' the *Transatlantic* made no such name as Ford's earlier review had done, for the prior existence of *The Dial* and *The Little Review* and of Bird's and McAlmon's presses made the discovery of new talent difficult. Even so, Ford was able to publish very early work by Hemingway, Djuna Barnes, William Carlos Williams, Cummings and Dos Passos and actually the first work of such writers as Donald Ogden Stewart and Ivan Beede.

While it is certain that the *Transatlantic* was not in the class of *The English Review*, it was still the best known of the Paris reviews of the 1920's. That it never gained widespread fame was probably due to over-specialization: it was too much a magazine of Paris, and it lacked the formula for success that strikes a balance between the work of unknown writers and the work of established authors. Yet there is no real need to cavil at it for, as Ford himself remarked, it fulfilled its purposes:

That then is the Movement . . . *a* Movement. And with a very definite complexion, so that, looking back, the record seems remarkably satisfactory. If the reader, being a man of good will, is questioned as to what good work is being done by, or what promise there is, in the young man of today he has only to cite the names above . . . [the names of contributors to the review]. Astonishingly satisfactory! For this is evidence that all over the Anglo-Saxon world from the West Middle West of the United States to the West Middle West of the London suburbs there is in motion a very definite creative impulse that is pretty well akin to the larger world movements. We have tapped as it were substrata in a great many parts of the world to find very much the same tide in motion everywhere. And we have not—at any rate consciously— done anything to falsify the issue.[30]

For the first number of the *Transatlantic* T. S. Eliot, who was then an editor himself, had written a hortatory letter in which he claimed that a 'review is not measured by the number of stars and scoops that it gets. Good literature is produced by a few queer people in odd corners; the use of a review is not to force talent, but to create a favourable atmosphere. And you will serve this purpose if you publish, as I hope you will find and publish, works of writers of whatever age who are too good and too independent to have found other publishers. . . .'[31]

If this statement is taken as a guide, then certainly *The Transatlantic Review* fulfilled Eliot's design. It contained much that was good and some that was not. 'Still,' as Sisley Huddleston said of Ford's review, 'it was his idea, as he would have said, of a magazine, and it does not much matter if it is anybody else's idea.'[32]

Because of his reputation as a writer and because of his position as editor of the *Transatlantic*, Ford soon became, along with Joyce, Gertrude Stein and one or two others, one of the leading literary figures in Paris during the 1920's. He therefore felt it his pleasant duty to provide a centre for other artists and writers. The review itself provided a formal outlet, but Ford also wanted to create a social milieu in which ideas could be exchanged and through which a definite movement in the arts might be started. He therefore arranged for the Thursday tea parties at the offices of the review, and to these functions came his new, and largely female 'discoveries'. Occasionally, these parties were laughed at by the hearty writers since for a number of people Ford was always a 'character' and sometimes a figure of fun. Norman Douglas, for example, said he was an 'animated adenoid', while Gertrude Stein called him the 'Golden Walrus' and Paul Nash dubbed him 'Silenus in Tweeds'.[33] The best summary, however, of Ford's appearance and rôle in Paris during the 'twenties was provided by Lloyd Morris:

He was then about fifty years old, and had the look of a friendly walrus, or a precursor of the still uncreated Colonel Blimp. Pink-faced, blue-eyed, with fine, pale blond hair that had begun to recede and diminish, he was tall, obese, stertorious, and spoke in the low, explosive mumble which well educated Englishmen often use to communicate with one another. But Ford's physical appearance mis-represented his spirit, just as his indistinct utterance disguised the shining distinction of his mind. I have known no man of letters whose conception of the literary vocation was nobler than Ford's; and his professional life consistently illustrated the high ideals which he held to be generally compulsive.[34]

In addition to the tea-parties, Ford gave many soirées in his large flat in the Boulevard Arago. A great barnlike place, this studio was decorated with elaborate gold frames containing ancient and indecipherable paintings, while its furniture consisted largely of intricately carved chests and cupboards. When lit by dozens of candles stuck in bottles, it looked dramatic and resembled the stage setting of La Bohème. Here the genial Ford gave parties which were attended both by the distinguished and by the young who had not yet made their reputations. In his reminiscences, Samuel Putnam has described them:

> Within its own vaguely precise boundaries the Quarter had a social-artistic life quite apart from the cafés. This life centred in certain salons. When I first came to Paris, it was to the studio apartment of Ford Madox Ford and Stella Bowen that those Americans went who were fortunate enough to be invited and who cared to listen to the one-time collaborator of Conrad and discoverer of D. H. Lawrence as he reminisced of his yesterdays or discussed, with equal enthusiasm, the new and promising talents of today for which he was constantly on the watch. By reason of the Transatlantic Review and his having published Hemingway, Ford rather dominated the picture at the moment, and, being kindly disposed and wholly free of literary snobbishness, liked to gather about him those who had some respect for writing as an art with a great and noble tradition behind it.[35]

Soon, however, these small evening functions got out of hand; and because there were so many people to entertain, 'the Leviathan of the Quartier Montparnasse, the gentle Gargantua of Lavigne's, the sophisticated Dr. Johnson of Notre Dame des Champs' as Herbert Gorman dubbed him,[36] decided instead to give a weekly party at a night-club called the Bal du Printemps. A very small place, with a tiny dance floor and music provided by a single accordionist who, though dressed in a Spanish costume played American jazz, it soon became popular with people like E. E. Cummings, Robert McAlmon, Nancy Cunard and Ernest Hemingway.[37] Although Ford and Pound danced with verve—Sisley Huddleston said that they looked like 'the elephant and the mule'[38]—Ford's main idea was not entertainment for its own sake. He thought, rather, that his parties might give a certain amount of publicity to the magazine and, more important, he wanted to provide a centre for the 'painfully shy' contributors to his review so that they might 'be drawn from their shells and establish contacts, not merely with those responsible for the review itself, but also with each other. Thus one might evolve an atmosphere of artistic friendliness and intimacy, such as is extremely beneficial to the population of an art centre on its aesthetic side.'[39]

Before long these *bal musettes* became well known amongst the tourists,* and they therefore had to be moved back to Ford's studio where they continued on a smaller scale until the review went out of business. They were, however, but one instance of Ford's devotion to his project for, as Natalie Barney has recounted, whenever Ford went to see her, he always reported on the new discoveries he was anxious to make known through the review.[40] That his energy was not wasted is proved by the quality of the *Transatlantic* itself for, although it only lasted a year, it was as Samuel Putnam said of it, 'essentially, the bringer of America to Europe.'[41] Thus, in the words of William Rose Benét, Ford really was 'an instinctively fine editor of literary publications. No older writer of whom I know has had a greater sympathy with brilliant young talent or done more in the way of its encouragement. . . . He was . . . the most remarkable appreciator and spokesman for the newer writers that they could have had. He should have remained the editor of a fully endowed international magazine for he was a great editor as well as a great writer.'[42]

Altogether, despite the disappointment occasioned by the demise of the review, the year 1924 was the real beginning of Ford's rebirth as a man of letters. Even before the move to Paris, his health had improved so much that he felt able to work again. He wrote H. G. Wells that he had at last recovered from the nervous tension he had undergone as a result of the war, and that he was both happy and able to write, which he had never thought he would be able to do.[43] The months in Paris consolidated these gains, for he soon found himself in the centre of a lively literary movement and on intimate terms with a number of the more important writers of this century. The long exile in Sussex was over, and the company of Gertrude Stein, Ezra Pound, Natalie Barney, James Joyce and others was proving beneficial to his morale. Ford's own writing never created the excitement that Joyce's and Hemingway's did, and the Shakespeare and Company bookshop did not sell his works as rapidly as it

---

* Chapter Three of Hemingway's *The Sun Also Rises*, for example, is placed in Ford's night-club.

did the works of others.[44] Yet enough people in his circle admired and supported him so that he felt more confident about his writing and his position than he had been for many years.

In addition to the task of editing *The Transatlantic Review*, Ford was able to do an extraordinary amount of writing in 1924. Twice during the year he had to leave Paris—once to attend his mother's funeral in England, and once to take care of the review's business arrangements in New York—but even so, he managed to republish an old collaboration written with Joseph Conrad, to finish the first and begin the second novel of his Tietjens tetralogy, to contribute a series of twelve 'Literary Causeries' to the Chicago *Tribune* and to write an entire book on Conrad. That such an output of work would be of high quality seems unlikely, but as the novelist Nathan Asch has written: 'We used to say in Paris in those days that Ford had several styles, his weekly style, his biweekly style for more serious stuff, his monthly style for considered material, and then his immortal style. . . . The only point is that while many writers have admitted they did hack work, Ford never did; and personally he could never be taxed with doing it. . . .'[45]

The collaboration, a short book called *The Nature of a Crime*, had originally been published under a pseudonym in *The English Review* and had subsequently been forgotten by both men. Then, years later, someone in Paris showed it to Ford who, after looking it over, decided that it was worth publishing simply as a document. Conrad agreed, and the preface he wrote for it was the last piece of writing he completed before he died. An odd psychological sketch on the theme of suicide, the book is an interesting sidelight to the Conrad-Ford collaboration, but is so slight that neither Ford nor Conrad appeared to like it.

The death of Conrad in August was a blow to Ford. It is true that, except for the work necessary to republish *The Nature of a Crime*, they had not written anything together for years and had only infrequently seen each other. But a friendly connexion had been preserved, and only three months before his death Conrad had written Ford to compliment him on *Some Do Not*. 'As to the novel,' he said, 'I think that, between us two, if I tell you that I consider it "tout à fait chic" you will understand perfectly how much that "phrase d'atelier" means to the initiated.'[46] Thus the death of Conrad who of all the writers Ford had known before the war was dearest to him, marked the closing of an era and served almost completely to isolate

Ford from his past. Out of respect and love for his friend, he therefore decided to write a memorial volume and, since their connexion had always been a literary one, to write down all he could remember about the years of the collaboration. The form he chose was novelistic: he did not want to write chronologically or factually but impressionistically, because he thought that the truth that comes from impressionism was the truth Conrad believed in and would have approved of had he been alive to speak.

'I wrote this book,' Ford said later, 'at fever heat and in an extraordinarily short time for I had, as it were, to get it out of my system. Nevertheless, I see very little that I want to change in it and I think it remains a very accurate account of our relationship— Conrad's and mine.'[47] That it was far from being accurate was claimed, however, by Conrad's widow who wrote to *The Times Literary Supplement* to say that Ford's book was merely an attempt to glorify himself at Conrad's expense.[48] The result of this letter and of subsequent editorial comment both in England and America was a literary controversy that was damaging to Ford's reputation. Everywhere it was assumed that Ford was a bounder who was cashing in on the attention given to Conrad on the occasion of his death by writing a book he never would have dared to write had Conrad still been alive.

Because of the controversy Ford felt obliged to produce the evidence upon which he based his book, and the result was an article called 'Working with Conrad' in which he took up, book by book, the various collaborations and semi-collaborations and, by referring to documents and manuscripts, substantiated what he had said in *A Personal Remembrance*. The writing of the article must have been a distasteful task, since it implied that he was on the defensive in an issue not of his own making.

What caused the difficulty in the first place was simply a difference of temperament. Although she was Conrad's constant companion, Mrs. Conrad demonstrates in her books of reminiscence that her approach to literature was quite different from her husband's. Ford, on the other hand, had actually worked day and night with Conrad and knew his mind in a way Mrs. Conrad never did. In these circumstances, it is not surprising that Mrs. Conrad's opinion that Ford's book was simply an attempt to steal her husband's glory, has not prevailed. Indeed, that Ford's version would ultimately be accepted might have been seen at the beginning of the controversy, for even then, one of Ford's estranged friends, Edward Garnett, admitted that 'there is a good deal of genuine atmospheric observation pervading these romantic pages,' and said that although Ford adds and suppresses, he then 'surprises you by telling you something really true, something that really happened.'[49] More to the point, however, is Christopher Morley's remark on another occasion. 'I have forgotten,' he writes, 'as most people have, the really extraordinary biography of Conrad that he wrote. It was probably unreliable as to facts but he went far behind facts in his brilliant suggestions as to Conrad's character as artist, as man, and as conundrum. When he said that Conrad threw teacups into the fire, I know perfectly well that Conrad did not actually do so. But he looked so gorgeously the desire of so doing that Ford conveyed it to us by what was probably an actual mis-statement and a shining intellectual veracity.'[50]

The really important part of *Joseph Conrad: A Personal Remembrance*, however, is not the part devoted to reminiscence, but the sections that deal with technique and the stylistic devices he and Conrad experimented with in order to achieve their effects. The exposition of these technical considerations must have been useful to Ford himself just at the time he was writing the Tietjens tetralogy, but to judge from the frequency with which it has been quoted by other novelists and critics, it must also be one of the most cogent and intelligent summaries ever written on the subject of the novel. From the time-shift to the *progression d'effet* and from the shading of dialogue to the use of *le mot juste* the whole array of technical knowledge painstakingly acquired during the collaboration is set down in a few short pages. No novelist has ever, with less fuss, revealed the workings of his professional mind so clearly and succinctly, and what is found there is still important for the craft of fiction. It is no wonder, then, that where it was understood, the book was appreciated. As Sinclair Lewis put it, it 'was the one great book on the technique of writing a novel that I have ever read.'[51]

Ford's first two years in France were, then, both happy and successful. The climate and ambiance of the country restored his health, his domestic life was peaceful and, as editor of *The Transatlantic Review*, he had both obtained a measure of confidence in himself and had found something deserving of his efforts. Most important of all, however, were the novels that he had begun to write in 1923 and which would eventually be considered as his principal contribution to English literature.

For I do not think
We ever took much stock in that Britannia
On the long French roads, or even on parades,
Or thought overmuch of Nelson or of Minden,
Or even the old traditions . . .
                                    I don't know,
In the breathless rush that it is of parades and drills,
Of digging at the double and strafes and fatigues,
These figures grow dimmed and lost:
Doubtless we too, we too, when the years have receded
Shall look like the heroes of Hellas, upon a frieze,
White-limbed and buoyant and passing the flame of the torches
From hand to hand . . . But today it's mud to the knees
And khaki and khaki and khaki . . .
                                    And love of one's land
Very quiet and hidden and still. . . .

What is love of one's land?
                                    Ah, we know very well
It is something that sleeps for a year, for a day,
For a month, something that keeps
Very hidden and quiet and still,
And then takes
The quiet heart like a wave,
The quiet brain like a spell,
The quiet will
Like a tornado, and that shakes
The whole being and soul . . .
Aye, the whole of the soul.

From 'Footsloggers' by FORD MADOX HUEFFER, 24/12/17–1/1/18

Chapter Nine

————《◆》《◆》————

PARADE'S END

————《◆》《◆》————

I

In 1909 Ford wrote a number of articles for *The English Review* which he later collected in a book called *The Critical Attitude*. These essays were designed to encourage his readers to take a rational attitude towards life and to make choices on the basis of intelligible standards. What he was promoting was, of course, a difficult task, for it is not always easy to discover the real worth of a particular act or to discriminate between values. Even the various impressions that are received in one day are often so contradictory or at least disconnected that it is hard to know anything more than that some are pleasing while others are not. Thus without a critical attitude it is almost impossible for the layman to make much sense out of modern life.

The function of the arts, and of fiction in particular, was, according to Ford, to make life intelligible to society at large. Because of his unspecialized concern for the subject, and because of his heightened powers of observation and his ability to see connexions between disparate events, the novelist is particularly suited to reveal patterns of human behaviour. For, starting with an observation of individuals, the novelist soon turns to the values that govern their lives, and these he examines critically. In so doing, he performs an act of great benefit for the ordinary man, for he presents a picture of life as a whole. He observes the various phenomena of modern life and draws from them a certain pattern. His task, as a novelist, is to present this pattern in a work of art.

Ford's own life had provided him with much material for the writing of novels, and gradually over the years he had begun to see an over-all pattern in life. But it was not until he began the Tietjens tetralogy that he was able to formulate it successfully. In his earlier novels, where his focus was more narrow, he had been able to present certain aspects of contemporary life with insight and intelligence. A number of these novels showed, for example, how impossible it is for the 'good man' to survive in a self-centred, hypocritical world. Christian goodness is hated everywhere and whoever professes it is always hounded out of society. Thus as early as 1907 Ford wrote this passage in *An English Girl*:

> There wasn't, in fact, in active England or elsewhere any room for what *he* called a decent man; the place of such men was gone from the world. What decent men there were in public life today did more harm than good, and they soiled themselves by mixing in pettinesses.[1]

Six years later, by the time he wrote *Mr. Fleight*, the good man had become an onlooker only:

> 'It's a nasty dirty business,' Mr. Blood said. 'It's the dirty comedy of life unrolled before your eyes. It's the thing that modern life has become. I'm trying to crush it all up into a short period so as to make the affair [the ascendancy into power by corrupt means of Mr. Fleight] all the more an object lesson—or, rather, all the more of a joke, because I don't care whether anybody learns anything from it or not. I'm not a social reformer.'[2]

The point Ford makes in these novels is, however, inhibited by the unlikeliness of certain of his situations and by the unreality of some of his characters. Violet Hunt put her finger on the weakness of much of Ford's early fiction by pointing out his failure to co-ordinate the emotional parts of a novel with its moral atmosphere.[3] Even *The Good Soldier*, which is certainly more complex and satisfactory than its predecessors, is too special, too much like a novel by Henry James reworked by Ford. For what Ford really wanted to produce was a novel which would be a general assessment of his times and which would also have a direct appeal to the ordinary reader who could understand what he had said in *The Critical Attitude*.

Parade's End did not come into being immediately, however, for in the years just after the war he made several false starts. One of these was a never-completed novel entitled *True Love and a General Court Martial*; another, *No Enemy*, was not so much a novel as fictionalized reminiscences of his own war experiences. The writer-hero, Gringoire, is seen through the eyes of an interviewer who comes to sit at his feet as he holds forth in his country cottage on his experiences during and after the war. Disillusioned by the war, Gringoire has at the same time benefited from it, for it has taught him what he could do without. He thus offers as a means of salvation for the world, the humble virtues of frugality and simplicity. Not intended as a novel, since it has neither plot nor dramatic conflict between characters, No Enemy is essentially a philosophic commentary on the theme of personal survival.

A highly biographical and personal book despite its fictionalized setting, it was not really the book Ford wanted to write about the war. It was useful to him, however, in so far as it helped him get the immediate effects of the war out of his system so that he could produce a more aloof account later on. Yet a third attempt was That Same Poor Man which has the alternative title of Mr. Croyd. Although never published, this novel is the immediate precursor of Some Do Not and also deals with the war. Set against the background of veterans returning to London from France, it is the story of Mr. Croyd, an improbably generous writer who is spurned (as is Moffat in The Benefactor and many subsequent Fordian heroes) by those who receive his bounty. Croyd stands for an older and more honourable tradition in the arts than the one obtaining in post-war London, and as a result, feels that the ingratitude and selfishness of young writers spell the downfall of the humaner letters in twentieth-century England.[4]

Although this novel contains a number of direct references to the war and is manifestly sincere, it is altogether too personal and mannered to be successful. Like Gringoire, Croyd is closely modelled on Ford himself, and therefore his attitude is very special. For at the time, as Ford later realized, his writing was full of bitterness and 'was even a little mad.' 'I was still bitter about the treatment of any ex-comrades in arms,' he noted. 'Those years come back to me as a sort of fog, in which people moved about dimly, forging one's cheques, losing one's manuscripts, sewing tares into one's potatoes and doing what they could to suppress one. In it one was completely isolated and forgotten.'[5] In this frame of mind, it was hardly likely that Ford could write a successful novel with a central character based on himself: for almost inevitably the bitterness would be tinged with self-pity. What was needed therefore for a good novel about the war was a central character based on somebody else, preferably someone who represented and was part of the tradition that had governed England since the times of Elizabeth.

In men like Galsworthy and Masterman, Ford had recognized this type, but the most representative heir of this tradition that he knew was Arthur Marwood whom he had first met while living in Winchelsea and with whom he founded *The English Review*. Marwood had been a brilliant mathematician as an undergraduate at Cambridge and was a Yorkshireman of ancient lineage. Ford was immensely impressed by him and called him 'a man of infinite benevolence, comprehensions and knowledges.'[6] Since Marwood had died in 1917, Ford felt free to use him as a model for the central character of *Parade's End*. Christopher Tietjens is of course more than a re-creation of Marwood, but there are remarkable similarities between fact and fiction. Mrs. Florence Wynne Finch, a niece of Arthur Marwood's, has pointed out that Groby, the Tietjens' manor house, is in reality Busby Hall near Middlesbrough in Yorkshire, and that a number of Christopher's relations are closely modelled on members of the Marwood family, including Mark who was based on Sir William Marwood, K.C.B. 'The really brilliant thing about Ford,' she notes, 'is the way he took an ounce of actual fact, and surrounded it with fiction, and yet made his characters re-act exactly as they did in real life.'[7]

One instance is so strangely true to life that it suggests Ford must have had second sight. For although Sir William Marwood did not die until seven years after *Last Post* was published, he died in exactly the same manner in which Ford described Mark's death in that novel. He lay for weeks without speaking and only died when a huge cedar tree that had begun to split the flagstones had to be cut down. His last words, like those of Mark, were 'Hold my hand.'

'All this is very strange,' Mrs. Finch writes. 'It seems as if Ford somehow so got himself under the Marwood skin that he knew them better than they knew themselves. The Marwood "spleen" was a by-word to us. The best bit in the book is the description of Arthur catching a train at the beginning of *Some Do Not*. This is so true that I laughed till I cried.'[8]

Yet Ford was sufficiently aloof from his subject so as not to be blinded by his faults. In general, he admired; but he could also perceive weaknesses:

I don't see what Yorkshire has to do with it—except that all Yorkshire people, as I have known them, are singularly lazy and singularly self-sufficient. . . . My friend Marwood, as you say, was a case in point; he had the clear intelligence of a poet, but, rather than trespass on his own shyness and shamefacedness, he would spend days making corrections on the Margins of the Encyclopaedia Britannica. He just—peace to his ashes—wanted to bolster up his self-conceit to himself (he didn't boast of his achievement to any other soul), and, of course, to remain très grand seigneur, Marwood of Busby, and so on. . . . That is at the bottom of most Yorkshire dislike of the Arts—a sort of shyness and love of ease! Your county folk see a Poet performing coram populo! They say to themselves: We dare not appear in public: they say aloud: That is a contemptible fellow! And gradually their public utterances become themselves and they end as sidesmen at the local Bethel! And conceal the Venus of Milo, as she used to be concealed in Leeds Art Gallery, behind Aspidistras![9]

Having thus chosen a figure who, like Marwood, was both intelligent and a member of 'the establishment', Ford then placed Tietjens in circumstances not dissimilar from those he had himself experienced. This simple procedure was to give the book the aloofness and relative impersonality that is necessary for superior art.

One further step was needed, however, and that was to relate his immediate story to what he later described as his general subject, 'the world as it culminated in the war.'[10] Apparently it was the death of Proust which brought this requirement to mind for, as he later remarked in *It Was the Nightingale*, 'The work that at that time—and now—I wanted to see done was something on an immense scale, a little cloudy in immediate attack, but with the salient points and the final impression extraordinarily clear. I wanted the Novelist in fact to appear in his really proud position as historian of his own time. Proust being dead I could see no one who was doing that. . . .'[11]

He had purposefully not read Proust lest he inadvertently adopt some of his methods, but the events of his stay in Paris in 1923, coupled with his general knowledge of Proust's contribution to fiction, set him on the road to writing *Parade's End*. At Notre Dame, standing before the war memorial to British troops, he had a chance reunion with a man called Evans with whom he had served in the Welch Regiment; in a French railway compartment he had a chat with a British officer who was returning to France to see in peacetime the country whose existence he had fought to save, and who was subjected to nothing but rudeness by French officialdom on his sentimental journey; and at the Amiens railway station he suddenly saw a woman standing in the shadows with the waiting passengers as the train came in: 'She was in a golden sheath-gown and her golden hair was done in bandeaux, extraordinarily brilliant in the dimness. Like a goddess come in from the forest of Amiens! I exclaimed: "Sylvia!" '[12] These and other experiences gave him the breadth he needed for a novel that was to deal not so much with the horrors of trench fighting as with the incessant worry which in wartime, whether at home or at the front, inexorably and remorselessly whittles away morale and either reduces men to a state of idiocy or forces them, if they are to survive at all, to seek new values.

Thus even the first two chapters of *Some Do Not* indicate that this work was to go much further than the customary Fordian study of a good man bedevilled by society. This note is also present, but is placed in the context of public events, so that early on, Tietjens is made to say: 'Well, war is as inevitable as divorce.'[13]

The novel opens with the passage mentioned in Mrs. Finch's letter:

The two young men—they were of the English public official class—sat in the perfectly appointed railway carriage. The leather straps to the windows were of virgin newness; the mirrors beneath the new luggage racks immaculate as if they had reflected very little; the bulging upholstery in its luxuriant, regulated curves was scarlet and yellow in an intricate, minute dragon pattern, the design of a geometrician in Cologne. The compartment smelt faintly, hygienically of admirable varnish; the train ran as smoothly—Tietjens remembered thinking—as British gilt-edged securities. . . .[14]

The key words in this passage are the adjectives—*virgin, immaculate, bulging, luxuriant, scarlet* and *yellow.* Through them the tone of the novel is set, and the paradox of a railway compartment that can be described as being both immaculate and scarlet is the paradox of modern England and the paradox of most of the characters in the Tietjens novels. For the point cannot be stressed too strongly that Ford does not moralize in this long novel; his heroes are not immaculate super-beings, nor do his villains wallow in opulent luxury.

For this reason, while still in the first chapter, Ford makes Macmaster, the self-made companion of Tietjens, think in these terms:

Macmaster congratulated himself again on his appearance. It was all very well for Tietjens to look like a sweep; he was of these people. He,

175

Macmaster, wasn't. He had, if anything, to be an authority, and authorities wore gold tie-rings and broadcloth. . . . Tietjens only caught the Rye train by running alongside it, pitching his enormous kit-bag through the carriage window and swinging on the foot-board. Macmaster reflected that if he had done that half the station would have been yelling, 'Stand away there.' As it was Tietjens, a stationmaster was galloping after him to open the carriage door and grinningly to part: 'Well caught, sir!' for it was a cricketing county.[15]

Thus, although it is clear from other passages that Macmaster is 'on the make' and using people for his private advantage in a way Tietjens never would, he is also an object of sympathy. It is not his fault that he was not 'of these people'; he was the son of a poor man in Leith and had risen to his present position through his own hard work. His final comment on the manner in which Tietjens boards the train is therefore almost pathetic:

> 'Truly', Macmaster quoted to himself,
> 'The Gods to each ascribe a differing lot:
> Some enter at the portal. Some do not!'[16]

While this may be an instance of Scottish 'wry' humour, it is also the *chose donnée* of the book as a whole. The dictum 'Some Do Not' is Ford's way of presenting the governing condition of life in pre-war England. At its best, it involves social responsibility, but it is also dangerously close to social snobbery and aloofness. Moreover, while it lends a certain stability to life, it also makes change inevitable. The phrase 'Some Do Not' is so loaded that it can only be viable so long as the institutions that support it are rooted in human values. Only in this way will the institutions themselves be respected by those outside of them. That Ford should casually state this vital concept in the form of a jingle is a mark of his artistry.*

The second chapter of *Some Do Not* strikes two other important notes in the book—those of religion and sex. These complement and complicate the themes of the opening section and mainly concern the relations between Christopher and his wife, Sylvia Tietjens. Intellectually and formally, Sylvia adheres to her Roman Catholic religious training, but she is emotionally unsatisfied and has frequent affairs with other men. By no means simply a lovely woman who has stooped to folly, Sylvia herself suffers as she bedevils her husband.

---

* The couplet, amusingly enough, is inspired by Ford's own *Mister Bosphorus*. In that book, however, the second line runs: 'Some rest on snowy bosoms! Some do not!'

To maintain an appearance of rationality, she balances her behaviour towards Christopher by good sportsmanship in other things. Thus none of the main characters of *Parade's End* is wholly good or wholly evil. Rather, they are all of them caught, like the characters of *The Good Soldier*, in a minuet that was really a 'prison full of screaming hysterics.' The world, in short, has not been corrupted by some immense and obvious evil, but human values have all been dislodged in a small way so that everyone has become slightly tainted. What makes the novel interesting is, that despite their extraordinary behaviour, the characters always remain real and their actions plausible.

After the groundwork is carefully laid in the first two chapters, the working out of the fates of Ford's characters begins. Their relationships are complex, but certain things shortly become clear. One incident, Macmaster's dishonest use of information given him by Tietjens to gain himself a knighthood, has many implications. It is significant to Tietjens himself because he is conscious of representing the old tradition of the Tory gentleman and of standing for the honour of the ruling class of England. When his protégé breaks the gentleman's code, Tietjens is therefore placed in a quandary. In a sense, he is responsible for what has happened, for he had shown Macmaster how figures could be juggled; he is also responsible because he had always been Macmaster's protector, had helped finance him through Cambridge and had procured him his government position. The choice presented to Tietjens is either to break with Macmaster and reveal his dishonsty, which would be both disagreeable and dangerous, or simply to ignore what had happened, which is also disagreeable and certainly dishonourable.

In the novel the issue is not presented so baldly, but it is there and Tietjens' inaction is inevitable. A denunciation of Macmaster by Tietjens would be an unthinkable violation of the gentleman's code; furthermore, as a worldly person, Tietjens is quite aware of the manner in which ambitious men rise to positions of prominence. Being himself wholly without ambition and occupying a social position in England that is far above his function in the government office, he looks with faintly amused contempt upon the judicious but corrupt methods by which small men gratify their petty ambitions. He knows, too, that scientific truth, here represented by statistics, can be manipulated for political purposes, but it would be contemptible of him to lower himself to a discussion of them. Like Mr. Blood before him, and like Ashburnham in *The Good Soldier*, Tietjens therefore chooses to remain uninvolved. The attitude is natural for one in Tietjens' position, and Ford uses it as a symbol of the ostrich-like attitude of the ruling classes as a whole, who had let their honour and position be whittled away by seemingly small corruptions so that by 1914 the entire country had become rotten.

Yet Christopher is not a completely passive character. The code which he refuses to impose on others he imposes on himself with great rigour. His ideals are virtually those of medieval chivalry, and he is fanatically responsible to them. The maintenance of this code makes life so difficult for him that he becomes eccentric. His troubles arise particularly in his dealings with his wife, Sylvia. Her scandalous behaviour in London ruins his reputation more than it ruins hers, for he is sneered at as a cuckold. He is quite aware of the reputation he has gained by refusing to fight back, but believes that since it is his privilege to be able to board moving trains, it is also his duty to accept without complaint the disagreeable behaviour of an unfaithful wife. Like Don Quixote, he is a sentimentalist. Yet while it may be vain and foolish of him to adhere to standards ignored by everybody else, his idealism raises him, just as Antigone is raised over Creon, or Hamlet over Laertes, to a higher and more endearing level.

If Tietjens were superhuman and if the novel were static, such a situation might endure for years; but having created a human character, Ford then proceeds, with Jamesian thoroughness, to remove the props that made it possible for Tietjens to maintain his individualistic attitude.

Driven by loneliness into a friendship with Valentine Wannop, the daughter of his father's oldest friend, Christopher soon finds himself thwarted even in this release. For hearing of this relationship, Sylvia tells her husband that his father has committed suicide because of Christopher's reportedly dishonourable behaviour with Valentine. The screw is also given another turn by means of a rumour that Valentine is really the bastard daughter of Christopher's father and Mrs. Wannop. As a result, Tietjens forces himself to behave with great reticence with Valentine and, distressed by his father's lack of faith in him, he refuses to touch a penny of his legacy even though he loves the Yorkshire place, Groby, better than any other place in the world. Another prop is removed when a fellow club member causes one of Tietjens' cheques to his club to be dishonoured. Christopher understands the man's motives, but when

178

through him the club seems to have been sullied, he resigns from it, even though it had formerly symbolized to him one of the few places where gentlemanly behaviour still obtained. By refusing to act against the man who insulted him, he thus passively contributes to the very force that served ultimately to dispossess his class as a whole. His code is both contradictory and incomplete, yet he persists in upholding it so far as his own behaviour is concerned.

Ford once noted that it was a characteristic of the modern age that, owing to 'the disappearance of Continence, Probity and the belief in revealed religion, Truth should have developed the bewildering faculty of the chameleon and have taken on, like Janus, two faces. ... So the novelist—the authentic and valid novelist whose duty it is to record his world in crystallized form so that it may be of advantage to posterity—the novelist seeing both sides of Truth can do no more than take one side at one moment and the other immediately afterwards. ...'[17] Thus Ford in *Parade's End* dispassionately presents not only the plight of Christopher, but equally the dilemma of Sylvia.

In his portrait of Sylvia, Ford produces the prototype of the chic society woman who arouses sympathy by her attractiveness and by her rather pathetic attempts to reconcile herself to her milieu. A product of her social class, she is something of a spoiled angel, basically a 'good girl' who has got off the rails and gone to the bad. She is something like Hemingway's Lady Brett Ashley in *The Sun Also Rises*, but her relationship with Christopher is far more harrowing than Brett's with Jake Barnes. Similar, too, in some ways to Mrs. Viveash in Huxley's *Antic Hay*, she is yet more thoughtful and, for all her casual wittiness, more seriously committed in her battle for her soul than either of these other women.

As Christopher's relations with society reveal much about the decay of public standards, so Sylvia's struggle represents the impossibility of reconciling the delicious freedom of society with a strict Roman Catholic upbringing. She respects the family priest, Father Consett, but because she is bitterly aware of Christopher's moral superiority, she acts as spitefully as she can towards her Christ-like husband and, even though it hurts her to do so, she rejects what she has been taught is good and decent. Her problem is a psychological study of a human heart torn between love and sex.

What really maddens Sylvia is her husband's imperturbability at her outrageous public behaviour. Instead of reacting harshly, he merely, like a long-suffering god, accepts her for what she is. Thus, driven from excess to excess in an attempt to make him recognize her as a human being, Sylvia devises the most excruciating mental tortures for Christopher. Ironically, she tortures him because she loves him, but as the novel progresses, her growing sexual jealousy makes her more and more violent. She knows her husband is omniscient and that he sees what she is up to, and this knowledge increases her fury. In *Some Do Not*, she says to him:

'. . . But in the name of the Almighty, how could any woman live beside you . . . and be forever forgiven? Or no: not forgiven; ignored! . . . Well, be proud when you die because of your honour. But God, you be humble about . . . your errors in judgement. *You* know what it is to ride a horse for miles with too tight a curb-chain and its tongue cut almost in half. . . . You remember the groom your father had who had the trick of turning the hunters out like that. . . . And you've horse-whipped him, and you've told me you've almost cried ever so often afterwards for thinking of that mare's mouth. . . . Well, think of *this* mare's mouth sometimes! You've ridden me like that for seven years. . . .'[18]

Yet Christopher, in adhering to his code, has been under the impression that rather than holding back his wife by a tight rein, he has let her run quite free and wild. This psychological blind spot, which rises from the failure to reconcile morality with human need, and to see that indifference is more deadly than hatred, is the source of the tragedy of Sylvia's and Christopher's relationship.

In the later stages of the novel, the situation between Christopher and Sylvia continues to deteriorate. Although in outward appearance still quite sane, Sylvia gradually reveals the toll her sexual jealousy has taken. Thus she even follows Tietjens to France, pulling strings in wartime so that she might meet him and sleep with him. Then upon arrival she resumes her torturing—both of herself and of her husband—in a mad colloquy with a regimental sergeant major which takes place in the presence of Christopher:

'Do you know what they used to say of the Captain? . . .' She said to herself: 'I pray to God the stiff, fatuous beast likes sitting here listening to this stuff . . . Blessed Virgin, mother of God, make him take me. . . . Before midnight. Before eleven . . . As soon as we can get rid of this . . . No, he's a decent little man . . . Blessed Virgin!' 'Do you know what they used to say of the Captain? . . . I heard the warmest banker in England say it of him . . .'

The sergeant-major, his eyes enormously opened said:

'Did you know the warmest banker in England? . . . But there, we always knew the captain was well connected. . . .'

She went on:

'They said of him. . . . He was always helping people' . . . 'Holy Mary, mother of God! . . . He's my *husband*. It's not a sin . . . Before midnight . . . Oh, give me a sign . . . Or before . . . the termination of hostilities . . . If you give me a sign I could wait.' . . . 'He helped virtuous Scotch students, and broken-down gentry . . . And women taken in adultery . . . All of them . . . Like . . . You know who. . . . That is his model. . . .' She said to herself : 'Curse him! . . . I hope he likes it . . . You'd think the only thing he thinks about is the beastly duck he's wolfing down.' And then aloud: 'They used to say: "He saved others; himself he could not save. . . ." '[19]

Thus by public humiliation and by every trick of the blackmailer, Sylvia tries to pull Christopher down to her own level. Of course she fails, because Tietjens simply will not admit reality: he plays the ostrich as he played it over Macmaster's dishonesty. His code permits of no other behaviour, for the Christist cannot play his rôle for a part of the time only. Sylvia in the meantime becomes increasingly debased and finally even loses her curiously sportsmanlike attitude towards life.

A situation like this cannot last for ever, yet it was a public event rather than a voluntary act that brought about a change. Indeed for humanity at large a world war was required to make it clear that the old code was dead because it was incomplete; and the fourth of August, 1914 ended a long tradition in English life.

That Tietjens had become aware of the public change is evident in his description to a brother officer of the orders for the ceremonial disbanding of a Kitchener battalion: '. . . the band would play *Land of Hope and Glory*, and the adjutant would say: *There will be no more parades* . . . Don't you see how symbolical it was—the band playing *Land of Hope and Glory* and then the adjutant saying *There will be no more parades?* . . . For there won't. There won't, there damn well won't . . . No more Hope, no more Glory, no more parades for you and me any more. Nor for the country . . . nor for the world, I dare say . . . None . . . Gone . . . Napoo, finny! No . . . more . . . parades!'[20]

Yet even though he realized how far public bankruptcy had gone, Tietjens had not yet been able to find a solution, either for the country or for himself. While at the front, however, he had begun to think of basic values and, in realizing that the old institutions like his club and even Groby were now meaningless, it was borne in on him that something deeper and more personal and hence more reliable was needed. In his spare time, he managed to do some reading and in the seventeenth century of George Herbert he found some measure of hope:

> The only satisfactory age in England!... Yet what chance had it today. Or still more, tomorrow. In the sense that the age of, say, Shakespeare had a chance. Or Pericles! Or Augustus!
>
> Heaven knew, we did not want a preposterous drumbeating such as the Elizabethans produced—and received. Like lions at a fair . . . But what chance had quiet fields, Anglican sainthood, accuracy of thought, heavy-leaved, timbered hedge-rows, slowly creeping plough-lands moving up the slopes? . . . Still the land remains. . . .
>
> The land remains . . . It remains! . . . At that same moment the dawn was wetly revealing; over there in George Herbert's parish . . . what was it called? . . . What the devil was its name? Oh, Hell! . . . Between Salisbury and Wilton . . . The tiny church . . . But he refused to consider the plough-lands, the heavy groves, the slow high-road above the church that the dawn was at that moment wetly revealing—until he could remember that name. He refused to consider that, probably even today, that land ran to . . . produced the stock of . . . Anglican sainthood. The quiet thing![21]

Here then was the dream, but Bemerton Parsonage is not easily accessible: a change of heart does not just happen. Tietjens' war experiences, like those of Ford himself, however, had begun to alter him. In the early months of the war, he had been indifferent in his usual way, but gradually his attitude hardens. Becoming embroiled in army life, he is forced for the first time to help himself, and he is even glad to get a command. This change is due solely to the war, for the war makes Tietjens realize that he cannot escape responsibility. When he refuses leave to one of his men, O Nine Morgan, on purely humanitarian grounds, he finds that he unwittingly causes his death, and when he carries the wounded soldier, Aranjuez, from a pile of earth where he fell, he discovers that he has accidentally caused him to go blind. Thus he learns that the Tory aloofness from the little nastinesses of life is no longer possible:

> The war had made a man of him! It had coarsened him and hardened him. There was no other way to look at it. It had made him reach a point at which he would no longer stand unbearable things. At any rate

from his equals! He counted Campion as his equal; few other people, of course. And what he wanted he was prepared to take. . . . What had he been before, God alone knew. A Younger Son? A Perpetual Second-in-Command? Who knew. But today the world had changed. Feudalism was finished; its last vestiges were gone. It held no place for him. He was going—he was damn well going! to make a place in it for . . . A man could now stand up upon a hill, so he and she could surely get into some hole together![22]

Yet Bemerton Parsonage was still not so easy to achieve, even with the new strength of manhood weirdly bequeathed by the war. For even with the end of his sentimentalism, Tietjens still had domestic complications with which he had to cope. By now, however, he was in a position to take action. (*A Man Could Stand Up* is appropriately the title of this third novel.) To return to a life with Sylvia was impossible because she had never really grown up or realized what the war meant. To her the war was merely an incident, and she was still tragically involved in fighting a code that Tietjens himself had abandoned. On the other hand, there was Valentine Wannop who represented to Tietjens all the best that had survived from the seventeenth-century world he idolized. Unlike Sylvia, Valentine had values deeply rooted in the past: she was, for example, an excellent classicist. But she also embodied the best of the new age: she was unpretentious, idiosyncratic, hard-working, honest and clean. She lacked the glamour of Sylvia, but by 1919 Tietjens had had his fill of glamour and knew how worthless it would be in a world of no more parades.

The working out of this personal affair occupies the final book of the tetralogy, *The Last Post*, and, like much that preceded it, is in part based on Ford's own experience with Stella Bowen. Tietjens and Valentine meet in London and then decide to bury themselves in a simple cottage deep in the country. On the face of it, this solution out of William Morris, a return to the Simple Life, might appear to be naïf, for this sort of escapism is hardly applicable to those who cannot afford bucolic solutions to their difficulties. Yet Ford was not being simple-minded. In the first place, his novel is the story of one man, and Tietjens' solution is in keeping with his character and position. Moreover, Ford himself, with little more than his mustering-out pay, had done the same thing. What is important about the incident, however, is that it suggests that the tradition of the English Tory can only survive by accepting what it would normally be expected to have scorned. Tietjens, in a word, is forced to abrogate the legal ways of man to gain his ends. He has to set up household with Valentine in an illegal fashion (for he was not divorced from Sylvia), he virtually leads the life of a peasant, and the hope that is promised for the future of England comes from Chrissy, his illegitimate son. This does not mean that Ford was preaching anarchy: it is only to suggest that laws, like statistics, are means, not ends, and that mankind may have to turn its back on old habits and customs if it is to restore decency to the world. Only in the manner of Antaeus returning to the soil can the governing classes become strong again and independent of the props and forms of their former greatness—the clubs, the great country houses, the carefully cultivated aloofness and the 'perfectly appointed railway carriage' in which Tietjens first appears in the novel.

There are strong indications in *The Last Post* that Ford considered political responsibility a necessary part of the rejuvenation of England. It is no accident that Christopher's son by Sylvia is a Communist while he is an undergraduate at Cambridge. Valentine herself is an active Leftist and is both a suffragette and a pacifist. Thus it is suggested that Tietjens' association with her, like the natural alliance between the aristocracy and the working classes who unite in their common dislike for middle class, will bring about a world in which the decent things of life are respected. Ford himself noted at the time that he was 'so fantastically old-fashioned as to see no salvation save in the feudal system as practised in the fourteenth-century—or in such Communism as may prevail a thousand years hence.'[23]

The need of a responsible return to old and tried values also underlies the religious portions of *Parade's End*. Ironically, it is Sylvia who is most concerned with religion throughout the tetralogy. Her adviser, Father Consett, is perspicacious and penetrating and, although his influence on Sylvia is relatively small, it is enough to worry her and to increase the violence of the vicious war that rages within herself. From time to time she goes to a Roman Catholic retreat near Birkenhead, but these attempts at reconciliation always fail, for Sylvia has never really understood what religion means. Father Consett and the retreat personify it and make it real to her, but beyond a childish sense of retribution, her understanding of religion is negligible. Indeed, she even uses it for blackmail, and pesters the Protestant Christopher by telling him that she intends

184

to raise their son, Michael Mark, as a Roman Catholic. Altogether, then, despite her profession of religion, Sylvia has never gone beyond its practical application or its form and, generally unaffected by the events of the war, she does not realize that in the post-war world, form is not enough.

Religion has a direct, if symbolic, place in Christopher's mind as well, for it is intimately connected with Groby, the Tietjens place in Yorkshire which had once been a monastery but which was later seized by William of Orange and given as a reward to an early Tietjens. Part of Christopher's early sentimentalism was that he always attached much importance to this place and to Groby Great Tree in particular. It was something stable in a world that was going to pieces. Sylvia's order that the tree should be cut down was therefore an act of spite against Christopher; later on, however, she realized that the destruction of the tree was perhaps a symbol that 'God was lifting the ban off the Tietjenses.'[24] Finally, Mark Tietjens, himself on the verge of death, sums up the situation:

> That then was over. The worst of it rolled up together. No suicide. No incest. No by-blow at Groby . . . A Papist there . . . Though how you could be a Papist and a Marxian-Communist passed his, Mark's comprehension . . . A Papist at Groby and Groby Great Tree down . . . The curse was perhaps off the family![25]

Thus the purification of Groby is like Christopher's retirement to a kind of Bemerton Parsonage. By returning to the faith of their fathers, the Tietjenses—and all the world—might be saved. The later adulterations of Protestantism are here seen to have weakened the core of Christianity in England and in the world. In an early book, *The Spirit of the People*, Ford had noted that while Protestantism was a 'nobler intellectual growth'[26] than Catholicism, the trouble was that no one could live up to it. The Civil War, he thought, 'doomed England to be the land of impractical ideals.'[27] *Parade's End* was Ford's way of saying, as Yeats also said, that the Christian religion had lost touch with the altar and had become merely a pulpit. It was therefore necessary to return to the fountainhead for greater strength and purer actions than middle class Protestantism had been able to provide. The tetralogy is not, of course, a sectarian work for, by using George Herbert, Ford indicates that Anglican sainthood would do as well as Catholicism, and Tietjens remains a Protestant. The Roman Catholicism of Groby is primarily a metaphorical concept.

185

Altogether, *Parade's End* is an immensely suggestive panoramic novel that at the same time provides a profound psychological analysis of a small number of human beings. Superficially, it has much in common with *Vanity Fair* and, in so far as it presents a study of the war between the sexes against a background of rising and falling social classes, it resembles Proust's *A la Recherche du Temps Perdu*. Yet comparison with these books or even with Joyce's *Ulysses* succeeds only in placing it in a class of literature. The success of *Parade's End* depends on Ford's skill in combining the intimate psychological techniques of James with a large social framework. This milieu is itself original in the sense that while the ordinary nineteenth-century novel seems to present an apparently static society with only an undercurrent of dissatisfaction and turmoil, and the twentieth-century novel shows a society whose institutions are wholly disrupted and discredited, *Parade's End*, standing half-way between these two, portrays the actual disruption as it took place during the war. Yet even in its psychological aspects, this tetralogy is not merely the sort of book James might have written had he attempted the 'big subject' of a Galsworthy or Balzac. For, as Granville Hicks remarked, Ford 'has done certain sorts of things that James could never have done and would not have attempted.'[28]

II

The substance of *Parade's End* would never have come through without the technical skill with which Ford treated his subject, and here the two are perfectly suited to each other. Hitherto, with the exception of *The Good Soldier*, Ford's work was uneven and his conception of his subject rarely lived up to the technical brilliance of his writing. Often his heroes were too extraordinary for belief, and sometimes, as Arnold Bennett wrote in a review of *A Call*, Ford endowed his characters 'with a comprehensive fineness of perception, and a skill in verbal expression which it is absolutely impossible that they, living the life they do live, could possess.'[29] Other faults like an excessive reliance on coincidence or an overpopulation of characters come from Ford's avowed notion that it mattered little what a man's subject was so long as the treatment was admirable. In his letters to other writers and during the long hours of conversation with Conrad, Ford had been concerned solely with the way in which a writer could best get his effects. For a novelist like H. G. Wells, this preoccupation was meaningless, and it is true that whatever may be the faults of Wells's work, it is strong where Ford's early work was weak: Wells's characters and situations were real; Ford's were not. Ford's devotion to technique, however, paid its dividends in such works as *The Good Soldier* and *Parade's End*, whereas much of Wells's later work suffers from the very sloppiness Ford was endeavouring to avoid.

In conceiving the characters of the Tietjens tetralogy, what Ford has done, as Melvin Seiden has pointed out,[30] is to make Christopher into an anti-hero who has affinities with Dostoievsky's *Idiot*, and to make his heroine the precise opposite of the typical British heroine. As the world has turned upside down, he seems to be saying, so also have people, so that a modern version of Pamela would necessarily have to be different from Richardson's. But the real point Ford makes is that Sylvia is neither extremely virtuous in the tradition of the British heroine of romance, nor fiendish in the manner of Lady Macbeth. Rather, she is merely a decent enough woman of the world. In an early essay, 'The Woman of the Novelists',[31] Ford criticized the English fictional heroine for always being an extreme— either a representative of the 'fair sex' or some sort of monster. Recognizing the falsehood of this notion, he tried in Sylvia Tietjens to create a real woman rather than a 'super-woman' of the type of Desdemona, Juliet or Sophia Western.

Thus in all his work Ford was a self-conscious writer who was always able to say, 'I know exactly how I get my effects as far as those effects go.'[32] Brought up in Victorian times when literature was more a matter of morality than of art, he found relief in the works of foreign writers lent him by his grandfather, Ford Madox Brown. And after reading such books as *Madame Bovary, Le Rouge et le Noir* and the *Lettres de Mon Moulin* of Daudet, along with all the usual classics of nineteenth-century English fiction, he perceived that the modern French novel was less amateurish than the English. He therefore strove to learn as much as he could from such Continental writers as Stendhal, Maupassant, Turgenev and Flaubert and from such writers in English as Marryat and Henry James who followed the same path. In the years of his apprenticeship, both alone and with Conrad, he gradually consolidated his method. The first product of it is *The Good Soldier*; the first detailed exposition of it occurs in his book on Joseph Conrad. The job of writing *The*

Good Soldier was doubtless hard enough, but for a psychological novelist like Ford, the effort of maintaining tension and interest for the eight hundred pages of *Parade's End* must have been extremely difficult.

In an article on Ford, Edward Crankshaw pointed out that both he and Conrad were rebelling against the traditional panoramic novel, preferring instead to limit their subject to an 'affaire'. In *Parade's End*, however, Ford goes beyond this limitation and adds what Crankshaw calls a 'mirror of society'. The result is a work that 'combines the intensiveness of the new school with the extensiveness of the old masters.'[33]

What made this achievement possible was Ford's attention to over-all form: every individual element of the book is subordinated to the central issue. The difficulty of achieving what Poe called 'unity of effect' is, of course, increased when the writer thinks not in terms of short stories but in sequels.[34] But even in his first trilogy, *The Fifth Queen* series, he took care to plan the work in terms of three books. The result, he found, was that the second volume was better than the first, as it was intended to be, because he had already got in his setting and descriptions in the earlier book.[35] In his later work, Ford's planning was necessarily more complex than simply deciding where to put descriptions and where to put action. He had, for example, to consider the rôle particular scenes would play in the book as a whole. The use of a strong scene is often tempting for a writer, since climactic moments are dramatic and exciting. They are sometimes also very false, however, and tend to stick out from the surface so that the reader remembers one particular scene, but not the book itself. The writer who considers his work as a progression in which motives and actions will be made clear only at the very end, must therefore suppress strong scenes. For however attractive they may be in themselves, they will interfere with his final effect.

Ford's willingness to obey this rigorous code so as to protect the architecture of his whole book is made clear in the suppression of the scene with which *Some Do Not* was to have ended. This scene, which now exists only in manuscript, depicts the last dramatic interview that takes place between Christopher and Sylvia before Tietjens leaves for the front; it stresses the sexual antagonism that has grown up between them and it contains a good deal of violence. Had *Some Do Not* been designed to stand alone, this ending would have been satisfactory, but as it was only a part of a tetralogy, it was suppressed, and Ford put its substance in the next novel in the form of Tietjens' reminiscences.*

Mention of form brings up the question of the final book of the series, *The Last Post*. It is clear from a letter Ford wrote in 1930, in which he said that he did not like this book and 'always intended the series to end with *A Man Could Stand Up*,' that *Parade's End* was intended as a trilogy.[36] In recent years, however, it has been twice published as a tetralogy. *The Last Post* differs from the preceding three novels in so far as the focus turns from Christopher Tietjens to his brother, Mark. Compared to the others, *The Last Post* is static and involves a certain amount of recapitulation of previously narrated events. Yet, as Robie Macaulay points out,[37] without this novel, the work as a whole would be 'sadly truncated,' for not only does one find out, as Ford wrote in his preface, 'what became of Tietjens,'[38] one also finds in this denouement that Tietjens is perpetuated as a symbol, thus making him not merely one man who walked a stage and was heard of no more, but a representative of a whole class. Those who live at Groby—Mark Tietjens and his retinue—constitute a kind of Greek chorus that serves to connect Tietjens with the Yorkshire soil, and indeed, with present reality. Artistically, it was also essential that the focus be changed; the Christopher-centred novel was designed for three novels, and to stretch it would have spoiled its form. A coda, then, was the only possible solution. †

With regard to the various techniques Ford employed in this book —the time-shift, the purposed *longueur*, *progression d'effet* and the others—enough has been said of them as they were applied to the collaborated works and to *The Good Soldier*. In a sense, it is remarkable that Ford knew for so long what Impressionism was supposed to do. Thus what he wrote in 1914 was wholly applicable to the Tietjens books of the 1920's. Not for a long time, however, did he succeed in doing himself what he had for so long set up as a model. The statement that appears below was the intention, but it was not really fulfilled until he wrote *Parade's End*.

For the first business of Impressionism is to produce an impression, and the only way in literature to produce an impression is to awaken

---

* The text of this suppressed ending is printed in my article 'A Conscious Craftsman: Ford Madox Ford's Manuscript Revisions', published in *Boston University Studies in English*, V, 3, Autumn 1961, pp. 182–4.

† It is worth noting that Ford's editor, Mr Graham Greene, disapproves of the inclusion of *The Last Post*, and that therefore *The Bodley Head Ford Madox Ford* contains only the first three volumes.

interest. And, in a sustained argument, you can only keep interest awakened by keeping alive, by whatever means you may have at your disposal, the surprise of your reader. You must state your argument; you must illustrate it, and then you must stick in something that appears to have nothing whatever to do with either subject or illustration, so that the reader will exclaim: 'What the devil is the fellow driving at?' And then you must go on in the same way arguing, illustrating and startling and illustrating—until at the very end your contentions will appear like a ravelled skein.

And then, in the last few lines, you will draw towards you the master-string of that seeming confusion, and the whole pattern of the carpet, the whole design of the net-work will be apparent.

This method, you observe, founds itself upon analysis of the human mind. For no human being likes listening to long and sustained arguments. Such listening is an effort, and no artist has the right to call for any effort from his audience. A picture should come out of its frame and seize the spectator.[39]

One technical change in *Parade's End* which increased the accessibility of Ford's prose is here worth noticing. Whereas much of the success of *The Good Soldier* had depended on Ford's use of a narrator whose very mannerisms contributed to the point of the book, in the tetralogy he returned to his own voice and emphasized dialogue. While this method may owe something to Hemingway, it differs from Hemingway in being far less abrupt and telegraphic, for Ford's greatest gift, as distinct from an acquired technique, was his mastery of flowing prose rhythms. Coupled with this new directness of manner is Ford's abandonment of the endlessly modified sentence of James and the highly coloured phraseology of Conrad. The result therefore is a novel that is at once complex in its over-all form and extraordinarily lucid in its language. The work as a whole has an individuality of style that makes it an original contribution to the world's literature. As Caroline Gordon said, in writing it Ford 'succeeded in doing the thing that Poe said could not be done. He produced a long work whose tensions are so nicely adjusted,whose tone is sustained as that of a short tale or lyric poem.'[40]

possibly thrice we glimpsed—
                        more likely twice
that (once crammed into someone's kitchenette)

wheezing bulgily world of genial plac
-idity (plus, out of much its misbutt-
oned trouserfly tumbling, faded five
or so lightyears of pyjamastring)

a (vastly and particularly) live
that undeluded notselfpitying

lover of all things excellently rare;
obsolete almost that phenomenon
(too gay for malice and too wise for fear)
of shadowy virtue and of sunful sin

namely (ford madox ford) and eke to wit
a human being
                —let's remember that
                                —E. E. CUMMINGS

Chapter Ten

─────《◆》《◆》─────

INTERNATIONAL FIGURE

─────《◆》《◆》─────

CONSIDERED in general terms, Ford's professional career prior to 1930 seems to be divisible into two main periods. The first began with the collaboration with Conrad, continued through the editorship of *The English Review*, and culminated in the publication of *The Good Soldier* in 1915. The second period, which began after the war, found Ford transformed into a new man: Hueffer had become Ford, and France, instead of England, had become his home. The achievement of this ten-year period consists largely in his editorship of *The Transatlantic Review* and the publication of the four novels that make up *Parade's End*.

In a sense, each of these periods represents a separate career, for each was geographically distinct from the other, and there were few friends common to both. In each, however, Ford was closely associated with the most important literary figures of the time and place, so that as he had once been the intimate of men like Henry James, Arnold Bennett, John Galsworthy and Joseph Conrad, he was in the 1920's continually in the company of writers like Ezra Pound, Ernest Hemingway, Gertrude Stein and James Joyce. Doubtless his continuing interest in new talent contributed to his perennial youthfulness as a writer and literary figure, but no other writer in modern times equalled his achievement in being a key figure in so many diverse literary movements. He was to continue the habit for the rest of his life. As Carl Van Doren said of him: 'Whatever new excellence appeared, he greeted it with quick and accurate pleasure. Excellence was always excellence to him, and he always recognized it as soon as he saw it. His accounts with literature were perennially open because he never closed his sensitive, retentive mind.'[1]

Of the two periods, the second—or middle phase—is probably the more important, and certainly the decade of the 1920's was the busiest in his life. Like Christopher Tietjens, Ford seems to have become a different man after the war and to have released a tremendous burst of energy. Perhaps it required a war to make this achievement possible. This second period is also special in Ford's life because it was the one time in which he enjoyed a certain amount of fame and standing, especially in the United States. He did not really begin to benefit from it, however, until the last years of the decade.

After the demise of the *Transatlantic* in 1924, Ford devoted almost all of his time to writing. For the most part, he and Stella remained in Paris, occupying in succession a small and unattractive flat in the rue Denfert-Rochereau, which is near the Montparnasse cemetery, and a large and roomy studio-apartment at 84 rue Notre Dame des Champs, where they were neighbours of Ezra Pound. As usual, neither place had much by way of *confort moderne*, but with her artist's touch Stella contrived to make them habitable. For weekends and longer periods during the summer, they would go to Guermantes where, at Gertrude Stein's suggestion, they had procured a small labourer's cottage. They had to repaint the interiors and have the walls papered, but as the rent was only 500 francs a year and the house was situated in a charming orchard, it was a good retreat.

Now freed from his time-consuming occupation as editor of the *Transatlantic*, and from the social pressures that accompanied it, Ford was able to concentrate on his own work and, since the novel he planned was immense, he was doubtless pleased to be once again his own master. Never at heart a recluse, however, Ford still remained very much in the centre of Parisian social and artistic life. With William Bradley and his wife, Jenny, Ford and Stella would discover new restaurants. Ford had first met Bradley in New York in 1906, and now Bradley was a literary agent in Paris. Like Ford, he was a serious connoisseur of good foods and wines. In the afternoons, when he was not himself at home to young friends, Ford would visit Gertrude Stein or attend the salon of Natalie Barney, the 'Amazone' of Rémy de Gourmont, whose little pavilion off the Rue Jacob was particularly favoured of French writers like Jaloux, Gide and Valéry. Altogether a literary man-about-town, Ford could always be seen at gatherings of writers or painters or at one or other favourite restaurant like Lavigne's where he would dine in the evenings in the company of friends.

As a person unusually conscious of the literary tradition, Ford strongly believed in the usefulness of these social gatherings. He enjoyed, moreover, the attention he received as a distinguished author and played the rôle accordingly. Proud of his calling, he moved about in Parisian artistic and social circles as one who had been a part of them all his life. Much of this was, of course, a pose, for he knew that his work was not widely appreciated. For this reason, as Stella Bowen noted, 'he often found it necessary to disguise himself as something very splendid and successful.'[2] Thus in the company of the wealthy men like William Bullitt, at whose home he sometimes dined, although 'bitterly aware that his best suit was nothing but a poor old has-been, and that standing his share of the drinks meant that he could not have the shoes he needed, [he] nevertheless talked the jargon of the rich as to the manner born. He presented a wonderful appearance of a bland, successful gentleman whose shabbiness was mere eccentricity and who regarded a preoccupation with the relative merits of Foyot and Larue, Vionnet and Poiret, the Ritz and the Hôtel George V, as very natural and necessary. . . . At the least hint of patronage, his pride would flare up, and he would metaphorically double the stakes.'[3]

At the same time, Ford was also paterfamilias, and Nina Hamnett, the English painter, has described him as she saw him in this rôle during one Christmas in Paris. 'We had Christmas lunch in the Boulevard Montparnasse,' she writes, 'at a restaurant called "Le Nègre de Toulouse". Ford had a small daughter, and in the afternoon there was a children's tea-party, with a Christmas tree and a real Father Christmas. Ford dressed up as le Père Noël. He looked magnificent as he was very tall. He wore a red cloak with cotton wool representing fur, and a red hood and a large white beard. He appeared with a large sack and spoke French, as nearly all the children spoke French better than they spoke English, and Ford's child did not speak English at all.'[4]

For the winter months of both 1924–25 and 1925–26, Ford and Stella decided to live in the South of France. At the suggestion of the Spanish painter, Juan Gris, they chose the old naval port of Toulon, a hundred miles west of Monte Carlo. Josette Gris produced rooms at a hotel for the whole Ford ménage, which included Julie and her nurse, Madame Annie, as well as an Alsatian puppy called Toulouse. From the moment of their arrival at the Hotel Victoria, they found Toulon immensely to their tastes. Close by Ford's beloved Provence, the town was not fashionable but it was very French. Prices were decent, living was simple, the climate delightful and there were no tourists. When they arrived Josette Gris told them: 'Il y a cinq cinémas et deux dancings. Ca fait juste la semaine!'[5] In the evenings after work, Ford and Stella would frequently join Juan and Josette at a café, and through them they met a number of painters living in the neighbourhood. One of them, Othon Friez, told Stella about an available studio, and she soon found herself in her element, for with Friez, Latapie and the others, she was able to talk about painting, whereas except for Francis Carco and, later on, William Seabrook, there were no other writers in the area. Gris found Ford eccentric and witty, but his Spanish soul was astonished at the 'terrifying quantity of alcohol' he consumed, and he wrote to a friend that he 'never thought one could drink so much.'[6]

Except for the months they spent in Paris and for a visit they paid to the Ezra Pounds in Rapallo in 1925, Ford and Stella lived quietly in Toulon. Much of Ford's time was devoted to the two middle books of the Tietjens series and to *A Mirror to France*, a book inspired by his love of French civilization and dedicated to Gertrude Stein. In the mornings he wrote, and in the afternoons attended to domestic arrangements and correspondence. He and Stella always dined out, and afterwards they usually went to one of the cafés along the port. For their second winter they were able to afford a room with a bath, and they spent some of their free time househunting on the outskirts of Toulon, where Ford was eventually to find a relatively permanent home. Sometimes there were also excursions to an outlying village or town in Provence, but on the whole, they stayed in Toulon. The life was hardly exciting, but it was the usual life of the artist who wishes to accomplish something.

Meanwhile, for the first time in his life, Ford was beginning to receive some reward for his labours. In New York his novel, *Some Do Not*, had been a success, while the second of the series, *No More Parades*, had sold between forty and fifty thousand copies. One result of his sudden fame was the visit of a group of American tourists who came all the way over from Nice to meet him and shake his hand. Shortly afterwards he was approached by James Pond, the leading American lecture agent, who asked him to go to the United States under his auspices. The proposal was for a ten-week tour of the East and Middle West.[7]

Despite his distaste for lecturing, Ford gladly accepted Pond's offer. After three years of unbroken work, he needed a change, and an opportunity to visit New York was always welcome. Moreover he had by this time formed a number of American connexions, having already published in magazines like *The Dial, Poetry* and *The Yale Review*, and he therefore decided to use his trip to strengthen his American associations as much as possible. That he had become a celebrity made the chance even more opportune.

After a brief farewell week-end in Avignon, Ford sailed for New York on the *Paris* in October of 1926. At first he was the guest of Herbert Gorman, the friend and biographer of James Joyce, but soon he had to leave on his lecture tour which took him, amongst other places, to St. Louis, Chicago and Boston. At Cambridge, he lectured to the undergraduates at the Harvard Union, recounting anecdotes about reading *The Red Badge of Courage* at the front in 1917, and telling them that Crane's imaginative powers had been so great that as he read the book he totally forgot he was within reach of the German artillery. As a lecturer, Ford was rarely dogmatic; he merely told quiet stories and let them make his points for him.[8] Everywhere he went on his tour he was fêted with receptions where he met American writers and critics and renewed old acquaintances. Equipped with letters of introduction, he looked up friends and relations of his American colleagues in Paris and, as he had once visited Nottingham in the company of D. H. Lawrence so as to discover at first hand the atmosphere of *Sons and Lovers*, he now went out to Oak Park, a suburb of Chicago, to call on Hemingway's father. A cumbersome, bulky man, with flaxen hair, and soft blue eyes and with a mouth always half open, he could hardly have appeared to his American hosts as the 'type' of the artist, but he soon demonstrated that underneath this bland exterior there was a keen and energetic mind. On at least one occasion during this trip he was able to give a vivid intellectual performance. When he called at the offices of *Poetry* magazine, he was asked by Harriet Monroe, the editor, to write a two thousand word article for the next number. One of the editors present has recounted how Ford then 'astonished us all by dictating it, without hesitation, then and there. It was an extremely good article, in his wittiest style. That was typical of the casual, seemingly effortless way in which he did important things.'[9]

New York, however, was the scene of his greatest triumphs. At the time of his arrival, *A Man Could Stand Up* had just been reprinted within three months of publication, and his *No More Parades* had been called 'far and away the finest book of the year' by the New York *Herald Tribune*, and 'the most highly praised novel of the year' by the *Saturday Review*. The ordinarily staid *Boston Evening Transcript* had even called him a 'genius'.[10] Very much then the literary man of the hour, Ford soon found himself discoursing on cooking and travel for *Harper's Magazine*, and writing articles and stories for *Vanity Fair*, *The Bookman* and the *Yale Review*. By January of 1927 he had been appointed visiting critic by the New York *Herald Tribune*. In October of the same year, when he returned for the second time, after spending the summer in Paris and Toulon, he was invited by Wilbur Cross and the librarian of Yale to lecture in New Haven, and he was honoured at a P.E.N. Club dinner along with two other English writers, Hugh Walpole and Osbert Sitwell.

Fond of quoting the old, and by then somewhat dated, phrase, 'Little old New York is good enough for me,' Ford managed to spend most of his time in Manhattan, and through Irita Van Doren and Herbert Gorman, managed to meet most of the American writers then living there. He liked New York because it was glamorous, kindly and incurious; but most of all he appreciated its 'casualness, its easiness, its sheer ordinariness.'[11] Finding its intellectual life keener than that of London, but with intellectual circles smaller than those of Paris,[12] he soon began to gather round him a group of friends like E. A. Robinson, Theodore Dreiser and Padraic Colum whom he entertained at a flat he had taken in lower fifth Avenue, and later on at 27 Bank Street, where he had an apartment in the same building as Allen Tate and his wife, Caroline Gordon.

His easy adaptability made him completely at home in New York and, as an international celebrity, he was seen everywhere. He was given a temporary membership to the National Arts Club and he knew his way in and out of speakeasies. An amusing instance of his urbanity is provided by Burton Rascoe who one day, in the company of E. E. Cummings, was out walking with Ford.

As we were walking down Fifth Avenue to my office . . . he excused himself and asked us to wait while he went into the Guaranty Trust

Company Bank, at Forty-fourth Street. Cummings expressed astonishment to me that Ford should have business with the bank. He asked Ford, when he came out, if he had an account there. Ford said, no, he didn't but that he had once gone there with John Quinn and had discovered that the bank had an *urinoir*; since then he had often used it, because, he said, 'American cities are not so solicitous of a man's comfort as Paris is.' Cummings said, 'It *would* take Ford to find an *urinoir* in a bank on Fifth Avenue and have the courage to use it without having an account there.'[13]

Thus, to quote Douglas Goldring, who had known Ford in *The English Review* days and who had met him again in New York, 'it was evident that he adored New York and that New York—or, at least, its literary circles—had responded by taking him to its hospitable bosom.'[14] Moreover, the thousands of dollars he was earning through the Tietjens books allowed him to adopt with impunity his favourite rôle as English Gentleman and successful literary personage. He had his portrait painted by Georg Hartmann and insisted that he be portrayed with a cigarette holder and top hat. Partly he meant the portrait as a joke, but it also represented that same quality in Ford which had made him, while editor of *The English Review*, drive about London in an open coach, while wearing an immense Inverness cloak that had once belonged to Dante Gabriel Rossetti.

Much of his time was spent with publishers and critics like H. S. Canby, Ernest Boyd and Carl and Mark Van Doren. The hospitality of these men he would then repay by squandering hundreds of dollars over them at expensive restaurants. Partly his dinner parties were the result of natural generosity, partly they allowed him to demonstrate his success as a writer. At any rate, they used up a great deal of the money he made from his writing, and what was left he invested in a stock market that was just then entering its wildest phase before the crash. Silly as his behaviour may seem to have been in retrospect, no other course was possible for a man of Ford's temperament. He reserved his greatest scorn for the prudent and the parsimonious—on the grounds that though secure they never really enjoyed life. A more serious result of his New York spree came from what may be called Ford's fatal swagger, for there is no doubt that in his moment of triumph he adopted a superior attitude towards a number of those whom he met. He had too much respect for the arts to be lofty with any other novelist or poet, but if the occasion arose, he would not hesitate to be so with some of the lesser breeds, amongst whom Ford included critics and publishers. So long as Ford remained a palpable success these men whose only indicator of character was worldly success, put up with him, but a number of them were waiting for the day when he would fall from glory.

It is worth drawing the distinction between these two types of literary men—the practising artist and the man of affairs whose business is literature, for during his stay in New York Ford went out of his way to be kind and helpful to young writers who had not yet made their reputations. He gave luncheon parties at the Arts Club for young men like John Dos Passos, Glenway Wescott, Van Wyck Brooks and Thornton Wilder, and he was always at home to hopeful young poets and novelists at his apartment in Bank Street. Douglas Goldring was later to recall going with Ford to a slum-like area where a party was being given by some young poets: 'The room was sparsely furnished and lit by one unshaded electric bulb. We drank home-made red wine, out of teacups. In these modest surroundings, Ford—who at that time was one of the most prominent and respected men of letters in New York and much sought after by socialites—was perfectly happy.'[15]

While his evenings were usually occupied by social gatherings, Ford also worked hard while in New York and devoted most of his mornings to writing. In a month's time, he was able to write ten thousand words of a new novel and to produce a number of articles as well.[16] Often these articles were the result of a chance request: thus on one occasion at a luncheon at Jack and Charlie's '21', he was asked by Burton Rascoe, the editor of *The Bookman*, to write a piece explaining what Conrad had intended to do with his unfinished manuscript, *The Sisters*. The result was his interesting article, 'Tiger, Tiger' which was later used as a preface when *The Sisters* was published in book form.[17]

That Ford in general made the best use of his opportunities is seen by the flurry of his own publications that accompanied his stay in New York. Two books of essays—*New York Essays* and *New York is Not America*—were issued in 1927, as was a volume called *New Poems*. *New York Essays* was issued in a limited edition of 750 copies signed by the author and is a collection of articles he had published earlier in American magazines. *New York is Not America* is, however, more of a book: meant partly as a tribute to what Ford calls 'My Gotham', it is also concerned, like so many of his books, with literature and, although he is polite and suave, he points out certain features of American life that have had an adverse effect on the literature of the country. He explains, as a foreigner can best explain, why American writers must often live abroad as expatriates, and he criticizes the teaching of writing and literature in the American universities. On both of these subjects he is practical and wise, and acts as a politer Ezra Pound towards his American hosts and audience.

Amongst the writers Ford met in New York was the American poetess, Elinor Wylie who, along with Irita Van Doren, urged him to publish a book of poems while he was there. The result was a thin book called *New Poems*. Although it contains the admirable 'A House', it added little to his reputation. One piece, 'Winter Night-song' is probably the worst poem he ever wrote. An unfortunate combination of sentimentality and colloquialism, it opens with these lines:

> My dearest dear, my honey-love,
> My brown-eyed squirrel, my soft dove,
> All tiny furred and feathered things
> Have long curled up or furled their wings.
>
> All taxi-lamps and street-lights too
> Grow dim along Fifth Avenue
> And in the doorways of the shops
> Slumber the dawn-awaiting cops.

Despite these lapses, the publication of *New Poems* showed that Ford was still very much interested in poetry, and during his second visit to New York he delivered a lecture on *vers libre*, which was a forceful statement of his views on poetic diction and verse rhythms.

None of these books is, however, of permanent interest. They were all, it would seem, rapidly put together to make the best use of an opportunity that was present. His real energies were going into writing the last section of *Parade's End*, much of which was dictated to Caroline Gordon during his stay in New York.

In December of 1927, Ford returned to Paris and announced to Stella, in her words, that he had formed 'a sentimental attachment to an American lady whom he proposed to visit every year.'[18] Stella was of course dismayed at his proposal that he maintain a ménage on either side of the Atlantic, and she naturally turned him down. Later on, after their separation, she realized that Ford's trips alone to the United States had been 'dress-rehearsals' for the years ahead when she would be without Ford. She realized moreover and had herself experienced Ford's tendency to fall in love with various beautiful women. Almost unique amongst women, she also understood his need. In her view, Ford's real passion was for letters; personal relations, she thought, meant little to him, except as a source of nourishment. Thus she wrote of Ford the artist: 'In order to keep his machinery running, he requires to exercise his sentimental talents from time to time upon a new object. It keeps him young. It refreshes his ego. It restores his belief in his powers. And who shall say that this type of lubrication is too expensive for so fine a machine?'[19]

In fact, of course, a great many people did hold it against Ford that he was one of that not uncommon type of man that requires fresh stimulus. The result to Ford himself was a somewhat tempestuous and often comic amorous life, full of new promise and ultimate disillusion. Yet his break with Stella was accomplished without bitterness or rancour and even in later years, they remained good friends. 'For the whole nine years of its duration,' writes Stella of their life together, 'we were never bored and I don't think anyone ever heard us utter an angry word. Even when we were on the brink of separating, we could still go out to dine together and have a grand argument about Lost Causes, or the Theory of the Infallibility of the Pope, or some such theme.'[20]

For most of the spring of 1928, Ford remained in Paris working on his new historical novel of the hundred days of Napoleon and then, instead of going south, he lent his house at Toulon to James Joyce and, in the early summer, sailed for New York to arrange for future publishing contracts. Because this was to be a business rather than a social trip, he decided to stay at the Hotel Carteret in West 23rd Street instead of taking an apartment.

All during his life Ford encountered difficulties with publishers, and even at this period of relative prosperity and success, he had continuous trouble. He realized that he would never be a popular author in England,[21] but the London sales of the Tietjens novels were almost insultingly low. Writing to a correspondent in England, he observed: 'Duckworth's statement informed me that just under 1,000 people had bought the English edition of *No More Parades* and just over 1,000 *A Man Could Stand Up*—and when you consider that 400 copies of each were ordered before publication by New

York purchasers of first editions and at least 100 by Americans in Paris—well, you perceive what feet of clay the image has in our country.'[22] Small as these sales were, after 1928 Ford received no income whatever from England for the Tietjens books, since he had signed over his English royalties to Stella Bowen.

In the United States, Ford's sales had been much larger, and thousands of copies of the Tietjens books had been sold. All the same, despite this seeming success, Ford was without funds. He had, of course, squandered much of his income in New York, but the principal reason for this situation was the sudden bankruptcy of his New York publishers. *Some Do Not* had been brought out by a new firm called Seltzer and had sold 40,000 copies, but shortly afterwards this publisher failed and Ford received nothing beyond his advance. He then secured an agreement with the A. C. Boni Company to publish both his future work and a collection of his past books to be called the 'Avignon' edition. Boni did in fact reissue *The Good Soldier*, but refused to bring out other books in the collected edition, publishing only the next two novels of the Tietjens series. Their failure to publish these other books doubtless cost Ford an immense amount of money, for at the time his reputation was at its height, and these books would probably have sold well. Ford turned the matter over to his New York lawyer, but it was clear that nothing could be done, owing to the time lag in the New York courts. An injunction would merely have held up Ford's work in the United States for years. He therefore had to take his loss.[23]

Up until 1928, Ford was able to survive these vicissitudes because of the continuing success of the Tietjens tetralogy. At the time of his arrival in June, the last volume of the series, *The Last Post*, had sold over fifty thousand copies and was being distributed by the Literary Guild of America. He was therefore in a very good position to recoup his losses and, during the summer of 1928, he was in fact approached by a great number of publishers for his next work. Within two months, he placed three new books, one of them, his new novel, with the Viking Press. On the face of it, Ford seemed on the verge of real prosperity, but as shall be seen, his hopes were misplaced.

Returning from New York in July, Ford decided to spend the balance of the summer of 1928 in the South of France. The separation from Stella and the death of Juan Gris in 1927 made Toulon seem cheerless, however, and so he moved to Carqueiranne, a quiet village near the sea. His American 'sentimental attachment' had come to nothing, and he was alone. His days were spent quietly divided between writing in the morning and swimming in the afternoon. It was a hermit-like existence, as he informed Gertrude Stein, but the rest was good for him after his hectic stay in America.[24]

This retired mode of living was also made necessary by his financial position, however, for in spite of the fame that had come to him in America, and the contracts he had signed on his trip to New York, Ford was almost penniless upon his return to France in 1928. Shortly after arriving in Marseilles, he wrote to his Paris agent, W. A. Bradley, to say that the American agents had broken their promise to pay him for his work and that as a result, he had only 312 francs to his name. He added that although he had written over 100,000 words during the course of his American trip, and had taken no holidays, he was continuously without funds because his New York publishers would not pay him the thousands of dollars they owed him.[25]

In September, however, some at least of these delinquents must have paid up, for Ford was able to take a brief trip to Monte Carlo and Corsica—the latter presumably to gather background material for his Napoleonic novel, *A Little Less than Gods*. He then spent a month in Toulon before returning to Paris where, subsequent to his separation from Stella, he had procured an attic apartment at 32 rue de Vaugirard. This flat was to be his Paris headquarters for the next six years. He had already turned over the week-end cottage at Guermantes to the Russian painter, Pavel Tchelitchew.

In the meantime, he had started to work on his next book, *The English Novel*, which was an outgrowth of the lectures he had been giving in America. Essentially a development of a number of points he had made in his memoir of Conrad, it is an impressionistic survey of English fiction from the point of view of the serious craftsman of letters, as distinct from that of the academic critic of literature. It is suggestive rather than definitive and, as he warned: 'The young, earnest student of literature for professional purposes should, if he desires good marks, write in his thesis for examination pretty well the opposite of what I have here set down.'[26] Ford was always separated by a vast chasm from the academic mind: not interested in presenting doctrine, he was only anxious to make his readers think and adopt what he had called as long ago as 1908, a 'critical attitude' towards literature. Although he was less violent than Ezra Pound, he hoped to make his reader think for himself and make his own objections when, for example, he found that Ford was dismissing the whole of nineteenth-century English literature as the work of amateurs. Yet Ford was not simply aiming to shock, for the views he expressed about the literature of the past are serious views, and as a man so frequently beset by private calamity, he believed that literature and the arts were the most important things in life.

Towards the end of 1928 his novel, *A Little Less than Gods*, was published in New York. This book, frankly written, as he wrote to a correspondent, as 'a straight narrative about the execution of Ney— to stretch my arms a little,'[27] appeared once to have been intended as a collaboration with Conrad. Both men had been interested in Ney, but before Ford went to the front in 1916, he met with Conrad and urged him to do the novel alone since he had done more reading for it than Ford had done. The result was *Suspense*, a book that was never completed because of Conrad's death. Because this novel is only a fragment, Ford presumably decided that he was at liberty to take on the once-projected collaboration. *A Little Less than Gods* is not a finished version of *Suspense* as Conrad planned it, but it is somewhat similar to what Ford elsewhere stated was to have been the subject of collaboration.

Certainly not one of Ford's more important novels, it does little more than provide an original and interesting portrait of one of Napoleon's great marshals. While it gave Ford a breathing space between *Parade's End* and his next serious work, it also served to enrage his publisher who, as a businessman, expected that Ford would be able to continue writing books of the calibre of the Tietjens novels without any lapses. The result was that the book was badly advertised, sold few copies and caused a good deal of bad blood between Ford and the publisher.

Thus when Ford returned to New York in May of 1929, he found the literary climate markedly altered. The purpose of his trip was to secure advances for his new novel and to renew acquaintances in American literary circles, and during his stay in New York, he wrote articles for *The Yale Review* and for *The Saturday Review*, while also contributing notes to the book collector, George Keating, who was preparing his bibliography of Conrad. He also continued his custom of writing prefaces for new books by young authors whom he admired. Altogether, between 1926 and 1930, he wrote no fewer than ten of these. Yet despite this flurry of activity, there were signs that Ford's days of glory were rapidly approaching an end. The first

9. James Joyce, Ezra Pound, John Quinn and Ford; Paris, 1923.

10. Ford Madox Ford, portrait by Georg Hartmann; New York, 1926.

11. Ford Madox Ford, portrait by Georg Hartmann; New York, 1927.

indication arose when certain reviewers observed that *A Little Less than Gods* was markedly inferior to the Tietjens novels. Others, sensing an incipient failure, began to recall incidents of a year or so earlier, when they had been patronized by the 'great English novelist'. A number of them, especially those who had met Stella Bowen on her trip to New York after her separation from Ford, revived stories of Ford's philandering. In 1926, similar tales had circulated as a result of the publication of Violet Hunt's *I Have This To Say*, and Ford had even been defrauded of his lecture contract on the grounds that his 'unsavoury reputation' was damaging to the good name of the agent. At that time, because of the success of *No More Parades*, Ford had been able to live down these aspects of his past, but in 1929, the situation was rather different.

But while these separate incidents all combined to hurt Ford's reputation badly, the real cause of his difficulties probably lay within his own temperament. He had become well known, but he had had to work at it, both as a writer and as a public figure. As one who had been so long neglected, he enormously enjoyed his success, and it went to his head. Feeling completely at home in New York, he imagined he knew all there was to know about its literary life. As a result, he was sometimes careless with his tongue and, most importantly, failed to treat publishers and reviewers with the respect they believed to be their due.

His decision to write *When the Wicked Man* as his next novel hardly improved the situation. Its literary reputation apart, this book helped to turn many a New York literary and publishing circle against him. For when the publishers that had commissioned it reported their dislike of it, Ford abused them for their commercial minds, pointing out, in a letter to his New York agent, that men whose sole business was to market other people's writing, had little right to tell him how to write his books. He concluded by observing that publishers never liked anything experimental or out of the ordinary, even though the experiments of today inevitably became the norm of tomorrow.[28]

In the course of this squabble Ford began to suspect, as he wrote in confidence to a friend, that the partners of his publishing house were privately trying to prevent his novel from being published, by themselves or by anybody else, because it told the truth about New York publishers. Altogether, the incident reveals Ford's tendency to sacrifice everything to his interest in literary experimentation. He admitted that he hadn't even thought of the publisher's reaction to his subject-matter when he had written the novel, and indeed said that it wouldn't have made any difference to him if he had.[29] Thus Ford's artistic conscience and lack of 'common sense' in terms of material once again embroiled him in difficulties.

In addition to these troubles, Ford began at this time to feel the effect of his months of work in New York. He told Bradley that he was exhausted from overwork, and doubted whether he would be able to keep it up in future. Then, towards the end of the summer, he sailed for Europe. A brief stop was made in London to see his agent, J. B. Pinker, but he was unable to place any new work there.

Settled in Paris for the winter, Ford suffered a mild heart attack in December which hindered him from doing any serious work for a number of months. As he had been badly hurt by the depression and had taken losses upwards of seventy per cent. on investments in New York, he wrote to H. G. Wells to make enquiries about procuring aid from the Royal Literary Fund. He told Wells that asking for money from the R.L.F. was almost as disagreeable as going to jail, and for that reason, perhaps, Wells simply lent Ford two thousand francs instead of sending on his application. Ford was of course grateful, but as he was unaccustomed to borrowing, he was embarrassed at having to cash Wells's cheque.[30]

Still alone, as he had been since leaving Stella, he found that the depression had cleared Paris of most of his English and American friends. The Tates were amongst the few who stayed on. They had sublet his flat during his absence in America and upon his return Allen Tate would act as a kind of major-domo for the Saturday night *bout-rimé* contests Ford held at this period. 'Subjects were handed out,' writes one of the participants, 'and a certain length of time was given in which to complete a sonnet, after which the respective efforts were compared and judged and prizes were awarded. It was all very exciting if you cared for that sort of thing, and, contrasted to what commonly passed as amusement in the Quarter, it was innocent enough. . . . The truth is, I suspect, that these were simply the genial pastimes of a lonely old man and that there were some who abetted him in them because they respected and were fond of him, while others had a canny eye to what his acquaintance might procure them.

'Ford was very lonely, that was plain to see.'[31]

Finally, even the Tates left and he felt more solitary and poor than ever. The book he was working on was not even sold, and he had little to live on in the meantime. As a result, he hardly ever went out, and whenever he did, as he confided to a friend, he felt exceptionally old and feeble. His only consolation was that his brain was still active and alert.[32]

Thus the decade of Ford's greatest fame and accomplishment ended on a note of solitary impoverishment, and in the winter of 1929–30, he reached the lowest ebb of his career. He had, of course, been through it all before—in 1911 when he lost *The English Review* and found himself ostracized because of his marital difficulties, and in 1918 when he returned from France a relatively forgotten man. And, like most men, he learned more from failure than from success. Thus as *The Good Soldier* was to emerge from the painful involvements of his personal life prior to 1913, and as *Parade's End* was possible only because of the experiences he had undergone during the war, so, in the 1930's he was to write books affected in large part by his experiences with the 'bitch goddess' Success and by his knowledge of what worldly prosperity does to the soul. As an artist who always experimented, his works of the next decade were to be presented in a form quite different from what he had already used and, since he was approaching his sixtieth birthday, they were to be somewhat more muted than they had formerly been. Nevertheless, as his last years went by, and as he stripped his life of non-essentials, he came to conclusions that are, in the long run, his most important message to the world.

THE MEDITERRANEAN

Quem das finem, rex magne, dolorum?

Where we went in the boat was a long bay
A slingshot wide, walled in by towering stone—
Peaked margin of antiquity's delay,
And we went there out of time's monotone:

Where we went in the black hull no light moved
But a gull white-winged along the feckless wave,
The breeze, unseen but fierce as a body loved,
That boat drove onward like a willing slave:

Where we went in the small ship the seaweed
Parted and gave to us the murmuring shore,
And we made feast and in our secret need
Devoured the very plates Aeneas bore:

Where derelict you see through the low twilight
The green coast that you, thunder-tossed, would win,
Drop sail, and hastening to drink all night
Eat dish and bowl to take that sweet land in!

Where we feasted and caroused on the sandless
Pebbles, affecting our day of piracy,
What prophecy of eaten plates could landless
Wanderers fulfill by the ancient sea?

We for that time might taste the famous age
Eternal here yet hidden from our eyes
When lust of power undid its stuffless rage;
They, in a wineskin, bore earth's paradise.

Let us lie down once more by the breathing side
Of Ocean, where our live forefathers sleep
As if the Known Sea still were a month wide—
Atlantis howls but is no longer steep!

What country shall we conquer, what fair land
Unman our conquest and locate our blood?
We've cracked the hemisphere with careless hand!
Now, from the Gates of Hercules we flood

Westward, westward till the barbarous brine
Whelms us to the tired land where tasseling corn,
Fat beans, grapes sweeter than muscadine
Rot on the vine: in that land were we born.

—ALLEN TATE

Chapter Eleven

——————⟨⟨•⟩⟩⟨⟨•⟩⟩——————

PROVENCE

——————⟨⟨•⟩⟩⟨⟨•⟩⟩——————

For the next four years, with the exception of a very brief lecture tour to the United States in the autumn of 1930, Ford remained in Europe. Yet although his movements were curtailed by lack of funds, he was not much bothered by having to remain in one place. He had begun to come to terms with the disagreeable fact of his public neglect, and as a result had started to work out a manner of living founded on a more substantial basis than popular fame. He was, moreover, busy with his own writings and with other literary chores. In June he was approached by William Carlos Williams and by H.D. to contribute to a new anthology of Imagist poetry, and responded by writing a reminiscential preface for the volume, entitled 'Those Were The Days'. Later in the summer, he contributed his verse to a new anthology of English poetry edited by Lascelles Abercrombie. Thus once again his devotion to writing came to his rescue. The true artist, Ford realized, 'supports with equanimity what would make a banker commit suicide.'[1]

In addition, there were windfalls. One of these occurred when his book *The English Novel* received a front-page review in the New York *Herald Tribune* by the then immensely popular English novelist, Hugh Walpole, with the consequence that the book was also published in England. This kind notice, the first Ford had received from an English writer in many years, led to an interesting correspondence between the two men: Walpole tried to find an English publisher for Ford's work and Ford, in return, dedicated the English edition of his treatise on the novel to Walpole. In his first letter to

210

Walpole, Ford claimed that he personally didn't feel neglected but admitted that because of his small sales and the taxes he paid by living abroad, he received only the equivalent of forty dollars for a year's work in England. It wasn't the fault of the reviews he received, for in fact his work was generally praised. Ford attributed his economic failure as a writer to the Americans' doubt as to whether he was really serious and to the Englishmen's knowledge that he was in dead earnest, which therefore discouraged them from reading him.[2]

Except for placing Ford's next book of reminiscences with the English firm of Gollancz, Walpole was not especially successful with the rest of Ford's work. Doubtless Ford's earnestness of purpose contributed to his unpopularity in England, but a further reason for his English failure may be traced to the hostility of powerful figures in literary London—men who could not prevent the publication of a decent review, but who would never give Ford that extra boost which raises a book out of the general run of well-reviewed books and brings it to the attention of the public.

By the early months of 1930, Ford had managed to straighten out the confusions of his personal life which had beset him for some time, for by that date he was joined by a young Polish-American painter called Janice Biala. In March, he moved to the South of France, and there he found a new house, a place called Villa Paul, which was located on the outskirts of Toulon at Cap Brun. A pink stucco house, with grey shutters, it had two small rooms on the ground floor, a sleeping alcove and a dark, primitive kitchen. The walls were a rough grey colour and the floors were of red tile. The upper storey of the house was occupied by a French officer and his wife, but Ford had the use of the garden and terrace, which was full of orange and fig trees. There was also a large oak tree which cast its shade on the stone terrace, and a fountain full of goldfish; the best feature of the place, however, was its immense view over the harbour to St. Mandrier.[3] Thus although it lacked amenities, it provided a picturesque background for the simple life Ford was then prepared to live.

Once again, he had returned to the soil for solace. This time, however, life was to be even simpler than it had been in Sussex, and there were to be no affectations about breeding prize pigs. Theodore Pratt, who visited Ford in 1931, has recalled the place: 'He had an old farmhouse with a piece of ground overlooking the Mediterranean; it was not a pretentious place but it was a good one, and Ford could live like a Frenchman. I remember his wry amusement when he asked me to buy something for him in town, and his learning the price I had paid, more than he would have paid. . . . I think he was a contented man then, even though his means were far from great. He enjoyed good food and preparing it; above all, he enjoyed French wine, the vin du pays; my job was to keep his glass filled from a big jar of it, and my arm got tired lifting the jar. . . . He was a good gardener, and raised vegetables. He was a true Bohemian, of course, without having to pretend to be, a rare and good state of affairs for some, not all, people.'⁴

Ford took his farming quite as seriously as any French peasant would have done and believed strongly in the effectiveness of hoeing and irrigation as against the use of artificial fertilizers. A glimpse of his gardening activity is provided in one of his prefaces:

> Then as soon as it was light I went down into the garden to plan out, in the pitiless Mediterranean drought, the irrigation of the day. The semi-tropical plants and trees—the oranges, lemons, peppers, vines and the rest can do without water for a long time. Musk- and water-melons must have a little water and the Northern plants that for his sins the pink Nordic has imported here—the peas, beans, string beans, cabbages, carrots and such gross, over-green matter, must have a great deal or incontinently die. It was a whole campaign of irrigation channels that I had mentally to arrange for a day given up entirely to writing and the affairs of the parched earth.⁵

In the quiet of Provence he was able to follow a method of writing as organized as his farming was. On a normal day he would be at work by nine o'clock, and for the first two hours he would sit at a table on his terrace, quietly playing patience. For all this time, however, he would be working out in his mind the next section of his book and then, say from eleven till one, he would go to his desk and write out the whole passage, ordinarily some two thousand words long. Because of his care in preparing every detail, he rarely made corrections and, especially in his last years, his first draft was his final draft. He preferred to write with pen and ink, but because of writer's cramp frequently had to use the typewriter. Only occasionally did he dictate, and then usually only short articles and letters.

After spending the summer in Villa Paul, Ford turned it over to Stella and Julie before returning to Paris in the autumn of 1930. There he settled down at 32 rue Vaugirard, and for the next year and a half, remained in France, wintering in Paris and spending the summer months at Cap Brun. Times were relatively quiet compared to the gay 1920's, and Ford devoted almost all of his energies to his own writing. Gertrude Stein, Joyce and some of the other figures of the earlier decade were still about, but Ford spent most of his time with younger writers. Katherine Anne Porter was one of those he saw a good deal of, and her husband, Eugene Pressly, who was then an official at the American Embassy in Paris, helped him in practical matters and in typing the manuscript of *It Was the Nightingale*, which book, in gratitude, Ford dedicated to him. The Presslys also sublet Ford's apartment in the summer of 1932.

At times, of course, Ford's spirits were very low. His income was negligible, and his name had fallen almost entirely from prominence. Whereas in the years 1927–28, he had published sixteen articles, in 1930 he published none, and in 1931 only two. Even in his years of relative success, as Stella Bowen later noted, 'He was all too ready, anyhow, to feel discouraged when things went wrong, and he found so many reasons for feeling frightened.'[6] So that, when things really did go wrong, he could sometimes be very morose. Katherine Anne Porter has said that she and her husband 'were probably nearest to him through the worst period of his life: he really clung to us as if he had nobody else; and it is true that he had exhausted the patience and resources of a good many.'[7]

Nevertheless, these periods would pass, for Ford never gave up. He had the extraordinary courage, as Allen Tate remarked some years afterwards, to continue at his writing when, to all appearances, it seemed to be a hopeless task.[8] Furthermore, his sojourns in the South of France always restored his spirits, and his resilience would reassert itself once he returned to Cap Brun. Thus, for example, after spending from May to July at the Villa Paul, he decided in August of 1932, to pay a visit to the Ezra Pounds in Rapallo. Pound who had by this time attained some prominence in Mussolini's Italy, made much of Ford upon his arrival, and even arranged to have a facetious interview published in the Rapallo newspaper, *Il Mare*. This interview, later translated by Olga Rudge and possibly entirely the work of Pound himself went on as follows:

Pound: What authors should a young Italian writer read if he wants to learn how to write novels?

Ford: (Spitting vigorously) Better to think about finding himself a subject.

213

Pound: (Suavely, ignoring Ford's irritation) Well, suppose he has already had the intelligence to read Stendhal and Flaubert?

Ford: A different curriculum is needed for each talent. One can learn from Flaubert and from Miss Braddon. In a certain way one can learn as much from a rotten writer as from a great one.

Pound: Which of your books would you like to see translated into Italian and in what order:

Ford: I don't trust translations; they leave nothing of my best qualities. Some writers are translatable.

Pound: What are the most important qualities in a prose writer?

Ford: What does 'prose writer' mean? The Napoleonic Code or the Canticle of Canticles?

Pound: Let us say a novelist.

Ford: (In agony) Oh Hell! Say philosophical grounding, a knowledge of words' roots, of the meaning of words.

Pound: What should a young prose writer do first?

Ford: (More and more annoyed at the inquisition) Brush his teeth.

Pound: (Ironically calm, with serene magniloquence) In the vast critical output of the illustrious critic now being interviewed (changing tone) . . . You have praised writer after writer with no apparent distinction (stressing the word 'apparent' nearly with rage). Is there any?

Ford: There are authentic writers and imitation writers; there is no difference between the authentic ones. There is no difference between Picasso and El Greco.

Pound: Don't get away from me into painting. Stick to literary examples.

Ford: Hudson, and Flaubert in 'Trois Contes'. Not all of Flaubert, let us say the 'Trois Contes'.

And so on. The 'interview' concludes with Ford's comments in praise of young writers like Richard Hughes, Caroline Gordon and Elizabeth Madox Roberts. On the following day, when again asked what a young novelist should read, Ford replied: 'Let him get a DICTIONARY and learn the meaning of words.'[9]

After returning from Italy, Ford was joined at Cap Brun by Allen Tate and his wife, Caroline Gordon, who stayed at a nearby villa Ford had found for them. One incident during their visit is worth recording for the insight it provides into Ford's sense of pleasure at simple things and, more importantly, the sense of tradition and history he attached to ordinary events in Provence. Mr. Tate has provided an interesting account of this event, an excursion for an evening shore dinner at a cove not far from Cassis:

It was a large party, about twenty I think and we had to get to the *calanque* in small fishing-boats. Our boat was manned by a typical Provençal fisherman called Marius. The dinner lasted seven or eight hours, with many courses, the *pièce de résistance* being a wonderful bouillabaisse into which thirty-two kinds of fish, caught that same morning, were cooked for about three hours. There was lively talk and a great deal of singing in French. An old man whose family had been vintners for about three hundred years came to the shore over the cliffs, with bottles of his own wine slung on his back. The *calanque* was very narrow, not more than a hundred feet wide and three hundred feet long: the channel led to a narrow, pebbly beach; and all round towered cliffs sixty to seventy feet high. In the course of the meal Ford said to me: 'In a cove like this the refugees from Troy must have stopped many times to eat and rest, and in such a place the Harpies must have descended upon Aeneas and his followers.' The next day in Toulon I bought a second-hand copy of the *Aeneid*, and read most of it in the following weeks. In September, I wrote 'The Mediterranean'.*[10]

The winter months of 1932–33 were once again spent in Paris, this time, however, at a different apartment in the rue Denfert-Rochereau, a move made necessary by the demolition of the old building in the rue Vaugirard. As usual, Ford was busy with literary chores, amongst them the writing of a preface for Ernest Hemingway's *A Farewell to Arms*. That he would go to considerable trouble to help promote the work of a man he admired may be seen in the pamphlet he organized in honour of the publication of Ezra Pound's *XXX Cantos*. On his own he wrote to a number of authors and critics like T. S. Eliot, Paul Morand, Carl Van Doren, Sherwood Anderson, Hugh Walpole, Ernest Hemingway, William Carlos Williams and Allen Tate, asking them for a few words for his pamphlet.[11] The result, *The Cantos of Ezra Pound, Some Testimonies*, was published in 1933 and assisted Pound's fortunes in both England and America. It was a typical act of generosity on Ford's part, for although he was himself very hard up, he would do all he could to help another if that man's work meant something to him.

In gratitude, Pound wrote to Ford asking if there were 'ANY logs I can roll for you?'[12] Evidently Ford urged him to take notice of the young French writer, René Béhaine, whose works Ford much admired. At any rate, this is Pound's reply:

* See epigraph to this chapter, p. 209.

Be/haine be/jabbers. I'll roll him if I can read him/ me conscience permits me not other. AND you by persistent settin on goose/eggs have occasionally hatched a swan/ but more often a one legged duck.[13]

To this remark Ford must have remonstrated, but Pound was not to be moved: 'Dowbtless yr/ reeward will be great upstairs and by the law of averages you DO discover 97 ducks to every swan and a half.'[14]

The balance of 1933 was divided, as had now become his custom, between Toulon and Paris, and except for a brief trip to Nice in July, passed without much incident, Ford spending most of his time writing. Since the beginning of the decade, he had published only two books, a volume of reminiscences called *Return to Yesterday*, and his novel on New York publishers, *When the Wicked Man*. During this same period, he was still working hard, however, and although perhaps not so prolific as he had been in former years, he had, by 1933, written a novel and a book of reminiscences and had started on a new novel. With a single exception, these were to be his last forays into fiction: nevertheless they contained his most mature analyses of the quality of international life after the depression of 1929.

Although *When the Wicked Man* seems to have been partly intended as Ford's revenge on New York publishers, it also had serious intellectual implications, and Ford himself considered it a very moral book.[15] The title was derived from Ezekiel: 'Again, when the wicked man turneth away from his wickedness that he hath committed . . . he shall save his soul alive.' The point is, of course, that the publisher does not turn away. This figure, Notterdam, is at once the ultimate heir of the great medieval prophet, Nostradamus, and the typical representative of American business. At heart a man of good will, Notterdam is beset by turmoil in both his public and private life, and he finds it difficult to reconcile his private friendship for his partner and alter-ego, Kratch, with his disapproval of Kratch's business ethics. Kratch, who almost seems to be a reincarnation of Kasker-Ryves in Ford's first novel, *The Shifting of the Fire*, is the real villain of the piece and is a model of commercial cupidity. Thanks largely to Notterdam's sense of decency, the publishing house is not intentionally evil, but its policies reflect the commercial instincts of the profession. The irony of the novel is that Notterdam neither accepts nor rejects these standards but becomes instead, through a series of ridiculous incidents, the great American hero of the moment. Ford thus only presents the first condition:

216

'When the wicked man'; and he omits the final phrase of the verse that concerns turning away from wickedness and saving one's soul. By breaking off Ezekiel's verse, Ford shows that even the ultimate heir of Nostradamus cannot overcome the stultifying effects of worldly success.

The main weakness of the novel is one of conception. As in some of his earlier novels, Ford here seems to be too close to his subject to be able to present a believable picture of his characters and their activities. It is, as he admitted, a lurid story,[16] and the gangsters and queer people that inhabit his world of high finance and publishing are unconvincing as people. One reason for this weakness may be traced to Ford's faulty use of Americanisms. Understandably, the foreigner often fails to perceive the nuances of another country's speech: especially conscious of the strange words, he forgets that these are only a part of that nation's vocabulary. At any rate, a number of the characters of *When the Wicked Man* use a language that bears little relation to that of Manhattan. A further shortcoming in the book is Ford's apparent indecision regarding satire. As one who saw many sides of human nature, Ford was not naturally inclined to satire, yet he wrote into this novel a number of sections that are clearly intended to be satirical. The result is an uneven book, for the satirical point of view is not maintained throughout.

The next two novels, *The Rash Act* and *Henry for Hugh*, also suffer from faults of conception, but because they are separated from Ford's personal preoccupations, they are more successful than their predecessors. Specifically, they are the result of Ford's concern with political and economic forces. 'The main point,' he said, 'is that public events play a principal part in the scheme of the novel as they do in our own lives . . . "The Rash Act" is the elaborately time-shifted story of a man driven to the very edge of suicide and almost over. The world crisis has ruined him. The writer's main impulse was what may be called historic.'[17] The two major developments of this period Ford took to be the commercial prosperity of the 1920's and the crash that followed in 1929. In much of his previous work, Ford had contrasted the 'haves' with the 'have-nots' and showed that the commercial instinct was incompatible with moral standards and probity. The pre-war pattern delineated in his books was that the commercially-minded rapidly gained power and control, while the uncommercial returned, like the poor but honest Tietjens, to the simple life of the country. During the 1920's, however, prosperity became possible for all: moral aloofness therefore seemed pointless in a world where the abuses of wealth were mitigated by general plenitude. Why then, came the crash? The answer Ford seems to be giving is, as Isabel Paterson pointed out, that people simply cannot endure general prosperity.[18]

Ford presents this issue and his analysis of the crash by means of two young millionaires, one English and one American. The American millionaire of *The Rash Act* is, however, quite a different sort from Don Kelleg, the pre-war hero of *An English Girl*. He realizes that there are no abuses he can rectify without destroying economic abundance and therefore finds himself caught in a morally frustrating situation. Life is pointless, and all his wealth is meaningless. He is therefore Ford's 'lost generation' hero. Caught in a world whose forces seem too strong to be altered by individual action, he simply exists in an extended state of inaction. He is thus a typical product of his age, charming enough and agreeable, but lacking in courage of any kind. He plays with the idea of suicide, but the rash act is beyond him. His life is thus a meaningless drift which Ford equates with the world at large.

The Rash Act and *Henry for Hugh* present then, not the fortune-makers Ford and Conrad had already dealt with in *The Inheritors*, but their heirs, one English and one American, both possessors of enormous industrial wealth. Both are distressed by the immorality of the business world, but neither is responsible enough, or courageous enough, to put his anti-materialistic views into action. In a fat and comfortable world, it is much easier not to make a fuss.

At first sight, the way in which the situation is worked out seems utterly preposterous, for both the American and English millionaires have the same name, H. M. A. Smith, both had been up at Oxford, had been in the same regiment and have suicidal tendencies. When the English Smith, Hugh Monkton, actually commits suicide, only to have the American Smith exchange clothes and documents with him, so that the world thinks Henry Martin is dead, the situation becomes so ludicrous that the reader may perhaps be excused from thinking that he is reading a fairy-story, and that Ford in his dotage has returned to the literary forms of his youth. The only explanation, therefore, seems to be that Ford was here attempting yet another 'new form' for his writing.

On frequent occasions, when discussing literary methods, Ford lamented the necessity of having a concrete subject for the writing of fiction. He often compared prose to painting or music and observed that where a canvas or a sonata could abstract meaning from an experience without detailing the experience itself, prose writing almost of necessity had to deal with particular situations and characters. In 1914, he stated that he believed that Impressionism was capable of attaining 'to the sort of odd vibration that scenes in real life really have. . . .' It gave the 'reader the impression that he was witnessing something real, that he was passing through an experience. . . .' He then went on to state that the effect produced was 'very like a Futurist picture—not a Cubist picture, but one of those canvases that show you in one corner a pair of stays, in another a bit of the foyer of a music hall, in another a fragment of early morning landscape, and in the middle a pair of eyes, the whole bearing the title of "A Night out".' [19]

But as painting moved beyond Futurism, and as music became increasingly less dependent on melody and a familiar combination of chords, so Ford wished writing to move beyond Impressionism. In the work of Gertrude Stein and James Joyce, writing had indeed moved beyond representationalism, and Ford was amongst the first to welcome their achievements. But their methods were not Ford's methods, and the principal difference lay in the matter of emphasis. The prose of Joyce, like that of Gertrude Stein, called attention to itself; the puns, the parodies, the newly manufactured vocabulary emphasized the witty and clever personality of the writer. Their language is often beautiful, but it is almost always obvious to the reader that it is contrived. Ford also wished his prose to be beautiful, but he did not want it to be noticeable: his ambition was to have it exist as an actuality as natural and as unobtrusive as experience itself.

It is probably impossible to write a prose that is at once abstract and actual, and Ford never really succeeded in doing so. He had noticed, however, that certain poets, and particularly the Troubadours in their *canzos* and *tenzos*, had come very close to combining these seemingly antagonistic elements. They had, after all, only one subject or theme—that of unrequited love, but they experimented continually with images and metres. 'So their work,' as Ford noted, 'came nearly into the category of that heart's desire of all true *literati*—absolute imaginative literature, using the word "absolute" in the sense that it is used by musicians. For if you could read the secrets of the hearts of writers, you would find that every one of them in the end, in the spirit either of wariness or of aversion, craves enormously to write versified or cadenced words that shall have beauty and be almost without significance. You get tired of having to tell stories or to treat of subjects; the thought of words set in due order and of unchanging meaning seems to you fatiguing. You long to express yourself by means of pure sounds as the musician can impress you and nothing else can impress you, by a fugue that consists of nothing but notes.'[20]

In their different ways, both Gertrude Stein and James Joyce seem to have been motivated by this same desire. Yet, for all their remarkable success, they could never succeed completely because of the very nature of the tools they used, since words, for better or worse, have meanings. Recognizing this limitation, Ford seems to have attempted a compromise between the impressionistic manner of his early fiction and the 'absolute' prose of, say, *Finnegans Wake*. Joyce, he believed, was 'riding his method to death'[21] which was a useful undertaking in so far as it showed how far a method could be pushed, however much it limited Joyce as an influence on others. Ford's compromise consisted in retaining the familiar elements of ordinary impressionism—the use of dialogue, realistic detail and so on— while at the same time converting his characters into representational types and his situation into something resembling allegory.

Thus *The Rash Act* and *Henry for Hugh* must be approached from a different critical stance from that taken for *Parade's End* or *The Good Soldier*. They are novels which lie half way between realistic fiction and abstract fiction. In semi-allegorical works of this sort, the coincidental similarities of the two Smiths are of less importance than they would be in purely representational novels. What counts is what they symbolize, and in these two books, Ford has presented in fictional form the result of his political and social observations during the early years of the decade. The American Smith, a character suggested to him in part by Hart Crane,[22] represents the product of American prosperity, while the English Smith is a portrait of what had become of the responsible class in England since the World War.

When Henry Martin, the American Smith, takes the place of Hugh Monkton, he assumes, for a time, an entirely new personality, but in the end his own identity is forced on him, and he can neither avoid his own responsibilities nor those he has recently adopted. The bluff he has perpetrated is no real solution to his dilemma, and the experiences he subsequently undergoes make him realize that he

12. Olivet College Library.

13. 329½ Cottage Street, Olivet, Michigan. Occupied by Ford intermittently, 1937-1939.

14. Ford Madox Ford, circa 1938.

cannot for ever avoid putting into action his own vaguely humanitarian instincts any more than he can dodge the tradition of responsibility that has been bequeathed him by Hugh Monkton. An important element in this pair of transatlantic novels is the rôle of the Continent, and of France in particular. These books are full of people of all nationalities, and all types from Communists to movie actresses are represented. In the end, however, all of them appear to be excessive in their modes of life except Eudoxie, who stands for the peasant soul of France which in other books Ford had always extolled. By marrying her to Henry Martin, Ford seems to suggest that the flabby commercialism of America and the irresponsibility of the governing classes of Great Britain could be overcome only by infusing some of the simple virtues of the Provençal peasant into the consciousness of England and the United States. Only with a vigorous union of the decent elements of the three great powers—England, France and America—would men everywhere be given the strength to oppose men like Hitler, Franco and Mussolini who were already, by the early 1930's, on their way to power.*

* It is only fair to note that Miss Caroline Gordon, who was well acquainted with Ford's working methods, disagrees with this theory of the semi-abstract novel. Her contention is that Ford never based his novels on a theory, but always began with human situations. With regard to these two books, Miss Gordon feels that Ford simply gave in to the temptation to write about mistaken identity—a subject she claims to be almost irresistibly attractive to novelists. Coming from someone of Miss Gordon's knowledge and experience, this view cannot be easily discounted, and there is indeed evidence for it in others of Ford's novels, as for instance his last work of fiction, *Vive Le Roy*. Moreover, as Ford himself recounted, a real event lay behind *The Rash Act*: 'The crux of the plot was suggested by an incident of the great storm of three Augusts ago in Toulon Roads. An unknown foreigner was actually wounded by his boat in the manner described in the book. Maddened by pain, he dashed, when he had succeeded in landing, through a small crowd that had waited on shore to help him. He disappeared into the woods of the island of St. Mandrier. The body of a suicide was afterwards found in those woods, and local opinion had it that that was the man who had rushed out of the boat. The local police, however, came to the conclusion that the man was a down-and-outer, whom, for unexplained reasons, they presumed to be an American.' (Ford, 'Autocriticism', *Week-End Review*, VIII, p. 249, 9 September 1933.)

These observations might seem to invalidate my interpretation of the two novels, but the question of artistic interpretation still remains, despite the actual source—or, in reference to Hart Crane, sources. I therefore leave my remarks to stand because I think they permit a seriousness of discussion which otherwise would not seem to be possible.

It is worth adding, I think, the following statement from Flaubert's *Correspondence*, a work certainly well known by Ford, in support of my view: 'What to me seems beautiful, what I would like to do, is a book about nothing, a book with no exterior link, which would hold itself together by the internal strength of its style, just as the earth hangs in the air without support; a book that would have almost no subject or at least where the subject would be nearly invisible, if such a thing would be possible.'

Yet as novels, *The Rash Act* and *Henry for Hugh* must ultimately be judged as failures. Ford's experiment with the semi-abstract novel is interesting, but the result is unsatisfactory. Most good novels start not with an idea but with characters and a situation, and in his effort to write stylized novels, Ford sacrificed both plausibility and human interest. Yet despite this fault in conception, the two novels are written with immense technical skill. Ford himself wrote that he considered them to be his two best books, even better than *The Good Soldier*, in both substance and method. What he presumably meant was that he had succeeded in taking the techniques of impressionism a good deal further than he had gone in his earlier books. He had attempted to produce a continuous present tense, not by using the stream-of-consciousness of Joyce, but by extending the ordinary impressionistic novel that derives from James and by developing to its limit the Conradian notion that an impressionistic novel was intended 'before all, to make you *see*.'[23] To make such a method work requires the strictest attention to form, and none of Ford's novels is so carefully planned as *Henry for Hugh* is. Although it is divided into four separate sections, it progresses seemingly without interruption, and each character moves forward with a vividness that simply would be unobtainable in a novel narrated chronologically.

Through his mastery of the time-shift and what he called 'working backwards and forwards in time,' Ford was able to give his novel an extraordinarily breathless quality, and the events of a given moment take on a richness and suggestiveness that hardly exist elsewhere in English fiction. Because Ford's writing is here as seemingly formless as life itself, it is impossible to provide an example of his technique in a short space. Every passage depends on other passages for its effect and this, in turn, is a simultaneous impression of past, present and future.

Thus, failures as they undoubtedly are as novels, *The Rash Act* and *Henry for Hugh* may be appreciated for the sheer skill with which they are written, and Ford himself must be respected for his effort. Few men in their sixties have dared to write sr far outside of their usual style.

The two other books Ford published in the early 'thirties are autobiographical reminiscences, the first, *Return to Yesterday*, being published in 1931 while the second, *It Was the Nightingale*, appeared in 1934. In a sense they are both continuations of the reminiscences of his childhood which Ford had published in 1911 under the title of *Ancient Lights*. From the first he had a special attitude towards books of this sort which derived from his belief that the usual book of reminiscence was extraordinarily uninteresting. 'The memoir of today,' he wrote earlier in the century, 'is a loosely strung necklace of anecdotes without, as a rule, any attempt to give a view of the subject's personality, or to render the atmosphere of the world in which he lived. It panders, in fact, almost wholly to that love of "ana"—of tit-bits—which has always been the distinguishing feature of the English reader.'[24]

Ford's own intention, therefore, was to present a unified picture of his period and to record anecdotes not for their own sake but only in so far as they were relevant to his theme. He believed that a book of memoirs required the same treatment as that demanded in a novel. If it was to be an intelligible portrait of an age it needed attention to form so that people and events would not merely be catalogued but would be used in the creation of an over-all impression—in the same way a novelist uses his materials to create a picture of life.

Thus Ford was not interested in facts for their own sake. In his preface to *Ancient Lights*, he wrote: 'This book, in short, is full of inaccuracies as to facts, but its accuracy as to impressions is absolute. . . . My business in life, in short, is to attempt to discover, and to try to let you see, where we stand. I don't really deal in facts, I have for facts a most profound contempt. I try to give you what I see to be the spirit of an age, of a town, of a movement. This cannot be done with facts."*[25]

Yet despite his warnings, Ford was frequently considered a liar because of what he put down in his memoirs. Almost every bit of reminiscence he wrote created trouble for him, either in the public press or in creating a private irritation in the mind of some self-important literary figure who would subsequently do his best to do Ford a disservice. These difficulties stemmed largely from Ford's notion that truth was relative, and that factual and impressionistic truth were not always the same. On one occasion, for example, when

---

* It is worthwhile noting that Ford's books of reminiscence were written in much the same spirit adopted by Henry Adams, and Ford would have agreed with Adams, who reported of a trip to Washington that, 'This was the journey he remembered. The actual journey may have been quite different, but the actual journey has no interest for education. The memory was all that mattered. . . .' Henry Adams, *The Education of Henry Adams*, Boston, 1918, p. 43.

Ford and Edward Garnett were going to lunch together, they stopped at Ford's publishing house to enquire about the sales of Ford's latest book. There they were pleased to learn that one thousand copies had been sold. Later on, at the restaurant, they were introduced to an American journalist who enquired about Ford's sales. Ford replied that he and Garnett had just asked about the sales and that *ten* thousand copies of his book had been sold. Afterwards, when angrily accused by Garnett of lying, Ford explained that truth was relative: they had both been pleased and impressed by Ford's sale of a mere thousand, but the American journalist, accustomed to much larger figures, would not have received the same impression if he had been told the actual sales; therefore Ford had merely adjusted the figures to create that same impression.[26]

A large part of Ford's romancing simply came from his lively imagination, without which he could never have been a writer. 'For,' as he and Conrad wrote in *The Nature of a Crime*, 'a lie is a figurative truth—and it is the poet who is the master of these illusions.'[27] Since another of Ford's artistic aims was to please and amuse, he also never hesitated about adjusting his facts for an effect. Not everyone appreciated this point of view, but Richard Aldington, when speaking of Ford said that the world was full 'of dull unimaginative creatures who are only too palpably and sincerely their own dreary selves. We ought to be grateful to an artist who in our own lifetime so successfully revived the tradition of the *commedia dell'arte*.'[28]

While *Ancient Lights* deals mostly with Ford's childhood and the Pre-Raphaelites, *Return to Yesterday* covers the years from 1894 to 1914 and treats of the various forces of Edwardian England which combined to move England towards the World War. Largely devoted to literary life, it contains the story of *The English Review*, an account of the collaboration with Conrad, and references to Henry James and many other figures of the era.

The sequel to this book is *It Was the Nightingale*, and here Ford deals with his post-war experiences and life in Paris. More artistically contrived than its predecessor, *It Was the Nightingale* has as a *leit-motif* Ford's experience of standing on a kerb in Campden Hill and realizing that he must say farewell to London. Here the techniques of the impressionistic novelist come fully into play, and these reminiscences have the unity and form of a novel. In a letter to Ford, Gerald Bullet congratulated him especially for succeeding in the art of *causerie*: 'In this book,' he said, 'the art of digression can be seen at its best—and it is all done not impudently (as Sterne did it) but quietly and without a wink. Your hinges never give the smallest squeak. It all looks very easy, and it *may* be easy to you, but I feel pretty certain it wasn't always so.'[29] In both style and tone, *It Was the Nightingale* leads directly towards his last books of reminiscence and philosophy, *Great Trade Route* and *Provence*.

Thus in the early years of the 1930's, Ford was still moving forward in his development as an artist. Despite poverty and neglect, he pushed his novels into regions where he had hitherto not gone, and he brought his reminiscences up to the technical level of *Parade's End*. In the few years that remained in his life, he was to progress even further, as only the most dedicated artists ever do.

It is certain that we must have patina and dust.
We are the sort that must, because our brain
Will not work in atmospheres of the perfect drain
And cellophane . . . And we must
Have irregular perspectives in crumbling stone
Dying upwards into times long past
And yet so passionately here. . . .

From 'Buckshee' by FORD MADOX FORD

Chapter Twelve

————《◆》《◆》 ————

GREAT TRADE ROUTE

———— 《◆》《◆》 ————

IN April of 1934, for the first time in many years, Ford journeyed to London to be on hand for the publication by Heinemann of his book, *It Was the Nightingale*. Upon his arrival, he moved to 31 Southampton Street, near Fitzroy Square, and there he took a pair of barely-furnished rooms. 'I am sitting,' he later wrote, 'writing in the garret of a gloomy, fog-filled, undignifiedly old London house. I have no fire, having lost in Provence the very habit of fires. A purplish phantom of sunlight filters, on the most depressed day of the London year, beneath the black-purple pall of the upper sky across the view from my elevated casements. It is Good Friday, and this is a cavern of draughts.'¹

Another man might have found it impossible to return in relative misery to a city where once he had possessed an elegant flat decorated with Pre-Raphaelite paintings and furnished with desks that had originally belonged to the Rossettis, but Ford cared little about possessions and didn't even own copies of his own books. Like most poets, he preferred either splendid luxury or extreme simplicity to the ordinary humdrum comforts. Thus when he wrote to his old sub-editor, Douglas Goldring, asking for information about a place to stay, he had requested 'a bed-sitting room—if possible with kitchen . . . [and] without attendance for we shd. do our own cooking . . . It doesn't matter *how* Spartan the place is. Since the crash we mostly live on beans and do our own washing. Personally I shd. love a garret!'² In any event, Ford was soon inviting round Walpole, T. S. Eliot and other older friends as well as some of the younger

228

writers in whom he had an interest, like Richard Hughes, Edward Crankshaw and Anthony Bertram. There were also parties out, and he was the guest both of his publishers and of writers like the Compton Mackenzies.

In a sense, the move to Fitzroy Square was a reversion to his past, for his grandfather, Madox Brown, had once lived there, and the streets near by were all familiar to his memory. In fact, however, much had changed in the intervening years, and the remembered London was not the same as that of 1934. Undaunted by these differences, or by his own relative obscurity and poverty, Ford made a point of dining out at restaurants which in former years had been famous as literary haunts, even though in reality they had long ceased to have any connexion with the arts.

Thus for the most part, the London trip was depressing. The food, as expected, was almost inedible, but what was more distressing were the endless advertisements strung up round Piccadilly Circus and Trafalgar Square which offered liver salts and other medications as cures for indigestion. Anxious to explore the London he had known and loved so well, Ford visited the National Gallery, and was once again impressed by its magnificent collections. On the other hand, he was disappointed by the low calibre of contemporary painting in England. Later on he visited the British Museum, where he had so often taken tea with Mr. Richard Garnett, but when he arrived, he was not recognized, and the attendants treated him rudely. Finally, London seemed to be entirely given over to a kind of maniacal religiousness: it was not the true religious spirit, but merely what Ford called 'Christism' and largely took the form of signs pasted on the hoardings and displayed in neon saying, 'God is Love.'

Altogether, the weeks spent in London were rather disagreeable and flat: Bloomsbury neither appealed to Ford nor did Ford particularly appeal to Bloomsbury. The year before he had been scurrilously attacked by Archibald Marshall in his memoirs,[3] and two years before that an anecdote concerning King George which he had published in *Return to Yesterday* brought a violent reaction from the London press. 'MONSTROUS STORY ABOUT THE KING,' ran the front-page headline of the *Daily Herald*.*[4] Depressed by the

* The anecdote, which had originally been told him by Masterman, concerned King George's threat to abdicate unless his ministers would hold a conference in an effort to solve the Irish question. Ford considered it a fine example of Kingship. However, the

generally wearisome atmosphere of the place, Ford soon decided to return to Toulon, but before leaving he spent a pleasant week-end with the Bertrams in Sussex, at a place not far distant from his old house at Bedham.

The South of France was doubtless a pleasant change after London, and Ford was soon busy with his garden and with writing *Provence*. In the late summer and autumn he took a number of trips through Provence, and attended several bullfights along the way. At Nîmes he watched the famous Chicuelo, whose performance particularly fascinated Ford, perhaps because he found a parallel between it and his own career. The crowd had attended the bull-fight fully prepared to give Chicuelo a bad time because on a previous occasion he had not performed well. This time, however, before an actively hostile audience, he displayed himself as a master of his art: he was so good that the onlookers could not bring themselves to hiss him.[5]

Most of Ford's time was taken up with agricultural pursuits, however, and for once, despite a late start on the garden and the dryness of the season, he had a bumper crop of tomatoes and eggplants. He told a correspondent that if he wanted to he could get five crops a year, but that in fact three were enough. During the autumn he also received a pleasant surprise in the form of a dedication to himself of a book by his young friend, Anthony Bertram. He was obviously pleased, but half-facetiously warned Bertram not to be overly eulogistic in his dedication lest the critics take revenge by damning the book as a whole.[6]

In December, after spending Christmas in Paris with Katherine Anne Porter and her husband, Ford left France to go to New York. The purpose of the trip was to arrange for the publication of some of his books, including *Provence*, but this time Ford was returning in a less hopeful mood than he had gone in 1927. Yet, as destiny would have it, this last period in America, though not so glittering as the years of his success in the 1920's, was to be in the end more satisfactory and enduring than his earlier stay.

Established in an apartment at 61 Fifth Avenue, he was soon taken up with invitations and commissions. Perhaps most pleasing,

---

Daily Herald printed these headlines: 'Indignant Denial of Any Pre-War Threat to Abdicate' and 'Court Official Says it is Not True.' For his part, Ford considered the official denials to be very lame, but agreed to the suppression of the story in any future editions of the book.

in view of the losses he had incurred through the collapse of Horace Liveright's publishing house, was the arrangement he made with the Philadelphia publishers, Lippincott, who agreed to bring out *Provence* and who also reissued *Ladies Whose Bright Eyes*. Ford also had a circle of friends in America with whom he was quite at home, and he appreciated the attention given him there as compared to his reception in Britain. He expressed his attitude on this point in a letter written in 1933 to Gerald Bullett in which he again reiterated his realization that no one in England liked what he wrote. He said that his unpopularity was quite understandable, however, since he did not deal with typical English subjects such as country life but placed his novels in France and America. Moreover, since he did not use subjective description or present his story chronologically, he could quite understand that his use of the time-shift and his impressionistic manner of writing would be wholly incomprehensible and certainly tedious to an English audience. In America, on the other hand, these techniques were readily understood—they were already, indeed, somewhat old-fashioned—but at least he was appreciated for what he had done.[7]

The experiences of 1933 and 1934 had begun to harden Ford's view both of his own position and of the situation in the world at large. In 1933 he had written: 'Heaven knows nobody could be further away from the English governing-class frame of mind than I am.'[8] In a sense, this assertion was true, but as he admitted, many of his automatic reactions were prescisely those of that class. Moreover, for a long time he had been concerned to re-establish his English reputation, and in 1926, when he was at the top of his fame in New York, he made a point of writing his London publisher, Duckworth, asking him whether his American success had improved his position in England.[9] The London trip of 1934 seems, however, to have brought about a definite change.

Returning to Cap Brun with his perceptions sharpened, he noticed once again the many examples of simple domestic art with which his villa was decorated. The naval quartermaster who had built it had also frescoed its walls with scenes from the local life of fishermen and farmers, while his wife had painted flowers on the walls of the interior. 'But imagine,' Ford noted, 'an English retired naval quartermaster in the suburbs of Portsmouth building, along with his lady and with their own hands, a house of Roman cement, tiled with Roman S-shaped tiles . . . And then frescoing it!'[10]

As a symbol, the house was indicative of the change in Ford, and from 1934 onwards he was more and more to side with the life and methods of Provence as against the depressing gloom of Bloomsbury. One of Ford's favourite sayings was that 'It is hypocrisy to seek for the person of the Sacred Emperor in a low tea house.' By 1934, he had begun to believe that England contained nothing but such houses and so, as his attitude towards England hardened, he accepted without reservation the implications of his earlier remark, 'Wherever there were creative thinkers was my country.'[11]

Letters from one of his most candid critics, Ezra Pound, must also have contributed to this gradual shift of point of view, for upon reading *It Was the Nightingale*, Pound wrote as follows to his friend:

> Wall, yew ave got a funny kind ov'a mind. BUT the opusculus throws a bit'er (meaning *bit of*) light onto some of its underbrush.
> Vurry readable/ vurry readable// less wildly inaccurate detail . . .
> Thank god I was born ten years later than you were. Escaped a lot of goddamed nonsense. Not sure that the beastly word gentleman hasn't caused you more trouble in yr/ bright l'il life than all the rest of the lang. (lang = langwidg) . . .
>
> [Next day]
> I was about to remove the paragraph about the 'gent' or at any rate rewrite it thinking it would make you pewk over the floor/
> First idea of softening it was:
> Fordie, you AVE got a rummy job lot of 'idees recues' and I come back to it that you HAVE bitched about 80% of yr/ work through hanging onto a set of idees recues.[12]

After spending Christmas with Theodore Dreiser at Mount Kisco, Ford returned to New York and a round of activities. As usual, his apartment lacked amenities. 'My surroundings are incredibly mouldy,' he wrote, 'the radiator in the studio does not function at all; that in the living-room broils you. The refrigerator in the night makes sounds like the Yeth hounds passing overhead on Exmoor; the bath water appears to come through the refrigerator; I am warned that I had better not use the gas-stove for fear of explosions.'[13] Despite these hazards, Ford was soon seeing and entertaining old friends like the Van Dorens and Katherine Anne Porter. On week-ends he would go out to New Jersey to see William Carlos Williams. Soon, too, he was finding literary work: H. L. Mencken's successor on *The American Mercury* signed him up for a series of articles starting in the autumn of 1935 and running through most of 1936. In February, he was asked by the New York *Times* to cover the then world-famous Hauptmann trial as a special reporter, and for this purpose he twice visited Flemington. Altogether, he was both busy and appreciated, and the sort of praise he received from Dreiser who, in the course of a letter, characterized him as 'a Poet as well as a master observer'[14] was as commonplace amongst his literary friends in America as it was rare in Great Britain.

With the coming of spring, Ford started on a trip through the South. Travelling by train as far as Philadelphia, where he stayed with a friend, he then transferred to a bus and continued the rest of his trip by that rigorous mode of transportation. For a day or two he stopped in Washington and also visited Gunston Hall, Mount Vernon and various other Virginia mansions on his way to his ultimate destination in Tennessee. Preoccupied as travellers always are by food and living conditions, Ford saw in the Middle Atlantic states very much the same sort of conflict he found between the life of Provence and that of metropolitan London. On the one hand were the forces of industrial 'progress' whose hallmark was standardization; on the other was the less pretentious individualism of the local artisan or farmer. Industrialization seemed to mean bad food, pointless bustle and jittery nerves, whereas the other meant good digestion and serenity.

At length, he arrived in Tennessee where he stayed with Allen Tate and his wife at 'Benfolly' their country house outside of Nashville. It had been largely through the Tates that Ford had met a number of young writers from the South, and by the mid-thirties, he had come to believe that the best writing in America was coming not so much from the Middle West (which had been his contention in the 1920's) as from the South. He was therefore pleased to accept Robert Penn Warren's invitation to attend the Southern Writers' Conference that was to be held at Louisiana State University in April and, at the suggestion of the Tates, he drove south with them to attend it. At the conference itself, Ford was considered the most distinguished visitor, and he was asked to speak on 'Provincial Literature' to an audience that included writers like John Peale Bishop, Randall Jarrell, John Gould Fletcher, Hodding Carter and the Tates. In his address, Ford criticized the commercialism of the New York publishers and booksellers and while applauding the establishment of *The Southern Review* as one result of the conference, urged the Southern writers to set up their own publishing and distribution centre as well. Moreover, he expressed the hope that through a folk art, akin to that of the troubadours, the Southern regionalist writers might one day be able to bring about a change in the whole course of civilization. His concluding remarks reveal his enthusiasm for the topic:

> The dominance, material and figurative, of the other provinces of this Continent is passing away and its equivalents are passing away all the world over. Seventy years ago you stood for the fruits of the earth and the treasures of the craftsman, means of wealth that alone can be coterminous with the life of this earth. During those seventy years of the obscuration of your traditions the industrial system rose, dominated humanity, called itself a civilization. It is now crumbling into its final decay. You on the other hand continued unmoved to follow out the pursuits and earnings of the husbandman—and measured by human lives, the pursuits and earnings of the husbandman constitute the only wealth that is and must be as durable as humanity itself. And you possess the richest tract of soil that the earth holds on its surface.
> Your survival is therefore inevitable: nothing shall put an end to it till this planet falls back into the sun from which it issued. And if you survive, alone endowed with wealth and an undisturbed tradition, your dominance of a hemisphere is as inevitable as your survival.
> So the future of the civilization of this hemisphere must lie in your hands as in other continents it will lie in the hands of men similarly minded and of similar traditions. It is for you alone to say what aspect that civilization shall assume.[15]

These brave words, the result of a direct transferal to the American south of his feelings for Provence, represent what Ford had come to believe in as the only hope for a world threatened as much by industrial materialism as by Hitler. But what is interesting here is to see the influence Ford was now beginning to exercise over some of the leading writers of the South. Osbert Sitwell presumably thought it amusing to dub him 'Freud Madox Fraud',[16] but to men and women like John Crowe Ransom, Robert Penn Warren, Allen Tate, Caroline Gordon, John Peale Bishop and Eudora Welty, Ford was esteemed and honoured as a figure of some stature.

The reasons for this respect are various. In the first place, Ford had personally encouraged a number of Southern writers in their work: some he had talked to about their manuscripts; others he had helped to find publishers in New York. Elizabeth Madox Roberts and Caroline Gordon particularly benefited from literary discussions with Ford, and later on, in 1938 and 1939, he was to be of considerable assistance to Robert Lowell,[17] Eudora Welty and Jean Stafford. In addition to his kindness and friendliness, Ford was much respected for his proficiency as a novelist. The South was one of the few places in the world where Ford's books were taken seriously, and *The Good Soldier* and *Parade's End* were much admired and read by young Southern writers both for the technical skills they exhibit and for their depiction of the conflict between the old order and the new which had its counterpart in the South. Through his own writings Ford had a direct influence on a few novelists like Caroline Gordon, but his indirect influence was probably far greater. In the work of Andrew Lytle, Peter Taylor and some others the influence seems to have come by way of the Tates, for they more than anyone else championed Ford's methods, Allen Tate having said, for example, that 'The English novel now would be much more solid had it followed Ford instead of E. M. Forster.'[18] Thus through them Ford indirectly influenced many people who probably never heard of him.

Finally, Ford's natural affinity for Southern life also contributed to his sympathy for the literary movement first becoming prominent there in the 1930's, and he had much in common with the economic views of the Nashville Agrarians. It is pleasant to note, in contrast to the many others whom Ford helped during his lifetime, that no Southern writer ever afterwards attacked him privately or in print.

Following the Louisiana conference Ford returned to New York in the late spring of 1935 and while there he made arrangements with the Oxford University Press to publish his *Collected Poems* in the United States. This book, which appeared in 1936, included some new poems he had written in 1931. Since for some years prior to that date he had not written any verse, he called this group *Buckshee* because, as he explained in a note, they had come to him as something 'unexpected, unearned—gratifying.'[19] Dedicated to Biala under the name of 'Haïtchka', they are love poems intermixed with a philosophical assessment of Ford's own position and the age in which he lives. In the first poem, modern life is seen as ambivalent:

> Our globe compact of virtues all half virtue
> Of vices scarce half-vices, made up of truth
> Blurred in the edges and of lies so limping
> They will not spur the pulse in the utterance. . . .[20]

235

And in this complex world, the ordinary man—Ford himself—is a compound of contradictions:

> I have neither foe nor friend,
> I stand neither erect nor stoop
> I am neither enslaved nor wield power.[21]

The familiar contemporary note struck in these lines produces no easy resolution; nevertheless, as a collection of poems written by a man in his last years *Buckshee* is an attempt to find some final meaning in life. In a sense, these poems are similar to those that Yeats wrote in his old age, but Ford is too full of doubt and humanity to come down as solidly as Yeats does on the side of art. Time for Ford seems to exist on two levels: there is the ordinary time of day-to-day living and there is the eternal time of pure thought and the immortality of at least some art. Yet who is to know whether his own art is immortal, and who can say that love and the daily round are not important?

In the course of his own life Ford had never neglected human relationships entirely, but they had always played a rôle secondary to his art. By the early 1930's, however, he began to reconsider this emphasis and to strike a balance between his private life and his art. *Buckshee* records this new attitude by asserting the necessity of both spheres and demonstrating how the two can be mingled. These poems are not didactic, but they picture the sort of life the wise man chooses to lead. Ford uses his simple farm near Toulon as an example of the kind of place where a man of industry and probity can find the good life. *Buckshee* then is a love poem, but it is a love poem that is also addressed to life itself.

A new technical development discernible in this collection is Ford's extensive use of the techniques of the novelist. Although he was capable of writing regular verse, he preferred a loose form dictated by the nature of the subject. One of the poems from *Buckshee* called 'Fleuve Profond' is, for example, an attempt to render in verse the experience of a literary party in Paris attended mostly by Americans. Here the challenge was to make the party seem alive and, at the same time, to indicate the poet's love for Haïtchka and his relationship to other writers attending the party. The method Ford adopted may be called 'poetic impressionism'. He places bits of literary gossip beside images of Haïtchka and sounds of singing next to a discussion of the Tietjens novels and, by using the fictional technique of the time-shift, continuously moves the focus of attention from one to the other. The method is similar in some ways to what Pound uses in his *Cantos*, but Ford's allusions are more limited than Pound's are and his poems are also more unified. This unity is achieved partially through repetition which, in turn, gives reality to the poem. Just as people tend to repeat themselves at parties, so the same snatches of conversation are repeated in Ford's poem, but the interesting point is that each time they take on a different shade of meaning.

In June of 1935, at the height of the tourist season, Ford decided to return to France. The only passage he could secure was Tourist Class on an Italian liner sailing by way of Madeira and Gibraltar. It was a dismal crossing: the ship was full of admirers of Mussolini, it was hot, it was crowded, the ship's officials treated the passengers abominably and the food was 'fantastically barbarous.'[22] Worst of all was the pressure of humanity: 'to travel without privacy is,' Ford later noted, 'let us be exact—Purgatory.'[23] Altogether, despite the pleasures of Funchal and Malaga, the trip was a nightmare and, in Ford's mind, seemed the epitome of machine-age horror.

It was a relief to return for the balance of the summer to Cap Brun and to enjoy fresh fruit and vegetables in the privacy of the villa. But by September, he was off again, this time to Switzerland where he stayed for the most part in Geneva. The experience of observing the world's political leaders at the Palais des Nations proved to be discouraging. They seemed, Ford thought, 'as degenerate, physically and mentally, as any body of men the world has ever seen. Physically almost more than mentally, since they are at least capable of a sufficiency of mental activity to plunge the world into war. But if you took all the Cabinets of the Western world and set them, provided with enough tools, in any rural solitude, they would starve and freeze and soak to death without the physical or mental imagination to plant a brussels sprout or to gather reeds for the thatching of a primitive shelter . . . And these men govern . . . Us!'[24]

All in all, Ford's travels along what he later called 'the Great Trade Route'—from France to England and on to America and then back, by way of Spain and Switzerland—markedly broadened his perspective. He had always been a firm internationalist, but the sense of 'enlargement' he had originally experienced many years before when he left Sussex for France, now became a permanent element in his make-up and affected both his literary and political views. He had already, before leaving New York in the summer of 1935, begun to look back on his own life and to pull together his views of the world. He had issued statements to the press listing his favourite books,* and had written a notice about himself for a book of portraits of public figures that had been gathered together by George Schreiber. What Ford says about himself is half-facetious, but provides an autobiographical assessment at the age of sixty-three:

> The life, then, is one of frustrations; if I had not so constantly travelled, I should have reaped better harvests and written more and better books; if I weren't, when travelling, constantly impeded by the desire to settle down somewhere and start growing and write something, I should have travelled more happily and farther.
>
> That, then, is my autobiography ... a man of action. My mental autobiography could be disposed of in about twenty words. *In my hot youth*—which wasn't really so torrid—*I yearned to be*—like Horace, Cervantes, Bunyan and others—*both poet and soldier : having been them, I find myself to have become pacifist and prosateur* ... which makes twenty-two words.[25]

During the course of his travels, encountering Italian fascists, Nazis and American nationalists and racists, Ford had observed how widespread the spirit of hatred had become in the world. This spirit seemed mainly to be the result of provincialism, an evil which Ford was to attack with increasing fervour in his last years. When it appeared in literature, he could be very outspoken, as he was when he wrote to Anthony Bertram about the latter's new novel *Men Adrift*. Chiding him for using the Christ story as background for his book, Ford points out that this not only reduces the inventiveness of the novel, since the author already has the legendary framework upon which to hang his plot, but—and this was the more severe criticism—it cheapened the story of Christ itself by perpetuating the middle-class illusion of a personal Christ who would always come to one's aid in time of trouble. 'We as Englishmen,' he wrote, 'have

---

* His statement in the New York *Herald Tribune* for 10 December 1935 was that 'the six classics I wish I had with me today' were Turgenev's *Récits d'un Chasseur*, Flaubert's *Education Sentimentale*, Hudson's *Nature in Downland*, Doughty's *Arabia Deserta*, Crane's *The Third Violet*, Clarendon's *History of the Great Rebellion* or Maine's *Ancient Law* and James's *Four Visits*. Always anxious to give a boost to his contemporaries, he also mentioned 'living authors I should like to re-read or have lately re-read for pleasure and improvement.' These were Hughes's *High Wind in Jamaica*, Cunninghame Graham's *Mogreb el Acksa*, René Béhaine's *Les Nouveux Venus*, Hemingway's 'story about trout fishing', Caroline Gordon's *Aleck Maury*, Graham Greene's *It's a Battlefield* and Dreiser's *The Lost Phoebe*.

gone on for long imagining that if we as individuals model ourselves on the English ideal of the Redemeer we shall have a good time—for so long that we expect the Redeemer to touch his forelock like a good footman and give us supernatural market tips and advantages even when we are doing no more than write a novel. The process is wanting in respect for the Son of God. . . . You must give up being a Christist and become a Christian or something else that is fierce and bitter as Christians have to be. Christianity isn't you know a Sunday supper with the maids given the evening off: it is eating flesh and drinking blood.'[26]

While letters like this and other occasional remarks indicate aspects of Ford's general attitude towards world conditions, his energies in 1935 and 1936 were largely devoted to the writing of *Great Trade Route* as a loose sequel to *Provence*. These two books were supposed to be, as Ford himself indicated, part of a trilogy in which he would present what might be called his world view.[27] The message of the proposed trilogy is at once simple and complex and comes, more than from any other single source, from Ford's admiration for the spirit of France. His appreciation of this spirit began with his love of French literature, especially the prose of the nineteenth-century novelists, and when he actually moved to Paris in the 1920's, he directly encountered the quality of French character that makes such books as the *Education Sentimentale* and *Le Rouge et le Noir* possible.

As an Englishman he was immediately impressed by the respect given to the arts by the ordinary Frenchman. Whereas the social position of an English writer is negligible unless he is otherwise a gentleman, the French artist cuts a far wider swathe than a cabinet minister or millionaire industrialist does. In one of the last pieces he ever wrote, Ford noted that the election of a new member to the Académie Française had occasioned more excitement in Paris than even sports or the latest move by Hitler had done.[28] Ford's sensitivity to this difference between England and France was doubtless increased by finding himself addressed as 'cher maître' by the townspeople of Toulon, whereas in England he was virtually unknown. In the case of the Academy there was also an element of contradiction, for although Ford used to say in a joking manner that what he would most have liked in the world would have been to be a member of the French Academy, he also knew the academician as a type and realized his deleterious effect on the arts in general.[29]

Nevertheless, it seemed to Ford that any country which puts so much stress upon artistic achievement must have other qualities worthy of close attention. He had early discovered that the French peasantry had a more intelligent attitude towards life than was found in most places: they were realists whose philosophy could be summed up in one phrase: *'La vie, voyez-vous, n'est jamais si bonne ni si mauvaise que l'on ne croit.'*[30] That they could endure the hardships—and governments—with which they had been beset for generations was due, in Ford's opinion, to their immense sense of rectitude and their love for the soil.[31] These conclusions Ford reached largely through his own observations, especially after moving to Toulon, when he himself virtually became a French smallhold farmer. In a world in which the half-lies of political and literary life were not only debilitating but dangerous to civilization, the French peasant represented the 'proper man' whom Ford described in another place as a person who built a house, planted a tree, wrote a book and begot a child.[32] Ford observed that more than any other place Provence produced this ideal man who was literate, active, frugal and responsible to his race.

The French themselves have always considered that Provence and the Mediterranean shore represented reason and order, for through them came the Roman and Greek inheritance.[33] Ford expanded this concept and used Provence as a symbol for civilization itself. In an earlier book, he had expounded the thesis that 'chivalric generosity, frugality, pure thought and the arts are the first requisites of a Civilization—and the only requisites of a Civilization; and then that such traces of chivalric generosity, frugality, pure thought and the arts as our pre-war, European civilization of white races could exhibit came to us from the district of Southern France on the shores of the Mediterranean where flourished the Courts of Toulouse, olive trees, the mistral, the Romance tradition, Bertran de Born, the Courts of Love and the only really amiable Heresy of which I know.'[34]

But by the 1930's this civilization had become seriously threatened. France was surrounded by the ruthless dictatorships of Franco, Mussolini and Hitler, and the deluge appeared to be fast approaching. Ford's message, then, was a desperate one: it was designed to save, before it was too late, the sort of proper man that he admired and the civilization that he loved.

In order to explain exactly what he meant by civilization, he took

Provence as a starting point. Then, having expounded the virtues of the 'magic triangle', he proceeded in a sequel called *Great Trade Route* to enquire whether the same spirit of Provence existed elsewhere in the world. The purpose of both books was to encourage all men of good will to unite in following the example of Provence and like-minded places so that the extinction of civilization then being threatened might be averted.

The title *Great Trade Route* was chosen as a means of dealing with a type of civilization that was to be found along the fortieth degree north parallel, stretching from the eastern reaches of the Mediterranean across the Atlantic to the southern region of the United States. The civilization found along this band was united in its essentials: it was agricultural; it was renowned for the chivalry and bravery of its people; it gave importance to craftsmanship and good cooking; and it was sympathetic towards the arts. In short, this essentially Mediterranean civilization, whose style was determined mainly by its emphasis on the individual as against the mass, represented for Ford the best possible hope for the happiness of mankind. That it was menaced by mechanization and pluralism, by financially suspect politicians and military-minded dictators Ford knew only too well: in part, therefore, his book was a philippic against these very forces.

The phrase Great Trade Route also had another purpose, however, for not only did civilization come through trade—as from China—but economics, in Ford's view, lay at the bottom of most of the world's difficulties. For Ford the great evil—he even called it a 'mortal sin'[35]—was Protection. More than any other force, it encouraged a warlike spirit in those countries receiving too small a share of the world's goods, and it spread the poisonous doctrines of nationalism, xenophobia and acquisitiveness amongst all people—to the detriment of the arts and civilization.

Having experienced the result of the protective instinct in the first World War, Ford found in Provence a way of life in which this spirit did not exist at all. Instead, he discovered a society of smallholders and small-producers—men who supported their families from the work of their own hands. He concluded therefore that the Provençal farmer was 'the one human being whom currency, finance, tariff, the refrigerator, the machine—those arbiters of the destinies of all other mortals—cannot very much affect. Even wars cannot root him out.'[36] Since the rest of mankind was increasingly controlled by machines and corrupted by the complementary doctrine of protection, the only solution, Ford believed, was for the world to adopt a system of economics that would unite rather than separate mankind.

But the principle that each countryside should produce only that for which it is most fitted and that such products should circulate freely through the world—preferably by barter—that principle is so blindingly clear that no human being can miss it. . . . And the putting into practice of that principle must of necessity abolish wars, since no country could dispense with the products of any other country. . . .[37]

Ford was aware that his solution might be considered as sentimental Utopianism and that he might be accused of being a William Morris *redivivus*. His answer was a simple prophecy:

I ask to be regarded, from this moment, not as Moralist, nor as Historian, but simply as prophet. I am going to point out to this world what will happen to it if it does not take Provence of the thirteenth century for its model. For there seems to be a general—and universal—impression that our Civilization—if that is what you want to call it—is staggering to its end. And for the first time in my life I find myself in agreement with the world from China to Peru.

Do you happen to know Haydn's symphony? . . . It is a piece that begins with full orchestra, each player having beside him a candle to light his score. They play that delicate, cheerful-regretful music of an eighteenth century that was already certain of its doom . . . As they play on the contrabassist takes his candle and steals away . . . The music goes on—and the drum is gone, and the bassoon . . . and the hautbois, and the second . . . violin . . . Then they are all gone and it is dark. . . .

That is our Age. . . .[38]

Thus it follows, he continued, that the simple life of the self-sufficient farmer will inevitably come:

It will, however, come to that after the world has passed through the preparatory stages of Fascism or Communism of the Russian variety or the mutually exterminating contests of those two opposed world tendencies . . . We must go back to the Dark Ages . . . For if we do not go back to the Provençal Dark Ages we shall go back to those of the Teutoburger Wald with the poison gas clouds for ever above the appalled tree-tops . . .[39]

Ford's solution also bore in mind the pleasure and happiness of the individual, for modern industrial civilization as he saw it reduced the individual to a man of no stamina and no real pleasures. His thrills are all vicarious, his tastes entirely synthetic. A city-dweller of necessity, he lives and dies in crowds. 'It is appalling to think,' Ford wrote in *Great Trade Route*, 'that there are millions and millions of human beings today who never have and who never will taste pure food, sit in a well-made chair, hear good music played except mechanically—or use all their muscles, or so much as cook well or properly polish the woodwork of their homes.'[40]

Without a change of heart, the machine civilization would inevitably drive men to war, for automation would ultimately make man useless except as cannon fodder. But with a new sense of values, civilization could survive, and men could return to the soil for most of their lives, attending to the machines only at intervals. With a new idea of what constituted the good life they would then not flock to the public centres for cheap amusement but would occupy their leisure time 'with the agreeable and unhurried labour of their own soil or with their own benches, chisels, easels, fiddle bows, lasts . . . and with whatever form of night life they shall find agreeable when the day is over. Occasionally even they will take a read in a book.'[41]

Thus although Ford's warnings were not heeded in 1938, they still seem relevant today and have a practicality that Morris's Utopianism never had. In today's machine age, modern warfare is so destructive that, should the bombs fall, it will in any event force the remnants of the human race back to the land, after all the machines and factories are annihilated. Ford's advice, then, is merely that it would be wiser to avoid world-wide slaughter and misery by getting rid of the machine civilization beforehand. *Provence* and *Great Trade Route* are not, however, tracts for the times: they do not propose any doctrines or systems. They merely present a picture of the kind of life Ford would like all men to enjoy. By indicating the self-sufficiency of Provençal life, they also reveal Ford's own happiness and serenity, and the contrast that exists between the full life of the 'proper man' and the specialized, isolated, dependent lives of most of the rest of humanity. These books are, then, humane: they are written for the happiness of mankind.

The humanity of these books is best revealed through the techniques Ford employed in writing them. Using many of the devices of fiction, especially the time-shift and *progression d'effet*, he produced books that sound like somewhat disordered though entertaining and civilized conversation but which, by the time one finishes them, have an impact that a chronologically-ordered discussion could never have achieved. When *Great Trade Route* was submitted for publication, the publisher's reader noted these qualities in it:

> It takes Mr. Ford a whole book to make his case convincing—he never argues solidly and dully; he talks on and on in his endlessly entertaining, discursive manner and, suddenly, the picture is there . . . But he does make it convincing. This book, bland, ironic, humorous, discursive, trivial-seeming in places, always light in touch, always entertaining, yet always with an underlying passion that in the end is allowed only for a moment to reveal itself, has a simply tremendous power, the full weight of which one is scarcely aware of until the end. . . .[42]

By nature, *Provence* is more cohesive than its sequel, for much of it is concerned with providing information about the country. Yet the twentieth century is by no means absent, as Graham Greene noted in his review of the book, in which he examined especially the chapter called 'Courts of Love' in order to describe Ford's method. This chapter is really as much about London as about Provence and starts with a walk in memory from Fitzroy Square to Piccadilly, from the house of Madox Brown to a space illuminated by advertisements for liver salts. It is also made to be a trip from Madox Brown to Edmund Gosse and from Frédéric Mistral and Francis Hueffer to Ezra Pound and Ford himself. Mr. Greene wrote that the method had something in common with Pound's *Cantos*: 'simultaneity, but carried out with infinitely greater technical ability.'[43]

To Ford Madox Ford in Heaven

Is it any better in Heaven, my friend Ford,
    than you found it in Provence?

A heavenly man you seem to me now, never
    having been for me a saintly one.
It lived about you, a certain grossness that
    was not like the world.
The world is cleanly, polished and well
    made but heavenly man
is filthy with his flesh and corrupt that
    loves to eat and drink and whore—
to laugh at himself and not be afraid of
    himself knowing well he has
no possessions and opinions that are worth
    caring a broker's word about
and that all he is, but one thing, he feeds
    as one will feed a pet dog.

So roust and love and dredge the belly full
    in Heaven's name!
I laugh to think of you wheezing in Heaven.
    Where is Heaven? But why
do I ask that, since you showed the way?
    I don't care a damn for it
other than for that better part lives beside
    me here so long as I
live and remember you. Thank God you
    were not delicate, you let the world in
and lied! damn it you lied grossly
    sometimes. But it was all, I
see now, a carelessness, the part of a man
    that is homeless here on earth.

Provence! the fat assed Ford will never
    again strain the chairs of your cafés,
pull and pare for his dish your sacred garlic,
    grunt and sweat and lick
his lips. Gross as the world he has left to
    us he has become
a part of that of which you were the known
    part, Provence, he loved so well.

              —WILLIAM CARLOS WILLIAMS

Chapter Thirteen

—————⟨⟨◆⟩⟩⟨⟨◆⟩⟩—————

MARCH OF LITERATURE

—————⟨⟨◆⟩⟩⟨⟨◆⟩⟩—————

FORD'S long periods of residence in Provence during the early 1930's seem to have given him a certain serenity and calmness that is reflected in his work. He approved of the standard of values that his Toulon life represented and, although he was neither rich nor famous, he was happy. What a man drinks is often a good index of his well-being, and during this period Ford, who considered himself a connoisseur of fine wines, wrote these sentences: 'I should of course like to drink *Château Pavie* or even *Château Mouton-Rothschild*—once again. But I do not suppose I ever shall, and I am perfectly contented with what I do drink.'[1]

In the circumstances, it might have been expected of Ford that he would end his days in quiet retirement at Cap Brun, peacefully attending his garden during the day and, in the evenings, eating his own produce and drinking the humble but decent *vin du pays*. But the idea of 'retirement' never appealed to Ford, and furthermore he could not afford it. By September of 1936 he had so little money that he wrote to his New York agent saying that unless his finances improved, he would have to give up his Toulon house and move to a single room in Paris—an event which he feared would be injurious to his health.[2] On the other hand, Ford was a restless man who liked the excitement of city living. Whatever its other virtues, Provence provided little or no artistic or literary society and so for the last four years of his life, he spent little time there. The decision to abandon Provence was thus a combination of inclination and necessity.

Ford spent the winter and early spring of 1936 in Paris, living in a

246

new apartment he had taken in the rue de Seine. Katherine Anne Porter had written that 'the whole town is hollow,'[3] but the quiet was conducive to work, and here Ford finished *Great Trade Route* and worked on his series of articles for *The American Mercury*. These provided him with a certain amount of income, but as he had to contribute towards his daughter Julie's education, in addition to paying his own expenses, he decided to go to England to see whether he could secure publication there for some of his books. He had published nothing in London since *It Was the Nightingale*, which appeared in 1934, and his agents had been unsuccessful in placing any of his other work.

Shortly after his arrival in London, he met Edward Crankshaw who offered to lend Ford his own house so that he could finish his American articles. Ford gladly accepted the proposal and in July moved down to Sandhurst in Kent, while Crankshaw, in the meantime, set about finding him a publisher. The task was not easy, but at last he managed to induce George Allen and Unwin to take over Ford's work. While no agreement was ever reached—owing to the possession of copyright by other publishers—to reissue the Tietjens novels and other of Ford's books that have a permanent value, Allen and Unwin undertook to publish all of Ford's later books, including *Provence* and *Great Trade Route* and agreed to publish in the future whatever he sent them. Ford was immensely pleased with this arrangement, for the recognition that came with Unwin's acceptance of all his last books was more tangible than anything he had received from England in decades. In the summer of 1939 Edward Crankshaw specified this pleasure by observing that Unwin's acceptance of Ford's books had given him 'during all these last three years, and year by year increasing, a satisfaction and joy fuller and deeper than anybody could imagine who did not know his extraordinary humility and his passionate attachment to England. Nothing, I think, has ever given him greater happiness; nothing else at that stage could have given him so much. He used to tell people in America, proudly, that at last, after all these years, he was back with—impressionistic to the end—his first publisher of all.'[4]

Ford of course realized that his sales would never live up to the hopes of his publisher, but in a letter to Sir Stanley Unwin written in 1938 he tried to lighten his publisher's burden by claiming that he himself had always assumed that if his books were to sell at all, they would do so after his death. He believed you couldn't have it both ways, and reminded Unwin that complimentary obituaries sometimes produced sales.[5]

The months he stayed in England in 1936 were very quiet, and were spent almost entirely in Kent. Coming from Provence, he found England in many ways unattractive. He was distressed by the bad food, felt oppressed by the green lushness of the countryside and considered that all of the South of England had been transformed into an immense suburbia, referring to Tunbridge Wells in Kent as 'London, S.E.96.'[6]

He kept away from London as much as he could because he thought it had gone mad in an attempt to imitate New York. Furthermore, except for the proprietors of *The London Mercury*, he had few friends there. Mostly he was ignored, except by the few who still bore him ill will. One of these even tried to discourage Unwin from publishing Ford, on the grounds that he was unreliable. This trait, not infrequently mentioned by those with whom Ford did business, needs a certain amount of explanation. What would seem, to the business mind, to have been wilful unreliability was, in fact, merely a reflection of his own feelings of insecurity. The resulting touchiness, natural to many artistic people, made him competent in certain things and immensely incompetent in others. He was, for example, an excellent cook and was famous for the elaborate meals he often prepared. On the other hand, he was, in the words of one who knew him well, at times 'so simple minded that he should not be allowed out alone.' In practical financial matters, he was especially at sea, and as a result, whenever he dealt with publishers, he was often extremely nervous and suspicious, and therefore exasperating. The nervousness was never intentional, however; rather it was, according to a friend, of the kind 'that makes a thoroughbred horse shy at a bit of rag by the roadside.'

At any rate, Unwin did not withdraw from the agreement he had made with him, and with the book of portraits finished, Ford left England in November in order to have a month's rest in Paris before leaving for New York.

During all the time of these movements and business arrangements Ford was hard at work on his writing. The articles he had written on men like Hardy, Lawrence, Dreiser, Conrad and others for *The American Mercury* he later collected and published as a book called *Mightier than the Sword*.* The purpose of these essays was to

---

* In the United States, the title was *Portraits from Life*.

provide a portrait in the round of the subject, first by presenting him as a person, and then by evaluating his work. In this impressionistic method Ford had no rivals: some could write better criticism and some could write more accurate biography, but none could combine the two so well. Since Ford knew all the writers he dealt with, he included an autobiographical element, and began most of the articles by portraying the subject as he first appeared to Ford. Out of this first meeting Ford normally developed an anecdote designed to reveal both the character of the author and his particular method of writing. In the James chapter, for example, the anecdote is rendered in the sort of language frequently used by 'the Master' himself, which provides therefore an unobtrusive analysis of both the man and his work.

William Carlos Williams was so moved by the book as a whole that he wrote to Ford about it and, in passing, gave it the best assessment it has received.

> I wanted particularly to offer you my thanks for the portraits of Stephen Crane and Hudson in your book of portraits. I don't know what it is that you are offering in your book—something extremely old and very new. I think the portraits gather up a good deal of your best to say and present it to us in a manner to make us ashamed—if we can still feel any shame. I had much the same feeling from hearing Frobenius lecture last Thursday evening. But you are conscious of a living phase. I don't feel like growing rhapsodic but I do wish to offer thanks for a vigor and a sensitive recognition which has penetrated many taboos to come to its target and which sticks to the living and finds it still alive. It makes certain popular bitternesses seem *nouveau riche*. . . .[7]

Despite the pressure of other work, Ford still found time to write a detective novel called *Vive Le Roy*. He had long admired the economy with which 'mystery' novelists like Simenon planned and executed their books, and presumably he wanted to try his hand in the same medium. Using a somewhat comic-opera situation, not unlike that of his earlier novel, *The New Humpty-Dumpty*, Ford based this book on the possibility of a royalist revolution in France. But since the novel depends essentially on a pun whereby Mr. LeRoy, an agent of the American Communist Party, is mistaken for 'le Roi', it is altogether too unreal to succeed as a serious work or even as a good detective novel. It is, nevertheless, an agreeable and amusing literary lark.

During the same year, Ford was preparing a work which was

designed to amplify what he had already written in *Provence* and *Great Trade Route*. What he intended to write was a three-volumed *History of Our Own Times* from 1870 to 1930. Aware perhaps that the personal and discursive methods used in *Provence* and its sequel had not secured the widespread audience that he felt was due so important a subject, he decided to write a straightforward documentary account. Its purpose was simply to educate, for Ford felt that the events from 1870 onwards had not been dealt with properly either in books or in university courses. What he intended to do was to present not only the subjects dealt with in ordinary histories—diplomacy, politics and war—but to provide some idea of literary and artistic movements as well. The history was to deal in particular with Europe and North America, and the idea of the book was to trace the way in which the centre of civilization had shifted from the Mediterranean, where it had rested for centuries, to those countries bordering the North Atlantic. In short, it was a study of the effects of industrialism on the Western world. The first volume dealt in particular with developments in France and Germany after the Franco-Prussian war, with the Reconstruction period in the United States and with England's creation of an all-powerful industrial empire. This book was also concerned with imperialism in Asia and Africa and with the warlike spirit which resulted in the Boer War, the Spanish-American war, the Russo-Japanese war and the Sino-Japanese war. These Ford merely considered to be conflicts preparatory to World War I. The main figures dealt with were Disraeli and Gladstone, Bismarck, General Grant, Cleveland, Macmahon, Gambetta and Kaiser Wilhelm II, whom Ford looked upon as a precursor of Adolph Hitler.[8]

Of this immense project, only the first volume was ever written: from Ford's description of it, however, it is clear that it was to be a continuation of the attitude taken in *Great Trade Route*. Ford told W. A. Bradley that his book would be essentially documentary, but said that did not mean it would be dull. What he evidently wanted to do was to back up with historical facts the impressions he had rendered in the earlier book. Unfortunately, the first volume of this history was never published because no publisher considered it a commercial possibility, and as a result, the other two volumes were never written.

Arriving in New York at the end of December 1936, Ford was soon back in the literary milieu which had become so familiar to him over the years. He attended various literary luncheons, wrote articles on publishing and cooking for *The Forum*, gave a radio talk on 'The W.P.A. and American Civilization' and gave a course of lectures in Boston.[9] In the spring he went down to Tennessee to stay with the Tates, and there he started his immense *March of Literature*. Consorting with the Tates, he wrote to his Boston publisher, was an exhausting intellectual undertaking. Nevertheless, he did not allow a day to go by without producing his thousand words of prose.[10]

During this stay at 'Benfolly' Ford became involved in the various incidents that finally led to the departure of John Crowe Ransom to Kenyon College in Ohio. When Ransom first received the offer from Kenyon, he hesitated to accept it, and while he delayed, Allen Tate wrote articles to the newspapers to say that it was disgraceful that Vanderbilt and Tennessee should permit a man of Ransom's stature to be taken from their midst. A testimonial dinner was then proposed for Ransom, and Ford was asked to be toastmaster. Dressed in an ancient dinner jacket and white duck trousers bought specially for the occasion, Ford made it plain in the course of his remarks that Ransom should leave, if only to teach Tennessee a lesson, so that in future that state might give proper recognition to her writers. After this, as Mr. Ransom has remarked half-facetiously, he simply had to go to Ohio.[11]

Later on, Ford was asked by Ransom to contribute to the first number of the *Kenyon Review*, and, since he had earlier contributed to the opening issue of the *Southern Review* as well, Ransom's act of courtesy may be taken as a further indication of the esteem in which he was held by Southern writers in general.[12]

Other honours came to him when, in May, he was asked to be the guest speaker at the twenty-fifth anniversary dinner of *Poetry: A Magazine of Verse* in Chicago. The purpose of the celebration was primarily to raise funds, for the founder, Harriet Monroe had died suddenly during the previous year, and the continuance of the magazine was a matter of pressing concern. Ford had had connexions with *Poetry* from its early years, and many of his poems, including the last *Buckshee* sequence, were published in its pages. In his letter of invitation, Morton Dauwen Zabel, the editor, wrote: '*Poetry* is staging the dinner out of its own funds, and hopes to make it festive enough to be productive of the required responses among the guests. For that dinner we would like to have your presence. Your international fame in authorship would be one asset, and another would be your own experience in editing literary periodicals in London and Paris. You would know as few others what *Poetry* means to the literary world today, what honour it has brought to American literature and to Chicago these past twenty-five years, and as the guest speaker of the evening, you would be extremely effective in telling of your own life-work, your editorships, and the place *Poetry* has achieved—and what Chicago's citizens owe it in recognition and support.'[13]

As might be expected, Ford responded to this appeal for the benefit of good letters, and on the twenty-sixth of May he attended the dinner, gave the address of the evening and spoke urgently for the cause. On the following evening he also addressed the Renaissance Society at the University of Chicago, and made that talk a more personal one, relating episodes out of his own long life as an author and editor in London, Paris and New York. It was a strenuous programme for a man of his age, but for literary occasions and causes of this sort, Ford was always willing to do his part.

In the meantime, Allen Tate had been making summer plans with Joseph Brewer, an old acquaintance of Ford's post-war English days. In the early 1920's Brewer, an American, had been a student at Oxford, and when he was later appointed president of a small Michigan college called Olivet, he went there with the intention of introducing the Oxford system of individual tutorials. Another part of his plan was to bring to his college various artists and writers, so that the students might learn a taste for the arts directly from those who were responsible for them. A subsidiary scheme was his idea of establishing a special summer session for imaginative writers to which both established and neophyte authors might come in order to benefit from one another's company and instruction.

When Brewer heard that Ford might be available for this summer conference, he asked both Ford and the Tates to take part in the 1937 session. Ford who was at once attracted by the idea and in need of funds accepted the offer and in July, together with the Tates and Robert Lowell, who was then still an undergraduate, drove out to Michigan.

By now, summer writers' conferences have become commonplace in the United States, but in 1937 they were a novel institution, and that Olivet, a small Congregational college for three hundred students, lost in the depths of the Middle West, should so successfully have pioneered and have gathered to its faculty the distinguished writers it did, is a mark of Mr. Brewer's daring and imagination. As Robie Macaulay has written, Olivet under Brewer's presidency had 'an extraordinary life as a centre of education in the arts,'[15] for in addition to Ford and the Tates, it employed men and women of the calibre of Katherine Anne Porter, Sherwood Anderson, William Troy and Count Korzybski as residential instructors, and engaged writers like Carl Sandburg, Carl Van Vechten and Gertrude Stein to give occasional talks to the students.

At first, Ford delivered public lectures in comparative literature, but since his voice was weak, he changed his plan and instead gave small seminars attended by half a dozen students. In describing Ford's task at Olivet, Mr. Brewer has written: 'His work with students was largely informal and individual although he held, as it were, tea-party seminars once a week during some of the terms. His instruction could never have been termed formal although it was none the less precise and effective.'[16]

One of these students, Robie Macaulay, has described Ford's pedagogical manner:

> Ford's method of teaching was narrative and anecdotal. Almost any question could be answered or any idea presented in the form of a story and he was ill at ease in any more abstract conversation. . . . Usually his stories were not simple illustrations of the point: they contained a great many relative and tangential things. Thus, a student asking a question about drama, might get as an answer a quite involved and probably half-imaginary story about Goethe that seemed to end up a considerable distance from the original question. If he thought about it, however, he would realize that along the way Ford had introduced a dozen relevant ideas and, though he had never given a direct answer, he had given an extraordinarily complete one. After listening to Ford, I always found other teachers something like a human true-and-false test.[17]

Life in Olivet was an unsettling experience for Ford. He lived in what Macaulay described as 'a miniature house not much bigger than a hen coop. He was a large stout man and I was always surprised to see that he actually fitted inside.'[18] His office, moreover, was merely a dusty room in the basement of the college library with bookshelves filled with theological tracts. It was not, however, these personal inconveniences which dismayed him but the total absence of bookshops in the towns round about and the intellectual poverty he found to be characteristic of the Middle West. As a result, he felt completely out of touch with the rest of the world. He wrote his

English publisher that he was so isolated in Michigan that talk of international politics was virtually non-existent. All that occupied the minds of his fellow-citizens was a musical competition that was to take place at Olivet between the brass bands of sixteen Michigan cities.[19]

Yet for all its shortcomings, Olivet certainly did not make Ford unhappy. He was, in fact, so engrossed with his own writing and with his never-ceasing aid to young writers that he had little time to complain of his location.

In the last years of his life Ford found himself spending an increasing amount of time in the encouragement of talented but unrecognized writers. For years he had been a devoted supporter of youth, and the list of those he helped is not only immensely long but contains the names of many of the most prominent writers in contemporary American and British literature. As editor of two reviews, he had had a special opportunity to aid those not yet established, but even then he never stopped at purely editorial assistance, and when, for example, D. H. Lawrence submitted his first novel to a London publisher, the manuscript was accompanied by a laudatory testimonial written by Ford.[20]

Many who appreciated his kindnesses have recorded their debts to him. Richard Aldington, for one, noted that Ford 'took great pains and devoted much time to helping young or poor or neglected writers,'[21] while Herbert Gorman, speaking of the young writers in Paris whom Ford had helped, wrote: 'There are reasons for the paternal place which Ford occupies in their midst. He is, after all, "the good soldier" of literature, the understanding officer who encourages, suggests, and pushes his men forward. He is a man of sensibility, if the word may be used, and he is, in himself, a living example of the literary tradition.'[22] Thus it was, as Lloyd Morris said, that sooner or later every American writer in Paris during the 1920's came into his orbit. 'The nobility of Ford's attitude to his art was touchingly affirmed by his prodigal generosity to younger writers. Himself always beset by an acute need for money, he gave whatever he had, and badgered all his friends into giving; and he was unsparing of his time, effort, assistance and encouragement.'[23]

Ford always looked upon his help to the young simply as a matter of duty. He said that he would rather starve than know that his fellow artists were not doing moderately well, and he made it plain that he would in no way profit from his help to other writers.[24]

Thus whenever Ford heard of a receptive publisher he would write to him suggesting he take on one or other writer for publication. His help to Miss Eudora Welty, who has described what occurred, is typical: 'I never met him,' she writes, 'but Miss Katherine Anne Porter evidently spoke to him in New York about my stories; . . . and then he wrote to me out of a clear sky, overwhelming me with his offer to do his best to help me find a publisher —which, from all one hears of him, is highly characteristic. . . .'[25]

If he could be helpful to those he had never met, he was even more so to those he knew. Faith Compton Mackenzie has written of his 'kindness and troubletaking over a short story of mine which he had read at the Deux Magots one day and sent to N.Y. where it was accepted by a highbrow mag. long before I had shown any sign of producing anything in the way of literature (if I may call it that). It was like him. He was as you know always generous with young authors but I was neither young nor an author!'[26]

Ford did not, of course, confine himself to offering help for publication, and one writer who is grateful to him records that 'he was tireless in his efforts to help young writers. I shall never forget one day that I spent with him at his country place at Guermantes. We spent hours going over some manuscripts I had brought, at his suggestion.'[27] Sometimes in the act of helping young writers Ford made enemies of them for, in the heat of literary discussion, he could be so ruthless in his criticism, that some thought he was gratuitously insulting. Yet more than one writer has said that 'if you could take it' the criticism was of infinite value.[28]

By the time he reached Olivet, Ford's reputation as one who was always willing to help the young had grown to such an extent that literally hundreds of young writers turned to him asking for counsel or aid. Some of the letters written him are especially touching for what they reveal of the conditions young writers have faced in the United States. One of the more interesting of these came from Jean Stafford who wrote from a small college in Missouri asking for a recommendation for a fellowship which would allow her 'to live without the necessity of so many hours a day, etc. of classes and office hours and private lessons for the illiterate debutantes that throng our campus.'

I have finished the novel which you read. I am now working on a diary I kept while I was in Germany last year. I work on my own writing about six hours a day, and my duties as a teacher take up about seven

255

more hours. It is difficult to keep up both. Fortunately I have chosen to neglect the teaching rather than the writing, but I am afraid that next year I'll have most of the spirit taken out of me. I am twenty-two years old and I should hate to chain myself to teaching before I had tested myself fully as a writer.

My main trouble here is that there is no other writer in the town. If there were *one* person to read my stuff and tell me occasionally that I was good and sometimes I approached literature, or even to tell me I was no good at all, I would be almost content. Well, not quite, but it would be better. As it is I get only this: I get a patronizing sort of interest in my work (well, well, our Jean is writing a novel) and then I get the worship of illiterate undergraduates simply because I have a couple of degrees which I probably could have done well without. . . .[29]

To the writer of this letter and to those who wrote like them Ford gave all the assistance he could. If he was not always able to find publishers or secure fellowships for them, he would at the least offer encouragement in letters or hospitality in his own home. His motives as a teacher and assistant of the young were very simple: he worked with others solely out of a love of good letters. Katherine Anne Porter, who never herself became his student, observed this quality in a letter to a friend: 'He . . . has said somewhere, himself, that none of the young people he told how to do things ever went away and did as he told them, which was precisely right . . . but always did their work using his advice as a springboard. . . . He seemed pleased that this was so, and I think it is fair enough. . . .'[30]

Although his experience had long since taught him not to expect gratitude for his kindness, Ford had the pleasure and reward of receiving letters from at least some of those whom he helped. Edward Dahlberg, for example, wrote to thank him for an evening and said: 'I know of no literary man in America who has your goodness, who is what I from young manhood believed an artist to be. My gratitude to you: it is good to have a human being to whom I can offer my little flower.'[31] Graham Greene, who had first met Ford in 1938, later sent him one of his early novels. The letter of encouragement and praise that Ford then wrote meant so much to Greene that he replied in these words:

I can't tell you the pleasure your letter gave me. I have for so long admired you as so incomparably the finest living English novelist that your praise goes to my head. I had thought the book would probably be followed by a tactful silence. . . . I wish I could convey to you the excitement and joy your letter gave me.[32]

The best summary, however, of what Ford meant to young writers came from W. H. Auden who, in 1939, had just come to the United States and been put in touch with Ford. In the course of their correspondence, Auden wrote:

> I was very touched by your wishes at the end of your letter, because few people nowadays have any feeling for a writer's difficulties. It is disheartening to be praised by people who one knows have never read a line of one's work with understanding, but think one can be useful to their cause (which is usually a good cause). . . .
>
> Isherwood (whose novels and stories I hope you know) is also here, and we would both very much like to meet you, whose work we have both admired so much and for so long.[33]

After the conclusion of the Olivet summer session, Ford then decided to move on for a second writers' conference at the University of Colorado in Boulder. Other *litterateurs* like Whit Burnett and Howard Mumford Jones were also in attendance, but Ford was the leading writer present. At this conference one incident occurred that illustrates what Robert Lowell later called Ford's courage and 'abundance' as a literary figure. Scheduled to give a lecture before a large audience, Ford discovered upon entering the theatre that no public address system had been provided. He knew that his weak voice would make him inaudible to most of the audience, but instead of making a scene about the absence of microphones, he began his lecture. Soon the audience became restless: there were shouts of 'Louder!' and then those in the rear of the hall began noisily to leave. Unable to speak louder, Ford simply went on with his lecture, apparently oblivious of the scene before him. Although he was undoubtedly aware that the evening had been a disaster, he afterwards made no comment about it whatever.[34]

In August Ford returned to Olivet where he had been offered a permanent position. The salary was almost insultingly low, but Ford knew that the college could not pay more and he gladly accepted the offer especially as it did not bind him to continuous residence there. Staying on, then, until the late autumn of 1937, Ford worked both on his *March of Literature* and on a new novel. With the coming of the cold winter months, however, he decided to return to France, staying in Paris until the following spring. By this time, Ford's health had begun to deteriorate. His heart was troubling him and he was only able, as he wrote to Gertrude Stein, to move about with difficulty.[35] Returning to Olivet, then, as he did in the spring of

1938, was almost a desperate move, for Michigan was a harsh contrast to the balmy climate of Provence. Although he enjoyed his teaching, Ford was worried about his health, for he was so rheumatic that he couldn't even dress himself or brush his hair. The damp climate of Michigan gave him particular trouble, and he told a friend that he knew he wouldn't get better until he returned to Provence.[36] What prevented his immediate departure for France was, of course, lack of funds. Since his stipend from Olivet covered only current expenses, he was forced to consider the necessity of a lecture tour. He hated lecturing and was fearful of the results on his health of travelling in America during mid-winter, but at the time there seemed to be no alternative. All that gave him comfort was the prospect of finishing his *March of Literature*, which he planned to complete on Bastille Day, 1938.[37]

One pleasant interlude in this otherwise somewhat trying period was the decision of Olivet College to confer upon Ford the honorary degree of Doctor of Letters, an action which touched him considerably since it was the only academic honour he ever received. The ceremony of conferment took place in June of 1938, and a long citation was read which summarized with some exaggeration the activities of his lifetime and stressed his devotion and his spirit of humanity. Ford was very pleased by the gesture, and in writing to a friend, he commented on the splendour of his scarlet robes, saying that it was almost as good as being a Cardinal. The honour cut both ways, however, and Ford concluded his letter with the cautionary remark that if his correspondent ever addressed him as 'Doctor' he would have the Post Office return the letter.[38] In gratitude to Olivet for the honour received, Ford in turn dedicated his *March of Literature* to the two chief officers of the college.

The book itself was finished as promised on the fourteenth of July, and on that date he wrote the dedicatory note which explains its extent and purpose. As a teacher and writer, he had noticed an enormous discrepancy between the number of professors of literature and the number of copies of works of real literature that were sold. His conclusion was, that after leaving the university, few students ever bought a book.

'So it occurred to us . . .' he writes, 'that there must be something wrong with the way in which the attractions of literature and the other arts are presented to our teeming populations. The solution of the problem seemed to us to be that that presentation must be in the wrong hands—that, in fact, such tuition, whether by word of mouth or in books, should be, not in the hands of the learned, but in those of artist-practitioners of the several arts—in the hands, that is to say, of men and women who love each their arts as they practice them. For it is your hot love for your art, not your dry delvings in the dry bones of ana and philologies that will enable you to convey to others your strong passion.' Thus *The March of Literature from Confucius to Modern Times*, to give it its full title, was the 'book of an old man mad about writing—in the sense that Hokusai called himself an old man mad about painting. So it is an attempt to induce a larger and always larger number of my fellows to taste the pleasure that comes from always more and more reading. But that poses on me certain limitations—the first being that, contrary to the habits of the learned, I must write only about the books I have found attractive: because if I lead my reader up to unreadable books I risk giving him a distaste for all literature.'[39]

This immense, eight-hundred page work, the longest single book he ever wrote, was then, the culmination of Ford's literary career. It is his literary testimonial, the outgrowth of all his reading and writing and the fullest statement of his literary credo. Since it is the work of an accomplished novelist, it is also extraordinarily vivid and readable. By avoiding irrelevancies and keeping close to his avowed purpose, Ford makes the ancients as lively and important as the most recent writers whose views fill the Sunday supplements. In Ford's opinion, all good writers were contemporary if you took them seriously, and by connecting the works of the ancients to modern times, Ford makes them all interesting. Like most of Ford's books, *The March of Literature* is very personal—not because of its anecdotes, but because of Ford's own involvement with his subject and the excitement he is able to pass along to the reader.

If a book of this sort is to have some worth, however, it must have standards, and Ford in one short passage explains both his thesis and his standards for judgement.

It should be remembered that in so far as this writer and the reader are united in taste we do what the French call *faire école*. We stand for Homer and the Greek lyricists as against Virgil and the Augustan Romans; for the Middle Ages as against the renaissance; for the seventeenth as against the eighteenth century; for the realists as against the romantics; and, above all, for the conscious literary artist as against the inspired person who, having looked upon the wine when it was red, sets vine leaves in his hair, and seizing a pen, upon paper royal inscribes such stuff as it pleases—or perhaps does not please—God to send him.

That is, perhaps as much as to say that we stand for the Mediterranean as against the Nordic tradition. Nearly all Mediterranean writers and critics acknowledge that if you want to write you should have some —nay, as much as possible—knowledge of the technique of your art. Nearly all Nordic writers and critics contemn the idea.[40]

The writing of this huge book was in itself a tremendous achievement, for almost all of it was written from memory. Quotations were, of course, verified and examples provided for illustration,* but by and large the substance of the book came out of his head.

Since the book depends so much on memory, it is necessary to consider an evaluation of Ford's own power of recall made by Dame Rebecca West:

> I don't think Ford was a great critic, I don't think it was in his power to be so because of his transforming memory which altered everything. A man can hardly say anything valuable about the great works of literature if he cannot remember a single one of them as they were written. I had the fresh memory of youth when I talked with Ford, and I hardly remember a single occasion when he discussed a great book without it presently emerging that he had a totally false impression of its theme or that he had added or subtracted from the author's list of characters. But he was a wonderful editor, and he had a most beautiful sensitiveness to a work of art at the first glance.[41]

It is perfectly true that there are errors of fact in *The March of Literature*, though hardly so many as Miss West's comments suggest there might be, and there are also strange omissions. Thus the Victorian novelists are passed over, and there is no mention of Hölderlin, Kafka or Tchekov. All critics, however, are liable to errors and personal whimsy of this sort; therefore an absolute judgement on Ford as a critic is difficult to make. The best one can do is to balance Rebecca West's comment with a statement by Sir Compton Mackenzie, who wrote: 'When I consider the critical minds with which I have come into contact I find that I have no hesitation in declaring that of the many judgments I have listened

* The American edition of this book, published by the Dial Press, is far from perfect because the publishers cut many of Ford's illustrative passages, thus reducing parts of the book to nonsense. The English edition, however, is far closer to what Ford intended it to be.

to on literature, the least fallible of all were Ford Madox Ford's.'[42] The point to be made about *The March of Literature*, moreover, is that Ford had a definite thesis: he therefore omitted the Victorians because he found them unattractive. His objection, noted in a letter to his publisher, to the title *March* or *History* of literature also indicates that he did not consider the book to be an academically thorough survey of the world's literature.[43]

A number of writers were, moreover, quite consciously omitted or given only summary treatment. Ford's purpose was to attract attention to writers normally neglected in academic histories, and he believed there was no point in emphasizing what was already known. Thus he told his publisher that he was not going to pay much attention to Shakespeare, on the grounds that his work was well enough known already.[44]

Ford's criticism is therefore idiosyncratic and impressionistic: he exaggerates and suppresses and generalizes, but he does so only in order to be suggestive. This quality, indeed, gives the book its particular merit. Thus he draws parallels between Confucius and the Buddha on the one hand, and the late Hebrew writers including the authors of the New Testament, on the other, suggesting a possible influence of the East on Christianity. Thus, too, he makes a vivid comparison between Richardson and Fielding and, from the different approach of each, traces the whole pattern of prose fiction.

Ford assumed that the publication of the book would create a good deal of controversy because of its anti-academic tone, but in fact no violent professorial replies were forthcoming. He was disappointed by the lack of rebuttal, but in a sense, none was possible.[45] The reasons for this are set forth in what was undoubtedly the most understanding review the book received. It was delivered, strangely enough, over the Indian radio in 1940:

> There is a peculiar quality in this book, that might almost be defined as enthusiasm plus conviction plus an almost passionate exposition without however the faintest trace of the didactic. There is a highly individualistic approach but no intolerance, no bigotry. If we could conduct all our discussions on this level many of our modern troubles would disappear. Freedom might be defined as the unconscious admission and acceptance of equality, and in this book one can breathe its rare and stimulating atmosphere. . . .
>
> This is not a book one can summarize; nor can one offer a key; one can only guide others to it. It is in a way the apologia proclaimed

261

cheerfully, defiantly but never arrogantly, of one who sought and preferred always spontaneity and originality. . . .

There is something beautiful in this book despite its preconceptions and passions and inaccuracies, something of the charm and unity that sometimes but so rarely, informs the late work of old men. The word 'humane' he says means something that at once unites and belongs to all races of mankind. I cannot imagine a better or more pleasing definition of the word or a more desirable attribute for men to seek, and Ford himself had attained it.[46]

For most of the summer of 1938 Ford stayed on at Olivet. The task of completing *The March of Literature* had tired him out, but he was still busy. In August he went to Detroit to broadcast on his new book, and almost every day he had to spend hours in correspondence with young writers who wanted to send him their manuscripts.[47] By September, the pressure had grown worse, and he had embarked on a series of lectures organized by his publisher in connexion with the publication of *The March of Literature*. His tour took him to such places as Boston and New York Universities, the Detroit Library, Northwestern and the University of Chicago, and he lectured on a variety of subjects ranging from 'Literary Characters', which was a discussion of some of the famous writers he had known, to French literature and cooking, literary and artistic life in Paris and modern painting.

In October he was in New York to be present for the publication of *The March of Literature*, for which an elaborate publicity campaign had been organized by the Dial Press. There he moved into an apartment at 10 Fifth Avenue and was soon seeing old friends. Edward Dahlberg has described the 'pair of wizened rooms'[48] he took as being furnished with 'three or four secondhand Quartorze chairs, a poor spindly table, the scantest number of books, a jetty sphynxed cat, several of his wife's Biala's paintings of Paris rains . . . all of which was served to you with tea and Sutter's cake. . . .' A number of negligible hangers-on came there to see him, but 'you could also see about him,' as Dalhberg says, 'a gifted face, the poet William Carlos Williams, the rare painter, Marsden Hartley . . . or capture the flittering image of the gentle Brancusi.'[49]

A month after his arrival, Ford received an unexpected honour when he attended a dinner given in November by the New York P.E.N. club for the American Nobel Prize winners, Pearl Buck and Sinclair Lewis. In the course of his remarks, Lewis praised Ford most fulsomely and referred to him as the Dean of American Letters.[50] Ford was so touched that he wrote to thank Lewis for his kindness, to which Lewis in turn replied, saying:

> Any tribute that I have paid you was merely the most plain statement of fact, and if there are people who do not recognize your dukedom in English letters, the joke is on them and not on those of us who have so admired and profited from your books. ....[51]

The claim has been made that, largely because of his financial situation,[52] Ford had, by the end of his life, become extremely left-wing in his political views. The facts, however, do not entirely support this notion. In 1935 he was asked to join the 'left-wing writers of America at a national congress in New York City' but he turned down the request on the basis of his nationality.[53] The real reason for his refusal, however, was simply that he was neither a communist nor a socialist. His own study of politics, especially those of Provence, had made him, if anything, an old-fashioned royalist. Although it is not a main issue, this political attitude certainly appears in his last published novel, *Vive Le Roy*, and it seems to lie behind his request to a French writer that he send an article explaining his royalist views so that Ford could have it published in the United States.[54] Admittedly, Ford was strenuously anti-fascist and had many friends who were leftist in their views, but he saw the weakness of all political alignments even in a period when political action was an intellectual aim and, although he was sympathetic towards the left, he preferred to remain independent and aloof.[55] The most interesting exposition of his own political views appears in his last, and unfinished novel, which was to be called *Professor's Progress* or *Bullen*, after its central character. Although Ford never completed more than a few chapters of this book, he did write a synopsis of it which gives an idea of its intent.[56] The idea of the novel was to show the development of political consciousness amongst educated people who ten years earlier had been wholly indifferent to politics. This change had come about, Ford believed, because of a general concern for deteriorating social conditions in the world.

The hero, Godfrey Bullen, is a young professor who is tolerant of political discussion, but anxious to keep himself independent of party politics. In his earlier academic studies of politics, he had observed that in past political arguments, both sides were usually wrong because both sacrificed accuracy of observation to their momentary enthusiasms. In this way, Bullen is not unlike some of Ford's earlier aloof characters, such as George Moffat in *The Benefactor* and Mr. Blood in the novel entitled *Mr. Fleight*. Soon, however, Bullen is drawn into the whirlpool of political activity: his banking friends are suspicious of his methods of investing money, his wife becomes a Communist and he himself becomes disgusted and enraged by Hitler's treatment of the Jews in Europe and Chamberlain's indifference to their treatment.

Bullen thus finds himself caught in a struggle between his head and his heart, and his previous dispassionate attitude seems no longer tenable. The rest of *Professor's Progress* was to have traced Bullen's undoing and his departure to obscurity and loneliness, a Tietjens redivivus. Yet in the end he is not really unhappy, for having read all of Marx's *Das Capital*, he realizes that Marx's final message is one that suits him perfectly; for it will be remembered that Marx's ultimate goal was a world of quiet anarchy, in which political organizations would cease to exist.[57]

To judge from *Provence* and *Great Trade Route*, the views of Professor Bullen may thus be taken to be roughly those of Ford himself. The habits of a lifetime, not to mention the disillusionment experienced during more than forty years of political observation, could hardly be overthrown by the enthusiasm of a decade. Ford was aware of the problem of political allegiance, but his own solution was to deal with it in human terms in his writing and in his own life to be a one-man political party, to be, that is, himself.

One of his last efforts, as a man of action, was to organize a society which he called 'Friends of William Carlos Williams'. Ford believed that neither the press nor the book trade, nor even the general public, had given Williams the recognition Ford felt he deserved as a poet, and he wanted to redress the balance by gathering together fellow writers who would do him honour.[58] He believed, too, that once the society was formed, it could provide a like service for other unjustly neglected authors. Thus at its monthly meetings, this new 'Académie Goncourt' as Pound called it,[59] also recorded its support of writers like E. E. Cummings and Edward Dahlberg, whose work then wanted recognition. Twelve or fourteen people assembled by Ford would gather for dinner at the Downtown Gallery on Thirteenth Street with Ford and Williams seated at the head of the table. 'Ford would open the proceedings—after the meal would be well under way,' Dr. Williams later observed. 'Someone would recite an original poem. Someone would read another. Then there would be an essay or an article critical in nature on some subject pertinent to the time.'[60] Dr. Williams said that he felt embarrassed by the honour bestowed on him and thought Ford more deserving of it. Edward Dahlberg, in recalling these dinners, remarked: 'I must say a wonderful galaxy of genuine people in the arts attended these affairs. I say this because it could have been a piece of dada nonsense or worse, something for poeticules.'[61] Although the society was short-lived it was yet another instance of Ford's good will and eagerness to help his fellow artists, for he had organized the whole undertaking himself and solicited the members, amongst whom were Sherwood Anderson, Archibald MacLeish, Alfred Stieglitz, Ezra Pound, Marianne Moore, Henry Miller, Katherine Anne Porter and Christopher Isherwood.

Altogether, Ford's last months in New York were extremely busy. He was appointed fiction editor at the Dial Press and put in charge of a series of new works to be brought out under his imprimateur,[62] was recommended as literary editor for the newly reorganized *Saturday Review of Literature*[63] and, finally, planned to revive *The Transatlantic Review* under the aegis of Harper's.[64] But in the end none of these schemes came to much; after five months he broke with the Dial Press, and his own death in 1939 prevented the rebirth of the *Transatlantic*.

The pressure of all these undertakings was hard on his health, however, and his friend, William Carlos Williams, himself a physician, realized how weak he had become and that he 'was really at that time, a sick man—gasping often for breath on mild exertion—though he'd never if possible let you know it. One night, trying to get into a taxi, I thought his end had come.'[65]

His financial situation also remained precarious: the sales of *The March of Literature* were disappointing and he could find no publisher willing to take the completed first volume of his *History of Our Own Times*. He was thus forced to start *Professor's Progress*. Yet even here he encountered difficulty in finding someone who would give him an advance against royalties.[66] His dismal sales record over the years cost him much peace of mind and physical comfort. In the previous six years, for example, he had had five different publishers in the United States, and as a consequence had no one 'regular' publisher who could be counted on to take what he wrote as a matter of course. He therefore had to shop round like a beginner; indeed, in some ways his position was worse than that of a beginner since it was well known that his books rarely covered his advances.

The truth is that Ford's last years were grim. Unable to pay more than $65 for a small apartment in New York, he didn't even have any rich acquaintances who could come to his aid, most of his friends being impoverished poets and painters. He thus tried to make ends meet by writing magazine articles, a task he found increasingly difficult in his old age. In purely literary circles there were difficulties of another sort, for although his writings were respected in a vague way, they excited little interest. As Edward Dahlberg said: 'Ford had very little money, and I can say that I heard of no one who spoke of his books at all, saying that they were either good or ill. I never heard anybody mention the Tietjens books. I must freely own that I had never read them myself. It is a hard statement for me to make since I loved Ford, and never tried to exploit his outrageously generous heart. . . .

'Like Sherwood Anderson at that period Ford was a fabulous name in literature, but a forsaken one. I never even recollect that Anderson ever referred to a single book that Ford had written. Despite Ford's long essay on Dreiser in *Portraits from Life*, Dreiser never once spoke to me of any book by Ford.'[67]

Gratitude is a perplexing quality, but as far as Ford is concerned, and in spite of the statements of thanks printed earlier in this chapter, most of those who received his help ultimately turned against him or, at the least, made no effort to express their indebtedness to him. As early as 1932, Katherine Anne Porter had commented on this phenomenon: 'I have myself noticed for some time,' she wrote, 'that Ford has a special genius for nourishing vipers in his bosom, and I have never seen an essay or article about him signed by any of these discoveries of his. I can make nothing of this, except that I have learned that most human beings—and I suppose artists are that, after all—suffer some blow to their self-esteem in being helped, and develop the canker of ingratitude. As if, somehow, they can, by denying their debt, or ignoring it, wipe it out altogether. . . . If I could really understand this warp in most human minds, or hearts, I should be God, I suppose. . . .'[68]

What made this neglect worse, moreover, was Ford's failure ever wholly to overcome the collapse of his New York reputation. The young hopefuls who sent him manuscripts in Michigan knew little or nothing of that fiasco of 1929, but amongst the literary cliques of

New York, as Mr. Dahlberg notes, 'People either said he was fat or always lied.'[69] As has already been noted, these 'lies' were usually either naïve little boasts or simple fantasies, by means of which he made his poverty and neglect bearable. Sherwood Anderson has recounted Ford's tendency to invite people to be guests of his at a great southern manor which did not exist.[70] In many ways Ford was like Don Quixote. Yet many of those who listened to Ford's fantastic stories, having at first believed them literally, were furious when they found out they were not true. What people hate most of all is to be taken in, and many literal-minded people resented and hated Ford for having 'duped' them, even though there was rarely if ever any malice in his stories.

By February of 1939, then, Ford's financial situation had become so desperate that he had to ask his English publisher for a loan of £250. It is to Sir Stanley Unwin's credit that he agreed to this loan at a time when he probably realized it could never be repaid, for the money not only relieved Ford's most pressing burdens, but also gave him the opportunity to return to France, which he had longed to do ever since he had experienced the harsh climate of Michigan. After a brief lecture tour which took him to the Carolinas, and after toying with the idea of after all staying the summer in Virginia, Ford left in May for France on the *Normandie*. His intention was to stay in the neighbourhood of Havre until October, because his doctor had told him that his health required nothing but French cooking.[71] On board ship, however, he became seriously ill, and after arrival in France was unable to proceed further than Honfleur before becoming desperately ill from uraemia. Taken then to the Clinique St. François at Deauville, he seemed to be recovering from his illness when suddenly, late on the Friday afternoon of 26 June 1939, his heart failed and he died. He had been in the hospital for only two days before he died, and it is agreeable to know, in the words of one who saw the place, that it was 'the most pleasant hospital I have ever seen . . . run by the most charming and devoted nuns.'

After a requiem mass on the following Wednesday, July 1st, Ford was buried at the age of sixty-five at Deauville, in a cemetery behind the city and overlooking the sea. Only two people were in attendance, one of them his English friend, Edward Crankshaw.

Such an end, lacking all the pomp and grandeur of the funerals ordinarily given men of note and distinction, may be considered merely as the last and most dismal episode in a life that seemed ill-starred from the beginning. It may appear pathetic and sad and thus a reflection of both the life and career of a man who, in Pound's phrase, 'took in his time more punishment of one sort and another than I have seen meted to anyone else.'[72] In a superficial sense, this interpretation is just, and the brief and generally contemptuous obituaries given him appear to fortify it, but for all his misfortunes, Ford had a happy life and had in the end found a way of living that suited him.

On the occasion of Conrad's death in 1924, Ford wrote a brief memoir for a French journal, in the course of which he touched on the very essence of the artistic life:

> My dear, our profession is truly a dog's trade. You will write and write, but no one in the whole world will understand either what you mean or what it has cost you in pain, blood and sweat. And at the end, you will say to yourself: it's as though I have spent all of my life on a boat in the middle of an immense river, enclosed by impenetrable fog. For although you will row and row, you will never see anything on the river bank that will let you know whether you are going upstream or whether you are being carried along by the current. And all the time you will know fasting and cold nights for lack of covers, bitter viands and sleep tormented by regrets.[73]

These words, ostensibly spoken by Conrad, in fact clearly derive from Ford's own experience. They are the words of a man who has given over his life entirely to his art, and who has known both the inner loneliness of his profession and the public notoriety that also, half-comprehendingly, accompanies an author's career. Naturally enough, Ford did not attain this degree of understanding overnight. As a young man he had been unenthusiastic about the arts, and when he finally took up writing, as it were for lack of anything better, he did so half-heartedly. Only when he really became involved, as he did with Conrad and The English Review, did he begin to take it seriously; and with that seriousness came the lesson inscribed above. Yet in retrospect the experience of being buffeted about and of going down, like his creature Tietjens, seems to have been necessary before books like The Good Soldier and Parade's End could be written. At any rate, once he was committed to literature, he devoted all of his life to it. Once that decision was made, everything else, from The Transatlantic Review to a small house in Provence and even Olivet College, was somehow inevitable. And in the process, he became the last really rounded man of letters our century has known.

Yet even with this devotion, there remained the final gnawing doubt, which is also expressed in his obituary notice of Conrad:

And never, never in your entire life, will you know a single soul who will be able to tell you whether in the end you are the greatest genius in the world . . . or whether you are merely the latest and most vile imitation of . . . Ponson du Terrail.*[74]

Up to the end, this was the doubt that assailed Ford most strongly. It is, of course, a doubt that worries all artists, but despite the personae he sometimes adopted to give himself courage, Ford was never really confident that he had become the genius his Pre-Raphaelite forebears had commanded him to be. At the end of his life, he therefore turned increasingly to life itself, not for solace only but to discover, after scraping away the inessentials of modern civilization, a way of living that made life an end in itself. In his last years he celebrated his discovery in books like *Great Trade Route* and *Provence*.

Sherwood Anderson, a man similar in many ways to Ford, recognized that by the end of his life Ford had found a measure of serenity:

Ford Madox Ford was a rich man. He was rich in a way in which we would all secretly like to be rich. He was rich in good work done, in self-respect. He didn't go about in an over-commercialized world being half apologetic because he was the very type of the artist man.

He was a sophisticate. He had seen the wheels go around, knew something about how they turned, a man who had seen life closely in many places, in many kinds of people, a fellow of ours who knew truth from nonsense. The man was equipped with a full-bodied imagination and knew how to use it. He never used it to hurt anyone. He used it to give joy. The man and his name are both now part of a fine tradition. It is an old tradition. He knew what it was. He kept the faith. I take it as an honor to myself that I am asked to say these few words in honor of such a man.[75]

Thus his death and quiet funeral in Deauville was somehow the only appropriate end for Ford. A true man of letters, he died with a contract for a new book on his desk and with some two hundred manuscripts by young writers in his hotel room. His ghost might

---

* This and the preceding passage were originally written in French, and have been translated freely by the writer. Ponson du Terrail was a nineteenth-century hack novelist. The original French text may be found in the appendix of Ford's *Joseph Conrad: A Personal Remembrance*.

have enjoyed a full-dress requiem mass at Westminster Cathedral, but it would also have recognized it as a sham. As to the question of his genius, time alone will determine whether his work will last. At the moment, all one can say is that while the bulk of his work is certainly uneven, it contains books that now seem certain to endure.

BIBLIOGRAPHY

The recent publication of David Dow Harvey's massive bibliography, *Ford Madox Ford, 1873–1939*, Princeton, 1962, happily eliminates the necessity of a full bibliography here. For the convenience of the reader who may, and hopefully will, want to read various of Ford's books, I append here Mr. Harvey's short list of Ford's publications.

CHRONOLOGICAL LIST OF FORD'S BOOKS (INCLUDING COLLABORATIONS AND FORD'S OWN TRANSLATIONS)

Date given is actual year of publication, not necessarily year on title-page.

1891. *The Brown Owl*. Children's fairy-tale.
1892. *The Feather*. Children's fairy-tale.
1892. *The Shifting of the Fire*. Novel.
1893. *The Questions at the Well* [pseud. 'Fenil Haig']. Poems.
1894. *The Queen Who Flew*. Children's fairy-tale.
1896. *Ford Madox Brown*. Biography.
1900. *Poems for Pictures*. Poems.
1900. *The Cinque Ports*. 'A Historical and Descriptive Record' (half-title) of Kent and Sussex port towns.
1901. *The Inheritors*. Novel, written in collaboration with Joseph Conrad.
1902. *Rossetti*. Art criticism and biography.
1903. *Romance*. Novel (historical adventure story), written in collaboration with Joseph Conrad.
1904. *The Face of the Night*. Poems.
1905. *The Soul of London*. Sociological impressionism.
1905. *The Benefactor*. Novel.
1905. *Hans Holbein*. Art criticism.
1906. *The Fifth Queen*. Novel (historical romance; first of the 'Katherine Howard' trilogy).
1906. *The Heart of the Country*. Sociological impressionism.
1906. *Christina's Fairy Book*. Children's fairy-tales.
1907. *Privy Seal*. Novel (historical romance; second of the 'Katherine Howard' trilogy).

271

1907. *England and the English.* Sociological impressionism; published only in America; composed of the previously published *The Soul of London* and *The Heart of the Country* plus *The Spirit of the People.*

1907. *From Inland.* Poems.

1907. *An English Girl.* Novel.

1907. *The Pre-Raphaelite Brotherhood.* Art criticism.

1907. *The Spirit of the People.* Sociological impressionism; previously published, only in America, in *England and the English.*

1908. *The Fifth Queen Crowned.* Novel (historical romance; third of the 'Katherine Howard' trilogy).

1908. *Mr. Apollo.* Novel.

1909. *The 'Half Moon'.* Novel (historical romance).

1910. *A Call.* Novel.

1910. *Songs from London.* Poems.

1910. *The Portrait.* Novel (historical romance).

1911. *The Simple Life Limited* [pseud. 'Daniel Chaucer']. Novel (satire).

1911. *Ancient Lights.* Reminiscences; published in America in 1911 as *Memories and Impressions.*

1911. *Ladies Whose Bright Eyes.* Novel (historical fantasy).

1911. *The Critical Attitude.* Essays in literary criticism.

1912. *High Germany.* Poems.

1912. *The Panel.* Novel (farce).

1912. *The New Humpty-Dumpty* [pseud. 'Daniel Chaucer']. Novel (satire).

[1913] *This Monstrous Regiment of Women.* Suffragette pamphlet.

1913. *Mr. Fleight.* Novel (satire).

1913. *The Desirable Alien.* Impressions of Germany, written in collaboration with Violet Hunt.

1913. *The Young Lovell.* Novel (historical romance).

1913. *Ring for Nancy.* Novel (farce; adaptation of *The Panel*; published only in America).

1913. *Collected Poems.*

1914. *Henry James.* Critical essay.

1915. *Antwerp.* Long poem (pamphlet).

1915. *The Good Soldier.* Novel.

1915. *When Blood is Their Argument.* War propaganda (anti-Prussian essays).

1915. *Between St. Dennis and St. George.* War propaganda (pro-French and anti-Prussian essays).

1915. *Zeppelin Nights.* Historical sketches (told Decameron-fashion against the background of the War), written in collaboration with Violet Hunt.

1917. *The Trail of the Barbarians.* Translation of the war pamphlet, *L'Outrage des Barbares* by Pierre Loti.

1918. *On Heaven.* Poems.

1921. *A House.* Long poem (pamphlet).

1921. *Thus to Revisit.* Literary criticism and reminiscence.

1923. *The Marsden Case.* Novel.

1923. *Women and Men.* Essays.

1923. *Mister Bosphorus and the Muses.* Long narrative and dramatic poem.

1924. *Some Do Not.* Novel (first of the 'Tietjens' tetralogy).

1924. *The Nature of a Crime.* Novella, written in collaboration with Joseph Conrad; previously published in 1909 in *English Review.*

1924. *Joseph Conrad: A Personal Remembrance.* Biography, reminiscence, and criticism.

1925. *No More Parades.* Novel (second of the 'Tietjens' tetralogy).

1926. *A Mirror to France.* Sociological impressionism.

1926. *A Man Could Stand Up.* Novel (third of the 'Tietjens' tetralogy).

1927. *New Poems.*

1927. *New York is not America.* Essays in sociological atmospheres.

1927. *New York Essays.*

1928. *The Last Post.* Novel (last novel of the 'Tietjens' tetralogy; titled *Last Post* in England).

1928. *A Little Less Than Gods.* Novel (historical romance).

[1928. *Perversity.* Translation of a novel by Francis Carco; possibly not by Ford.]

1929. *The English Novel.* Essay in literary criticism and history.

1929. *No Enemy.* Disguised autobiography (concerning the war years; written shortly after the war).

1931. *Return to Yesterday.* Reminiscences (up to 1914).

1931. *When the Wicked Man.* Novel.

1933. *The Rash Act.* Novel.

1933. *It Was the Nightingale.* Autobiography and reminiscences (from 1918).

1934. *Henry for Hugh.* Novel.

1935. *Provence.* Impressions of France and England.

1936. *Vive le Roy.* 'Mystery' novel.

1936. *Collected Poems.*

1937. *Great Trade Route.* Impressions of France, the United States and England.

1937. *Portraits from Life.* Essays in personal reminiscence and literary criticism about ten *prosateurs* and one poet; published in England in 1938 as *Mightier than the Sword.*

1938.   *The March of Literature*. Survey of literature 'From Confucius to Modern Times'.

Note: Most of Ford's books are no longer in print, although in recent years several of his major novels have been republished in both the United States and Great Britain. Alfred Knopf, the New York publisher, has reissued *The Good Soldier* and *Parade's End*, which is a one-volume edition of the Tietjens tetralogy, and the Vanguard Press has brought out *The Fifth Queen*, a one-volume edition of that early trilogy. In England, four volumes of *The Bodley Head Ford Madox Ford* have been published under the editorship of Graham Greene. These include *The Good Soldier*, *The Fifth Queen* trilogy, a selection of poems and reminiscences, and the first three volumes of the Tietjens series.

Some original editions of Ford's works are also still in print, notably several of his last works published in London by George Allen and Unwin Ltd. In the United States, the Regnery Company has reissued *Portraits from Life*, and the University of Nebraska Press an edition of Ford's critical writings edited by myself.

NOTES

CHAPTER ONE: BROWNS AND HUEFFERS

[1] Johann Hermann Hueffer, *Erlebtes*, Münster (privately printed), 1854.
[2] Ford Madox Hueffer, *Ancient Lights and Certain New Reflections*, London, 1911, pp. 42–43.
[3] Ernest Sieper, ed., *Hermann Hueffer, Reminiscences*, Berlin, 1912. The quotation used was provided by Mr. M. S. Wilde, a distant cousin of Ford's, who also translated the passage from the German.
[4] William Michael Rossetti, *Some Reminiscences*, London, 1906, pp. 332–3.
[5] Limerick by Dante Gabriel Rossetti quoted in *Ancient Lights*, p. 44.
[6] *Ancient Lights*, p. 92.
[7] Ford Madox Ford, *Mightier than the Sword*, London, 1938, pp. 241–3.
[8] Mrs. Helen Rossetti Angeli to the writer, 23 February 1955.
[9] Ford Madox Ford, *It Was the Nightingale*, London, 1934, p. 121.
[10] *Ancient Lights*, pp. 41–42.
[11] Juliet Soskice, *Chapters from Childhood*, London, 1921, p. 201.
[12] *Ancient Lights*, p. 70.
[13] Ford Madox Ford, *Great Trade Route*, London, 1937, p. 19.
[14] R. T. Skinner, 'Oliver Madox Hueffer', *The Scotsman*, 27 June 1931.
[15] Talk with Dame Rebecca West, November 1953.
[16] Stephen Haweis to the writer, 22 August 1954.
[17] *Ancient Lights*, p. viii.
[18] *Ancient Lights*, pp. 76–78.
[19] *Ancient Lights*, pp. 51–52.
[20] *Ancient Lights*, p. 101.
[21] Helen Rossetti Angeli, *Pre-Raphaelite Twilight*, London, 1954, p. 145.
[22] *Ancient Lights*, p. 102.
[23] *Ancient Lights*, p. 102.
[24] Ford Madox Ford, *Return to Yesterday*, London, 1931, p. 113.
[25] Juliet Soskice, *Chapters from Childhood*, pp. 235–6.
[26] *Ancient Lights*, p. 156.
[27] *Ancient Lights*, p. 222.
[28] *Ancient Lights*, pp. 197–8.

CHAPTER TWO: MARRIAGE

[1] Ford Madox Hueffer, *Ancient Lights*, London, 1911, p. 120.
[2] *Ancient Lights*, pp. 267–8.
[3] *Ancient Lights*, p. 242.
[4] *Ancient Lights*, p. 242.
[5] Ford Madox Ford, *Collected Poems*, New York, 1936, p. 289.
[6] *Collected Poems*, p. 217.
[7] *Ancient Lights*, p. 175.

[8] *Return to Yesterday*, p. 141.
[9] *Ancient Lights*, pp. 154–5.
[10] *Return to Yesterday*, p. 152.
[11] *Return to Yesterday*, p. 154.
[12] *Return to Yesterday*, p. 154.
[13] Letter to Walter Jerrold, n.d. (1896). Quoted in Douglas Goldring, *The Last Pre-Raphaelite*, London, 1948, p. 262.
[14] David Garnett, *The Golden Echo*, London, 1953, p. 36.
[15] *Return to Yesterday*, p. 33.
[16] *Ancient Lights*, p. 227.
[17] Letter from Joseph Conrad to Ford Madox Hueffer, 29 September 1898.
[18] Letter from Conrad, 2 October 1898.
[19] Letter from Conrad, 6 October 1898.

CHAPTER THREE: CONRAD COLLABORATION

[1] Letter from Conrad, 6 October 1898.
[2] Letter from Conrad to W. E. Henley, 18 October 1898.
[3] Letter from H. G. Wells to Joseph Conrad, n.d. (May 1896). Quoted in G. Jean-Aubry, *Twenty Letters to Joseph Conrad*, London, 1926.
[4] Ford Madox Ford, *Joseph Conrad, A Personal Remembrance*, London, 1924, p. 36.
[5] *Joseph Conrad*, pp. 239–40.
[6] H. G. Wells, *Experiment in Autobiography*, Vol. II, London, 1934, p. 615.
[7] Henry James, *The Wings of the Dove*, New York, 1902, pp. 54–55.
[8] Letter from Conrad, November 1898.
[9] Letter from Conrad, 17 November 1898.
[10] *Joseph Conrad*, p. 23.
[11] Letter from Conrad, 23 November 1899.
[12] Letter from Conrad, November 1899.
[13] Letter from Ford to Walter Jerrold, 17 March 1900. Quoted in Goldring, p. 85.
[14] Letter from Conrad, 17 February 1900.
[15] Telegram from Conrad, 26 March 1900; letter 31 March 1900.
[16] Letter from Conrad, n.d.
[17] Letter from Conrad, 19 July 1901.
[18] Letter from Conrad to Edward Garnett, 26 March 1900. Edward Garnett, ed., *Letters from Conrad (1895–1924)*, London, 1928, p. 169.
[19] Letter from Conrad, November 1899.
[20] Letters from Conrad to Mrs. Ford Madox Hueffer, mostly undated.
[21] Jessie Conrad, *Joseph Conrad and His Circle*, London, 1935, p. 66.
[22] Letter from Conrad, n.d.
[23] Letter from Conrad, n.d.
[24] Letter from Conrad, 28 April 1901.
[25] Letter from Conrad to John Galsworthy, 30 November 1903. G. Jean-Aubry, *Joseph Conrad, Life and Letters*, London, 1927. Vol. I, p. 322.
[26] Letter from Conrad, November 1899.
[27] David Garnett, *The Golden Echo*, pp. 36–37, 63
[28] *Joseph Conrad*, p. 132.
[29] Letter from Conrad to the Editor, *New York Times Saturday Review*, 24 August 1901, p. 603.
[30] Ford Madox Ford, 'Working with Conrad', *Yale Review*, XVIII, No. 4, June 1929, p. 713. Facsimile of inscription in Mr. George Keating's copy.
[31] Thomas J. Wise, *A Conrad Library*, London, 1928, p. 6.
[32] *Joseph Conrad*, pp. 135–9.

[33] Letter from Conrad to *New York Times Saturday Review*, 24 August 1901, p. 603.
[34] George T. Keating, *A Conrad Memorial Library*, New York, 1929, p. 133.
[35] *Joseph Conrad*, pp. 204-5.
[36] Letter from Conrad, n.d.
[37] *Joseph Conrad*, p. 210.
[38] Letter from Conrad, 1902. G. Jean-Aubry, *Joseph Conrad*, Vol. I, p. 312.
[39] G. Jean-Aubry, *Joseph Conrad*, Vol. I, p. 168. *Note* (Conrad's inscription of T. J. Wise's copy of *Romance*, 1923).
[40] Letter from Conrad, n.d.
[41] Letter from Conrad, n.d.
[42] Letter from Conrad, September 1903. Quoted in G. Jean-Aubry, *Joseph Conrad*, Vol. I, pp. 318-19.
[43] Anon. (Actually Ford) '*Romance*, an Analysis', *The Transatlantic Review*, Vol. I, No. 2, February 1924, Paris, p. 84.
[44] Letter from Conrad, 30 August 1915. G. Jean-Aubry, *Joseph Conrad*, Vol. II, p. 169.
[45] Joseph Conrad and Ford Madox Hueffer, *The Nature of a Crime*, London, 1924. Appendix, pp. 115-16.
[46] Letter from Conrad to Ford as editor, *The Transatlantic Review*, Vol. I, No. 1, p. 99, January 1924.
[47] Letter from Conrad, n.d.
[48] Letter from Conrad, 15 April 1902.
[49] Conrad to H. G. Wells, 20 October 1905. G. Jean-Aubry, *Joseph Conrad*, Vol. II, p. 25.
[50] Ford Madox Hueffer, *The Cinque Ports*, Edinburgh, 1900, p. 163.
[51] Joseph Conrad, *Some Reminiscences* (the original title for the book), London, 1912, p. 7.
[52] Letter from Conrad, n.d.
[53] Pages 145-54 of the 1904 edition of *Nostromo*, Part II, Chapter 5 from the 12th paragraph onwards are, or appear to be, by Ford. Manuscript in Ford's handwriting in the Keating Collection, Rare Book Room, Yale University Library. The Manuscript was presented to Keating by Conrad.
[54] Letter from Conrad, 19 July 1904.
[55] Joseph Conrad, *The Sisters*, New York, 1928. Introduction by Ford Madox Ford, pp. 9-10.
[56] H. G. Wells, *Experiment in Autobiography*, Vol. II, p. 622.
[57] Conrad to Edward Garnett, 10 June 1902. E. Garnett, ed., *Letters from Conrad*, p. 180.
[58] Conrad to K. Waliszewski. Letter quoted in Jocelyn Baines, *Joseph Conrad, A Critical Biography*, London, 1959, p. 275.
[59] *Joseph Conrad*, pp. 198-9.
[60] 'Working with Conrad', *Yale Review*, p. 702.
[61] Ford to Herbert Read, 19 September 1920. Quoted in Herbert Read, *Annals of Innocence and Experience*, London, 1940, pp. 198-9.
[62] *Return to Yesterday*, London, 1931, p. 205.

CHAPTER FOUR: ESTABLISHED IN LONDON

[1] H. G. Wells, *Experiment in Autobiography*, Vol. II, p. 617.
[2] Ford to Wells, 1904. (University of Illinois Library.)
[3] William Michael Rossetti to Elsie Hueffer, 22 October 1904. Quoted in Goldring, p. 128.
[4] Letter from Conrad, 'Monday evening' (n.d.—1902).
[5] *Return to Yesterday*, London, 1931, p. 275.

[6] *Return to Yesterday*, p. 300.

[7] Letter from Conrad, 5 September 1904.

[8] Ford to Walter Jerrold, n.d. (1904). Quoted in Goldring, p. 131.

[9] Edward Garnett to John Galsworthy, 8 May 1905. Edward Garnett, ed., *Letters from John Galsworthy 1900–1932*, London, 1934, p. 59.

[10] Ford to Walter Jerrold, 1905. Quoted in Goldring, p. 131.

[11] *Return to Yesterday*, p. 236.

[12] *Return to Yesterday*, p. 236.

[13] *Return to Yesterday*, p. 347.

[14] Ford to John Galsworthy, n.d. (1900–1901) in H. V. Marrot, *The Life and Letters of John Galsworthy*, London, 1935, p. 123.

[15] Ford to H. G. Wells, dated by Wells as May 1905.

[16] Ford to H. G. Wells, dated by Wells as 1903. Quoted in Frank MacShane, 'Ford Madox Ford and his Contemporaries', *English Fiction in Transition*, IV, 1 January 1961, p. 7.

[17] Ford to Edward Garnett, dated by Garnett as 1901–4. Quoted in Frank MacShane, 'The English Review', *South Atlantic Quarterly*, LX, 3, Summer 1961, p. 312.

[18] Ford to R. A. Scott-James, 1906. R. A. Scott-James, 'Ford Madox Ford when he was Hueffer', *South Atlantic Quarterly*, LVII, Spring 1958, p. 239.

[19] Ford Madox Hueffer, *The Soul of London*, London, 1905, pp. xi–xii.

[20] Ford Madox Hueffer, *The Spirit of the People*, London, 1907, p. 67 (note).

[21] Ford Madox Hueffer, 'On Impressionism I', *Poetry and Drama*, II, 2 June 1914, p. 171.

[22] Ford Madox Ford, *A Little Less than Gods*, London, 1928, Introduction, pp. vii–viii.

[23] Conrad to John Galsworthy, 20 February 1908. G. Jean-Aubry, *Joseph Conrad Life and Letters*, Vol. II, p. 67.

[24] Notation on letter from Andrew Melrose to J. B. Pinker, 1909.

[25] This information has been supplied by John Lane, The Bodley Head Ltd., William Heinemann Ltd., Chapman and Hall, Ltd., Victor Gollancz, Ltd., William Blackwood and Sons Ltd., Penguin Books Ltd., Constable and Company Ltd., Martin Secker and Warburg, Ltd., Longmans, Green and Company Ltd., Hodder and Stoughton, Ltd., George Allen and Unwin, Ltd., Chatto and Windus, Ltd., Little, Brown and Company, Bobbs-Merrill Company, Inc., Alfred A. Knopf, Inc., Houghton Mifflin Company, J. B. Lippincott Company, Harper and Brothers, Doubleday and Company, Inc., and Oxford University Press, Inc.

[26] Letter from Brandt and Brandt to Eric Pinker, 12 May 1923. The letter concerns *The Marsden Case* which by that date had been rejected by seven of the leading New York publishers; it was never issued in America.

[27] Ford to J. B. Pinker, letter dated 1914. Quoted in Paul Alexander Bartlett, 'Letters of Ford Madox Ford', *Saturday Review of Literature* (N.Y.), XXIV, 15, 2 August 1941, p. 4.

[28] Correspondence between Constable and Company and Pinker.

[29] Letter from Hutchinson and Co. to J. B. Pinker, 13 September 1909.

[30] Ezra Pound, 'Ford Madox (Hueffer) Ford; Obit.', *Nineteenth Century and After*, CXXVI, 750, August 1939, p. 181.

[31] Ezra Pound, *Pavannes and Divisions*, New York, 1918, p. 131.

[32] Violet Hunt, *The Flurried Years*, London, n.d. (1926), p. 244.

[33] Pound exaggerates. Ezra Pound to W. H. D. Rouse. Letter 30 October 1937, D. D. Paige, ed., *The Letters of Ezra Pound*, New York, 1950, p. 297.

[34] Ford Madox Hueffer, *The Benefactor*, London, 1905, p. 214.

[35] Letter from Conrad, 14 October 1907.

CHAPTER FIVE: *THE ENGLISH REVIEW*

[1] Ford to Mrs. H. G. Wells, 29 January 1909.
[2] Letter from Conrad, 1924. Quoted in *The Translantic Review*, I, 1, January 1924, p. 98.
[3] Horace Shipp, ed., *The English Review Book of Short Stories*, London, n.d. Introduction by Ford Madox Ford, p. vii.
[4] Ford Madox Ford, *Mightier than the Sword*, London, 1938, pp. 100-3.
[5] Ibid., pp. 98-9.
[6] Hunt, *The Flurried Years*, p. 47.
[7] D. H. Lawrence, *Phoenix*, London, 1936, p. 253.
[8] *Return to Yesterday*, London, 1931, p. 408.
[9] Norman Douglas, *Late Harvest*, London, 1947, p. 45.
[10] Wyndham Lewis, *Rude Assignment*, London, 1947, p. 122.
[11] H. M. Tomlinson to the writer, 28 September 1954.
[12] Violet Hunt, *I Have This to Say*, New York, 1926, p. 56.
[13] Ford to Edward Garnett, 17 October 1908. Quoted in 'The English Review', *South Atlantic Quarterly*, p. 317.
[14] Sir Compton Mackenzie, *Literature in My Time*, London, 1933, p. 182.
[15] D. H. Lawrence to Edward Garnett, 11 June 1913. Quoted in Aldous Huxley, ed., *The Letters of D. H. Lawrence*, London, 1932, p. 125.
[16] Frank Swinnerton, *The Georgian Literary Scene*, London, 1950, p. 195.
[17] Ezra Pound to Michael Roberts, July 1937. Quoted in D. D. Paige, ed., *The Letters of Ezra Pound*, p. 296.
[18] Wyndham Lewis, *Rude Assignment*, p. 122.
[19] Edgar Jepson, *Memories of an Edwardian*, London, 1937, p. 149.
[20] Richard Aldington to the writer, 17 May 1954. Mr. Aldington agreed that Ford was probably right in this suspicion. 'They run vendettas . . .' he adds.
[21] Ford to Mrs. H. G. Wells, 29 January 1909.
[22] Conrad to Edward Garnett, 19 July 1909. E. Garnett, ed., *Letters from Conrad*, p. 232.
[23] Ford to George T. Keating, n.d.
[24] Joseph Conrad, *Some Reminiscences*, p. 7.
[25] Conrad to J. B. Pinker, dated July 1909 by Jocelyn Baines and quoted in his *Joseph Conrad, A Critical Biography*, pp. 350-1.
[26] Richard Aldington to the writer, 17 May 1954.
[27] Wyndham Lewis, *Rude Assignment*, p. 122.
[28] H. E. Bates, *Edward Garnett*, London, 1950, p. 32.
[29] Violet Hunt, *I Have This to Say*, p. 38.
[30] H. E. Bates, *Edward Garnett*, pp. 32-33.
[31] David Garnett, *The Golden Echo*, pp. 129-30.
[32] Violet Hunt, *I Have This to Say*, p. 60.
[33] David Garnett, *The Golden Echo*, p. 128.
[34] H. G. Wells to G. K. Chesterton (n.d., 1915). Quoted in Maisie Ward, *Gilbert Keith Chesterton*, London, 1944, p. 351.
[35] Quoted in John Berryman, *Stephen Crane*, New York, 1950, p. 251.
[36] D. H. Lawrence to Violet Hunt. Quoted in *The Flurried Years*, p. 158.
[37] Richard Aldington to the writer, 17 May 1954.
[38] E. O. Thomas (Ford's secretary) to H. G. Wells, 31 March 1909.
[39] *Return to Yesterday*, pp. 411-12.
[40] 'Jacob Tonson' (Arnold Bennett), 'Books and Persons', *The New Age*, VII, 13, 27 January 1910, p. 305.

[41] Ford to Violet Hunt. Quoted in *The Flurried Years*, p. 147.
[42] Violet Hunt, *The Flurried Years*, pp. 212–13.

CHAPTER SIX: POET AND NOVELIST

[1] Ford Madox Hueffer, *Henry James, A Critical Study*, London, 1913, p. 9.
[2] Henry James to Archibald Marshall. Letter quoted in Archibald Marshall, *Out and About*, London, 1933, pp. 273–4.
[3] Ford to Lucy Masterman, 23 January 1912. Quoted in Frank MacShane, ed., *Critical Writings of Ford Madox Ford*, Lincoln, Nebraska, 1964, p. 154.
[4] Ford Madox Ford, 'Notes for a Lecture on Vers Libre', manuscript, 23 June 1927, p. 5b. Quoted in *Critical Writings*, p. 157.
[5] 'Notes for a Lecture on Vers Libre', p. 10. Quoted in *Critical Writings*, p. 161.
[6] *Collected Poems*, New York, 1936, p. 132.
[7] *Collected Poems*, p. 129.
[8] Ezra Pound, 'Status Rerum', *Poetry*, I, 4, Chicago, January 1913, pp. 125–6.
[9] Ezra Pound, *Polite Essays*, London, 1937, p. 180.
[10] Pound, *Polite Essays*, p. 57.
[11] Ford Madox Hueffer, *On Heaven and Other Poems*, London, 1918, Preface, p. 9.
[12] T. S. Eliot, *On Poetry and Poets*, London, 1957, p. 37.
[13] Ford Madox Hueffer, 'Third Rate Poet', *The Golden Hind*, I, 1, October 1922, p. 18.
[14] Ford Madox Ford, *The March of Literature*, London, 1947, p. 45.
[15] Ezra Pound to Harriet Monroe, 13 August 1913, D. D. Paige, ed., *The Letters of Ezra Pound*, p. 21.
[16] Richard Aldington to the writer, 17 May 1954.
[17] *Some Imagist Poets, An Anthology*, London, 1915, Preface, pp. vi–vii.
[18] Richard Aldington, *Life for Life's Sake*, New York, 1941, p. 133.
[19] Ford Madox Hueffer, 'The Making of Modern Verse', *The Academy* (London), LXII, 1563, 19 April 1902, p. 413.
[20] *Ancient Lights*, pp. 293, 296.
[21] Violet Hunt, *The Flurried Years*, pp. 216–17.
[22] *Collected Poems*, pp. 3–4.
[23] *Collected Poems*, p. 9.
[24] *Collected Poems*, p. 17.
[25] 'Notes for a Lecture on Vers Libre' un-numbered page. Quoted in *Critical Writings*, p. 159.
[26] Ezra Pound, *Pavannes and Divisions*, p. 131. This statement was first published in *Poetry* in 1914.
[27] Conrad Aiken, 'The Function of Rhythm', *The Dial*, LXV, 16 November 1918, p. 148.
[28] Ezra Pound, 'Ford Madox (Hueffer) Ford; Obit.', *Nineteenth Century and After*, p. 179.
[29] T. S. Eliot, 'Reflections on Contemporary Poetry', *The Egoist*, IV, 10 November 1917, p. 151.
[30] *Collected Poems*, p. 18.
[31] *Collected Poems*, pp. 21–22.
[32] *Collected Poems*, p. 22.
[33] John Milton, 'L'Allegro'.
[34] W. B. Yeats, 'The Second Coming', *Collected Poems*, New York, 1951, p. 185.
[35] Ford Madox Ford, *The Good Soldier*, 'Dedicatory Letter', New York, 1951, p. xviii.
[36] *Return to Yesterday*, London, 1931, p. 270.
[37] *Return to Yesterday*, pp. 275–6.

[38] *The Good Soldier*, p. 7.
[39] *The Good Soldier*, p. 237.
[40] Graham Greene, quoted in Harold Strauss, ed., *Ford Madox Ford, Parade's End*, New York, 1950, p. 1.
[41] *Return to Yesterday*, 'Dedication', London, 1931, p. vii.
[42] Ford Madox Hueffer, 'Mr. Gilbert Cannan and "Old Mule"', *The Outlook*, XXXIII, 834, 24 January 1914, p. 110.
[43] Ford to Edward Garnett, n.d. (1908).
[44] *The Good Soldier*, p. 12.
[45] *The Good Soldier*, p. 183.
[46] Ford to Anthony Bertram, 14 August 1922. Quoted in *Critical Writings*, pp. 100-101.
[47] *Joseph Conrad*, London, 1924, p. 193.
[48] Ford Madox Ford, 'Introduction' in Ernest Hemingway, *A Farewell to Arms*, New York (Modern Library), 1932, p. xvi.
[49] *The March of Literature*, p. 562.
[50] John Rodker to the writer, 8 March 1954.
[51] 'Dedicatory Letter', *The Good Soldier*, p. xxi.

CHAPTER SEVEN: THE WAR AND AFTER

[1] Ford Madox Hueffer, *Thus to Revisit*, London, 1921, p. 137.
[2] Quoted in Violet Hunt, *I Have This to Say*, p. 211.
[3] *Thus to Revisit*, pp. 136-7.
[4] *Thus to Revisit*, p. 136.
[5] Ezra Pound to the writer, 11 February 1955.
[6] Account written by Ralph Cope and quoted in Goldring, pp. 164-5.
[7] Faith Compton Mackenzie, *As Much as I Dare*, London, 1938, pp. 271-2.
[8] Hunt, *I Have This to Say*, p. 241.
[9] Talk with Rebecca West, November, 1953.
[10] Ford Madox Hueffer and Violet Hunt, *Zeppelin Nights*, London, 1916, p. 306.
[11] *It Was the Nightingale*, p. 57.
[12] Ford to Lucy Masterman. Quoted in Goldring, pp. 164-5.
[13] Stella Bowen, *Drawn from Life*, London, n.d. (1940), pp. 61-62.
[14] Ford Madox Hueffer, 'A Jubilee', *The Outlook*, XXXVI, 910, 10 July 1915, p. 46.
[15] Thomas A. Lloyd to the writer, 21 August 1954.
[16] Ford to Lucy Masterman, Goldring, p. 187.
[17] Quoted in Douglas Goldring, *South Lodge*, London, 1943, p. 119.
[18] Ford to H. G. Wells, 22 March 1916.
[19] Letter from Conrad. Quoted in G. Jean-Aubry, *Joseph Conrad*, Vol. II, p. 169.
[20] Ford to Lucy Masterman. Quoted in Goldring, p. 188.
[21] Ford to Conrad, n.d. Quoted in Edward Naumburg, 'A Catalogue of a Ford Madox Ford Collection', *Princeton University Library Chronicle*, IX, April 1948, pp. 114-15.
[22] Ford to Conrad, 6 September 1916, quoted in Naumburg, p. 114.
[23] Ibid., pp. 114-15.
[24] Ford to Conrad, 19 December 1916. The quoted phrase is from the novel, *Romance*.
[25] Ford to C. F. G. Masterman, 5 January 1917. Quoted in Goldring, p. 194.
[26] Ford Madox Ford, 'I Revisit the Riviera', *Harper's Magazine*, CLVI, December 1932, p. 66.
[27] Ford to C. F. G. Masterman, 5 January 1917. Quoted in Goldring, p. 194.
[28] Ford to Katherine Hueffer, 10 December 1916. Quoted in Goldring, p. 196.
[29] Ford to Conrad, 19 December 1916.
[30] Ford to Edgar Jepson, 4 November 1917.

[31] 'Officers Record Services—Army Book—439, Ford Madox Hueffer.' See also *It Was the Nightingale*, p. 7.
[32] *It Was the Nightingale*, p. 64.
[33] Ford to Lucy Masterman, n.d. Quoted in Goldring, p. 188.
[34] Ibid., p. 191.
[35] Ibid., p. 198.
[36] *Collected Poems*, p. 81.
[37] Ford Madox Ford, *No Enemy*, New York, 1929, p. 268.
[38] Ibid., pp. 265–6.
[39] Stella Bowen, *Drawn from Life*, p. 63.
[40] Ford to Edgar Jepson, 15 August 1932. Quoted in Goldring, p. 216.
[41] Stella Bowen, *Drawn from Life*, p. 65.
[42] Ford to Herbert Read, 2 September 1919.
[43] Ford to J. B. Pinker, 29 June 1919. Quoted in Paul Alexander Bartlett, 'Letters of Ford Madox Ford', *Saturday Review of Literature*, p. 4.
[44] Quoted in *It Was the Nightingale*, p. 120.
[45] Stella Bowen, *Drawn from Life*, p. 69.
[46] Ford to J. B. Pinker, 17 May 1921. Quoted in Bartlett 'Letters', p. 4.
[47] Ford to Edgar Jepson, 9 July 1921. Quoted in Goldring, p. 212.
[48] Ford to Edgar Jepson, 20 July 1921.
[49] Quoted as epigraph in *Thus to Revisit*.
[50] Stella Bowen, *Drawn from Life*, p. 68.
[51] Ibid., p. 81.
[52] Ford to Anthony Bertram, 4 July 1923. Quoted in *Critical Writings*, p. 101.
[53] Ford to Herbert Read, 11 June 1920. Quoted in Herbert Read, *Annals of Innocence and Experience*, pp. 194–5.
[54] Ford to Herbert Read, 19 September 1920. Quoted in Read, *Annals*, pp. 197–8.
[55] Stella Bowen, *Drawn from Life*, p. 80.
[56] Ford to Alec Waugh, 26 July 1920. Quoted in David D. Harvey, *Ford Madox Ford*, Princeton 1962, p. 54.
[57] Ford to J. B. Pinker, n.d. (1921).
[58] Ford to Katherine Hueffer, 13 April 1918. Quoted in Goldring, p. 199.
[59] Ford to J. B. Pinker, 6 January 1918. Quoted in Bartlett, 'Letters', p. 4.
[60] Ford to Edgar Jepson, 8 September 1923. Quoted in Naumburg, 'A Catalogue', *Princeton Library Chronicle*, p. 192.
[61] *No Enemy*, p. 167.
[62] Stella Bowen, *Drawn from Life*, pp. 69, 70.
[63] Ford to Edgar Jepson. Quoted in Naumburg, p. 255.
[64] Ford to Harriet Monroe, 7 November 1921. Quoted in Harvey, *Ford Madox Ford*, p. 53.
[65] Ford to Edgar Jepson, 8 September 1923. Quoted in Goldring, p. 221.
[66] Ford to Joseph Conrad, 8 November 1923.
[67] Ford Madox Ford, *Mister Bosphorus and the Muses*, London, 1923, p. 103.
[68] Ford Madox Hueffer, *The Heart of the Country*, London, 1906, pp. 13–14.
[69] Stella Bowen, *Drawn from Life*, pp. 93–94.

CHAPTER EIGHT: PARIS AND *THE TRANSATLANTIC REVIEW*

[1] Ford to Edgar Jepson, 25 November 1922. Quoted in Goldring, p. 265.
[2] Stella Bowen, *Drawn from Life*, pp. 92–93.
[3] Ford to Anthony Bertram, 20 January 1923.
[4] Ford to Anthony Bertram, 20 March 1923.
[5] Stella Bowen, *Drawn from Life*, p. 107.

[6] Ford to Edgar Jepson, 28 January 1923. Quoted in Goldring, p. 223.

[7] *It Was the Nightingale*, p. 248.

[8] Quoted in Douglas Goldring, *South Lodge*, London, 1943, pp. 143–5.

[9] *The Transatlantic Review*, I, 4, 'Chroniques I', p. 196.

[10] Ibid.

[11] Stella Bowen, *Drawn from Life*, p. 117.

[12] Ford, 'Introduction' to Ernest Hemingway, *A Farewell to Arms*, New York (Modern Library), 1932, pp. xiii–xiv.

[13] *It Was the Nightingale*, p. 269.

[14] Ford to A. E. Coppard, 28 September 1923. Quoted in Frank MacShane, 'The Transatlantic Review', *The London Magazine*, VII, 12 December 1960, p. 53.

[15] H. G. Wells to Ford, 'Communications', *The Transatlantic Review*, I, 1, p. 94.

[16] *Selected Writings of Gertrude Stein*, New York, 1946, 'The Autobiography of Alice B. Toklas', p. 178.

[17] Ernest Hemingway to Gertrude Stein, 17 February 1924. Donald Gallup, ed., *The Flowers of Friendship*, New York, 1953, p. 195.

[18] Ernest Hemingway to Gertrude Stein, 14 September 1924. Donald Gallup, ed., 'The Making of *The Making of Americans*', *The New Colophon*, New York, 1950, p. 62.

[19] Ford to Gertrude Stein. Letter, 14 September 1924. Ibid., p. 61.

[20] Gertrude Stein to Ford, n.d. Ibid., p. 62.

[21] Ezra Pound to Sisley Huddleston, n.d. Quoted in Sisley Huddleston, *Bohemian, Literary and Social Life in Paris*, London, 1929, p. 103.

[22] *The Transatlantic Review*, I, 4, 'Chroniques I', p. 201.

[23] Sisley Huddleston, *Bohemian, Literary and Social Life in Paris*, p. 264.

[24] *The Transatlantic Review*, 'Chronique III, II, 2, p. 213.

[25] Carlos Baker, *Hemingway, the Writer as Artist*, Princeton, 1952, p. 264.

[26] Ford to A. E. Coppard, 17 February 1927. Quoted in 'The Transatlantic Review', *The London Magazine*, pp. 56–57.

[27] *The Transatlantic Review*, I, 6, 'Communications', p. 480.

[28] Ford to Ezra Pound, n.d. Quoted in 'The Transatlantic Review', p. 57.

[29] *The Transatlantic Review*, Paris Letter, II, 5, p. 551.

[30] *The Transatlantic Review*, II, 6, 'Editorial', p. 683.

[31] *The Transatlantic Review*, I, 1, 'Communications'—a letter from T. S. Eliot, p. 96.

[32] Sisley Huddleston, *Bohemian, Literary and Social Life in Paris*, p. 143.

[33] Norman Douglas, *Late Harvest*, London, 1947, p. 45; Talk with Miss Alice B. Toklas, January 1954, Paris; Paul Nash to Anthony Bertram, Letter, 2 March 1925.

[34] Lloyd Morris, 'A Remarkable Literary Figure of Our Era', *New York Herald Tribune*, 'Weekly Book Review', 22 May 1949, p. 1.

[35] Samuel Putnam, *Paris Was Our Mistress*, New York, 1947, p. 71.

[36] Herbert Gorman, 'Ford Madox Ford—A Portrait in Impressions', *The Bookman*, LXVII, 1, March 1928, p. 56.

[37] Burton Rascoe, *We Were Interrupted*, New York, 1947, p. 185.

[38] Sisley Huddleston, *Bohemian, Literary and Social Life in Paris*, p. 144.

[39] *It Was the Nightingale*, pp. 307–8.

[40] Natalie Barney, *Aventures de l'Esprit*, Paris, 1929, p. 223.

[41] Samuel Putnam, *Paris Was Our Mistress*, p. 220.

[42] William Rose Benét, 'Introduction' to *Collected Poems of Ford Madox Ford*, New York, 1936, p. vii and 'Homage to Ford Madox Ford', *New Directions Number Seven*, Norfolk, Connecticut, 1942, p. 460.

[43] Ford to H. G. Wells, 14 October 1923.

[44] Talk with Sylvia Beach, Paris, January, 1954.

[45] Nathan Asch to the writer, 29 November 1954.

[46] Conrad to Ford, 22 May 1924.

[47] Ford Madox Ford: Inscription written in a copy of *Joseph Conrad, A Personal Remembrance*, dated December 1926. Quoted in Edward Naumburg, *Princeton University Library Chronicle*, IX, April 1948, p. 154.

[48] Jessie Conrad, A Letter to the Editor, *Times Literary Supplement*, 4 December 1924, p. 826.

[49] Edward Garnett, 'Instructive and Amusing', *The Weekly Westminster*, 14 February 1925, p. 473.

[50] Christopher Morley, 'Homage to Ford Madox Ford', *New Directions Number Seven*, p. 476.

[51] Sinclair Lewis to Ford, 30 November 1938.

CHAPTER NINE: PARADE'S END

[1] Ford Madox Hueffer, *An English Girl*, London, 1907, p. 237.

[2] Ford Madox Hueffer, *Mr. Fleight*, London, 1913, pp. 193–4.

[3] Violet Hunt, *I Have This to Say*, p. 209.

[4] For further bibliographical details see Harvey, *Ford Madox Ford*, pp. 118–19.

[5] *It Was the Nightingale*, London, 1934, p. 138.

[6] Ibid., p. 188.

[7] Mrs. Florence Wynne Finch to Kenneth Young, February 1954.

[8] Ibid.

[9] Ford to Herbert Read. Letter, 19 September 1920. Quoted in Herbert Read, *Annals of Innocence and Experience*, p. 197.

[10] *It Was the Nightingale*, p. 195.

[11] Ibid., p. 180.

[12] Ibid., p. 191.

[13] Ford Madox Ford, *Some Do Not*, London, 1924, p. 30 (in Knopf edition of *Parade's End*, New York, 1950, p. 21).

[14] *Some Do Not*, p. 9 (*Parade's End*, p. 3).

[15] Ibid., pp. 31–2 (*Parade's End*, p. 22).

[16] Ibid., p. 32 (*Parade's End*, p. 22).

[17] *Mightier than the Sword*, p. 235.

[18] *Some Do Not*, pp. 215–16 (*Parade's End*, p. 173).

[19] Ford Madox Ford, *No More Parades*, London 1925, pp. 177–8. Ibid., p. 404.

[20] Ibid., p. 34 (*Parade's End*, pp. 306–7).

[21] Ford Madox Ford, *A Man Could Stand Up*, London 1926, pp. 100–1 (*Parade's End*, p. 566).

[22] Ibid., p. 266 (*Parade's End*, p. 668).

[23] Ford Madox Ford, Prospectus for *The Transatlantic Review*. Quoted in Douglas Goldring, *South Lodge*, p. 145.

[24] Ford Madox Ford, *Last Post*, London 1928, p. 233 (*Parade's End*, p. 802).

[25] Ibid., p. 329 (*Parade's End*, p. 832).

[26] *The Spirit of the People*, p. 115.

[27] Ibid., p. 81.

[28] Granville Hicks, 'Ford Madox Ford', *The Bookman*, LXII, 4, December 1930, p. 369.

[29] 'Jacob Tonson' (Bennett), 'Books and Persons', *The New Age*, VI, 20, 17 March 1910, p. 471.

[30] Melvin Seiden, 'Ford Madox Ford and his Tetralogy', *The London Magazine*, IV, 8, August 1959, pp. 45–55.

[31] This essay appears in *The Critical Attitude*, London, 1911.

[32] Ford Madox Hueffer, 'On Impressionism—I', *Poetry and Drama*, II, 2, June 1914, p. 167.

[33] Edward Crankshaw, 'Ford Madox Ford', *National Review*, CXXXI, August 1948, p. 166.

[34] Ford to Gerald Bullett, 8 October 1933.

[35] Ford to J. B. Pinker, n.d. (1906).

[36] Ford to a Mr. Barton of the firm of J. B. Pinker, 17 August 1930. Quoted in Bartlett, *Saturday Review*, p. 14.

[37] Robie Macaulay, 'Introduction' in Ford, *Parade's End*, New York, 1951, p. xxi.

[38] Ford Madox Ford, 'Dedicatory Letter', *Last Post*, London (Penguin Books), 1948, p. 11.

[39] Ford Madox Hueffer, 'On Impressionism—II', *Poetry and Drama*, II, 4 (December 1914), pp. 327–8.

[40] Caroline Gordon, 'Homage to Ford Madox Ford', *New Directions Number Seven*, Norfolk, Connecticut, 1942, p. 475.

CHAPTER TEN: INTERNATIONAL FIGURE

[1] Carl Van Doren, 'Homage to Ford Madox Ford', *New Directions Number Seven*, Norfolk, Connecticut, 1942, p. 470.

[2] Stella Bowen, *Drawn from Life*, p. 153.

[3] Ibid., p. 152.

[4] Nina Hamnett, *Laughing Torso*, New York, 1932, pp. 188–9.

[5] Stella Bowen, *Drawn from Life*, p. 137.

[6] Juan Gris to D. H. Kahnweiller, 4 January 1926.

[7] Ford to Gerald Duckworth, 9 March 1926.

[8] Talk with Professor Sterling Dow, July 1961.

[9] George Dillon, 'Homage to Ford Madox Ford', *New Directions Number Seven*, p. 469.

[10] Quotations taken from dust-jacket of *A Man Could Stand Up*, second printing, New York, 1926.

[11] Ford Madox Ford, *New York Essays*, New York, 1927, p. 7.

[12] Ibid., p. 10.

[13] Burton Rascoe, *We Were Interrupted*, New York, 1947, p. 230.

[14] Douglas Goldring, *South Lodge*, 1943, pp. 179–80.

[15] Ibid., p. 182.

[16] Ford to Gerald Duckworth, 28 November 1927.

[17] Rascoe, *We Were Interrupted*, pp. 227–30.

[18] Stella Bowen, *Drawn from Life*, p. 169.

[19] Ibid., p. 165.

[20] Ibid., p. 165.

[21] Ford to Gerald Duckworth, 13 February 1928.

[22] Ford to Percival Hinton, 13 February 1938. Quoted in Goldring, pp. 244–5.

[23] Talk with Ford's lawyer, Mr. Arthur Spingarn, New York, December 1954.

[24] Ford to Gertrude Stein, 8 September 1928.

[25] Ford to W. A. Bradley, 13 August 1928.

[26] Ford Madox Ford, *The English Novel*, Philadelphia, 1929, pp. 13–14.

[27] Ford to Percival Hinton, 1 February 1928. Quoted in Goldring, p. 245.

[28] Ford to Miss Baumgarten of Brandt and Brandt, 10 July 1929.

[29] Ford Madox Ford. Letter, 2 April 1930.

[30] Ford to H. G. Wells, 28 July 1930.

[31] Samuel Putnam, *Paris Was Our Mistress*, pp. 124–5.

[32] Ford. Letter, 2 April 1930.

CHAPTER ELEVEN: PROVENCE

[1] *It Was the Nightingale*, p. 124.
[2] Ford to Hugh Walpole, 2 December 1929.
[3] Stella Bowen, *Drawn from Life*, pp. 191–2.
[4] Theodore Pratt to the writer, 1 May 1954.
[5] *It Was the Nightingale*, p. viii.
[6] Stella Bowen, *Drawn from Life*, pp. 79–80.
[7] Katherine Anne Porter to the writer, 9 May 1961.
[8] Talk with Allen Tate, July 1961.
[9] Ezra Pound, *Pavannes and Divagations*, New York, 1958, pp. 153–5.
[10] Allen Tate to the writer, 24 July 1961.
[11] Ford to Hugh Walpole, 25 October 1932.
[12] Ezra Pound to Ford, 7 September 1933.
[13] Pound to Ford, 11 October 1933.
[14] Pound to Ford, 3 November 1933.
[15] Ford to T. R. Smith, 14 March 1931.
[16] Ford to J. B. Pinker, 17 August 1929.
[17] Ford Madox Ford, 'Autocriticism', Weekend *Week-End Review*, VIII, 9 September 1933, p. 249.
[18] Isabel Paterson, 'The Heir of All the Ages', New York *Herald-Tribune*, 'Books', 26 February 1933, p. 4.
[19] Ford Madox Hueffer, 'On Impressionism—I', *Poetry and Drama*, II, 2, June 1914, p. 175.
[20] *The March of Literature*, p. 301.
[21] *Thus to Revisit*, p. 64.
[22] Ford to Ray Long, 2 July 1932.
[23] Joseph Conrad, 'Preface', *The Nigger of the 'Narcissus,'* New York, 1925, p. xiv.
[24] Ford Madox Hueffer, *The Critical Attitude*, London, 1911, p. 60.
[25] *Ancient Lights*, p. xvi.
[26] Talk with Jonathan Cape, London, 8 December 1953.
[27] Joseph Conrad and Ford Madox Hueffer, *The Nature of a Crime*, London, 1924, p. 66.
[28] Richard Aldington, *Life for Life's Sake*, p. 156.
[29] Gerald Bullett to Ford, 4 December 1933.

CHAPTER TWELVE: GREAT TRADE ROUTE

[1] Ford Madox Ford, *Provence*, London, 1938, p. 79.
[2] Ford to Douglas Goldring, 15 February 1934. Quoted in Goldring, *South Lodge*, p. 192.
[3] Archibald Marshall, *Out and About*, London, 1933.
[4] *The Daily Herald*, 2 November 1931, p. 1.
[5] Ford to Anthony Bertram, 14 September 1934.
[6] Ford to Anthony Bertram, 27 September 1934.
[7] Ford to Gerald Bullett, 24 August 1933.
[8] *It Was the Nightingale*, p. 39.
[9] Ford to Gerald Duckworth, 9 March 1926.
[10] *Provence*, p. 235.
[11] *It Was the Nightingale*, p. 59.
[12] Ezra Pound to Ford, 27 December 1933.
[13] Ford Madox Ford, *Great Trade Route*, London, 1937, p. 65.

[14] Theodore Dreiser to Ford, 1 June 1935.

[15] From 'Transcript of the Meetings of the Conference on Literature and Reading in the South and South-west', held under the auspices of Louisiana State University, Baton Rouge, Louisiana, 10 and 11 April 1935.

[16] Sir Osbert Sitwell to the writer, 17 April 1954.

[17] Not, of course, a Southern writer, but by reason of his attendance at Kenyon College, a friend of J. C. Ransom and other distinctly Southern writers.

[18] Allen Tate to the writer, 20 November 1952.

[19] Collected Poems, p. 293.

[20] Ibid., p. 292.

[21] Ibid., p. 295.

[22] Great Trade Route, p. 408.

[23] Ibid., p. 406.

[24] Ibid., p. 102.

[25] Typically, it doesn't: it makes twenty-four. Quoted in George Schreiber, Portraits and Self-Portraits, Boston, 1936, p. 39.

[26] Ford to Anthony Bertram, 15 October 1935. Quoted in Critical Writings, p. 102.

[27] Ford to Stanton Campbell, 24 August 1938. See David Harvey, Ford Madox Ford, p. 8.

[28] Ford Madox Ford, 'Paris Letter', Kenyon Review, I, 1, Winter 1939, pp. 18–31.

[29] Talk with Allen Tate, Rome, 1954.

[30] Ford Madox Ford, A Mirror to France, London, 1926, p. 33.

[31] Ford Madox Ford, 'Preface' in René Béhaine, The Survivors, London, 1938, p. iii.

[32] Ford Madox Ford, 'Hands Off the Arts', The American Mercury, XXXIV, April 1933, p. 12.

[33] Paul Morand, statement in The Cantos of Ezra Pound, Some Testimonies, New York, 1933, p. 12.

[34] A Mirror to France, p. 14.

[35] Great Trade Route, p. 432.

[36] Ibid., p. 188.

[37] Provence, pp. 362–3.

[38] Ibid., p. 261.

[39] Ibid., p. 319.

[40] Great Trade Route, p. 234.

[41] Ibid., p. 196.

[42] Reader's report on Great Trade Route, 17 August 1936. Edward Crankshaw was the reader. (Edward Crankshaw file, 1936, Allen and Unwin Ltd., London.)

[43] Graham Greene, 'The Good Life', The London Mercury, December 1938, pp. 217–218.

CHAPTER THIRTEEN: MARCH OF LITERATURE

[1] Provence, London, 1938, p. 344.

[2] Ford to Ruth Aley, 7 September 1936. The letter was not actually sent.

[3] Letter from Katherine Anne Porter, 15 January 1936.

[4] Edward Crankshaw to Sir Stanley Unwin, July 1939.

[5] Ford to Stanley Unwin, 15 March 1938.

[6] Ford Madox Ford, 'London Re-visited', The London Mercury, XXXV, 206, December, 1936, p. 177.

[7] William Carlos Williams to Ford, 1 May 1937.

[8] Ford to W. A. Bradley, n.d. (1936).

[9] Ford to Stanley Unwin, 29 May 1937.

10 Ford to Dale Warren, 11 June 1937.

11 Talk with John Crowe Ransom, Poughkeepsie, New York, May 1959.

12 I am indebted to Mr. Ashley Brown of Columbia, So. Carolina for much of the information contained in this and earlier sections dealing with Southern writers. I am also indebted to Mr. Robert Penn Warren for information received in December 1959, and to Mr. Allen Tate and Miss Caroline Gordon for material given me in the summer of 1961.

13 Morton D. Zabel to Ford, 9 May, 1937.

14 Ford to Stanley Unwin, 29 May 1937.

15 Robie Macaulay, 'The Dean in Exile', *Shenandoah*, IV, 1, Spring 1953, p. 47.

16 Joseph Brewer to the writer, 27 January 1954.

17 Robie Macaulay, 'The Dean in Exile', *Shenandoah*, pp. 45–46.

18 Ibid., pp. 46–47.

19 Ford to Stanley Unwin, 16 April 1938.

20 D. H. Lawrence to William Heinemann, 15 December 1909. Aldous Huxley, ed., *The Letters of D. H. Lawrence*, London, 1932, p. 1.

21 Richard Aldington, *Life for Life's Sake*, p. 156.

22 Herbert Gorman, 'Ford Madox Ford, A Portrait in Impressions', *The Bookman*, LXVII, 1, March 1928, p. 58.

23 Lloyd Morris, *A Threshold in the Sun*, London, 1948, p. 217.

24 Ford to Stanley Unwin, 23 March 1939. See also *New York is Not America*, p. 105.

25 Eudora Welty to the writer, 3 February 1954, and four letters from Ford to Miss Welty, dated 3 November 1938 and 7 January, 19 January and 25 May 1939.

26 Lady Mackenzie to the writer, 27 November 1953.

27 Ellen Alix duPoy (Taylor) Daniel to the writer, 23 March 1954.

28 Talk with Edward Crankshaw, London, 4 February 1954.

29 Jean Stafford to Ford, 1 February 1938.

30 Katherine Anne Porter to Caroline Gordon, 12 July 1935.

31 Edward Dahlberg to Ford, 14 April 1939.

32 Grahame Greene to Ford, 18 December (no year—1938).

33 W. H. Auden to Ford, n.d., 1939.

34 Talk with Robert Lowell, Castine, Maine, August 1961.

35 Ford to Gertrude Stein, 1 March 1938.

36 Ford to George Keating, 20 June 1938.

37 Ibid.

38 Ford to George Keating, 28 June 1938.

39 *The March of Literature*, pp. 5–6.

40 Ibid., p. 486.

41 Rebecca West to the writer, 19 November 1953.

42 Compton Mackenzie, *Literature in My Time*, London, 1933, p. 183.

43 Ford to Stanley Unwin, 13 October 1938.

44 Ford to Grenville Vernon of The Dial Press, 6 November 1937.

45 Ford to Stanley Unwin, Letter, 13 October 1938.

46 M. W. Yeatts, C.I.E., I.C.S., Census Commissioner, Government of India, New Delhi. A review of *The March of Literature*, broadcast from All India Radio, 16 February 1940.

47 Ford to Stanley Unwin, 4 August 1938.

48 Edward Dahlberg to the writer, 9 July 1961.

49 Edward Dahlberg, 'Homage to Ford Madox Ford', *New Directions Number Seven*, Norfolk, Connecticut, 1942, p. 468.

50 Ford to Stanley Unwin, Letter, 16 February 1939.

51 Sinclair Lewis to Ford, 30 November 1938.

52 Ford to Stanley Unwin, 16 February 1939.

[53] Orrick Johns to Ford, 19 April 1935; and Ford to Johns, 24 April 1935.

[54] Ford to René Béhaine, 10 August 1938.

[55] Ford to Stanley Unwin, 23 September 1938.

[56] Ford Madox Ford, 'Synopsis of *Professor's Progress*'—Manuscript.

[57] 'Synopsis of *Professor's Progress*'—Manuscript.

[58] Ford to Theodore Dreiser, letter, n.d., 1939.

[59] Ezra Pound to Ford, 31 January 1939. D. D. Paige, ed., *Letters of Ezra Pound*, p. 321.

[60] William Carlos Williams to the writer, 7 February 1955.

[61] Edward Dahlberg to the writer, 9 July 1961.

[62] Ford to Stanley Unwin, 12 October 1938.

[63] Edward Dahlberg to Ford, 14 April 1939.

[64] Various letters dated 14 March 1939 to H. G. Wells, Maxim Litvinoff, Ernest Hemingway, etc.

[65] Williams Carlos Williams, *Autobiography*, New York, 1951, p. 299.

[66] Ford to Stanley Unwin, 16 February 1939.

[67] Edward Dahlberg to the writer, 9 July 1961.

[68] Letter from Katherine Anne Porter, 6 May 1932.

[69] Edward Dahlberg to the writer, 9 July 1961.

[70] Sherwood Anderson, 'Legacies of Ford Madox Ford', *Coronet*, VIII, 5, August 1940, pp. 135–6.

[71] Ford to Stanley Unwin, 25 May 1939.

[72] Ezra Pound, 'Ford Madox (Hueffer) Ford: Obit.', *Nineteenth Century and After*, CXXVI, 750, August 1939, p. 178.

[73] *Joseph Conrad*, appendix, pp. 255–6. (Writer's translation.)

[74] Ibid., p. 256.

[75] Sherwood Anderson, 'Homage to Ford Madox Ford', *New Directions Number Seven*, p. 459.

INDEX